Seasoning

For Leon and Janet

sent for Leon's birthday

May 15, 1999

with love
from

Lenore and Frank

Seasoning

A POET'S YEAR

With Seasonal Recipes

David Young

OHIO STATE UNIVERSITY PRESS
COLUMBUS

Copyright © 1999
by The Ohio State University.
All rights reserved.

Library of Congress Cataloging-in-Publication Data

Young, David, 1936–
Seasoning : a poet's year : with seasonal recipes / David Young.
p.   cm.
Includes bibliographical references.
ISBN 0-8142-0803-7 (cl : alk. paper)
1. Young, David, 1936–   .   2. Poets, American—20th century—
Biography.   3. Months—Poetry.   4. Cookery.   I. Title.
PS3575.O78S43   1999
811'.54—dc21   98-42429
CIP

Illustrations by Melissa Ehn.
Text and jacket design by Christine Taylor.
Type set in Perpetua with Nicholas Cochin Black
by Wilsted & Taylor Publishing Services.
Printed by Thomson-Shore, Inc.

The paper used in this publication meets the minimum
requirements of the American National Standard for
Information Sciences—Permanence of Paper
for Printed Library Materials.
ANSI Z39.48-1992.

9   8   7   6   5   4   3   2   1

Contents

. . . .

Preface

．　．　．　．

I walk around, aware and unaware, seasoning the familiar with the unfamiliar. Time holds me in giant, invisible arms everywhere I go. My attempts to understand it season me, temper me. Ripen me. My knowledge of the world, a steadily enlarging store, is chastened again and again by revelations of my ignorance. I am *in season,* then just as suddenly *out of season,* even *seasonless.* I think I know each season, the year's colossal quadrants, but every successive spring, summer, fall, and winter is a set of new discoveries.

Word-picker, phrase-gardener, I think I know a word like *season.* An old verb, for example, derived from the act of sowing (*sationum,* root of *serrere*). *Stages and stations, seeding and kneading, knowing and sowing.* I reflect that *season* was used to mark not only the predictable wedges of the year's slow wheel but special times, predictable or not—periods of festivity (the Christmas season), fertility (mating season), inclemency (rainy season).

George Herbert tells me that a sweet and virtuous soul is "seasoned timber," good for building or for firewood. Flourishing my pepper mill on a winter morning in the kitchen, or rubbing thyme between my hands as I drop it on a summer evening's salad, I think I know how to season food, but there are always new combinations, new thresholds, surprises. Time turns a corner, opens another vista.

Food plays an eventful part in my yearly journey through the seasons. When I cook and serve new dishes, am I trying to eat time, consuming what slowly consumes me? When I write a poem, am I hoping to speak through time that speaks through me? Is time a fruit we pick, an apple of knowledge? Ending a poem about memory, I once called time a pomegranate. The many-chambered fruit of the dead, a little red leather globe that feels and looks like the archaic orb of a Florentine prince, filled with glistening seeds—it was a good metaphor, but a bit exotic for my locale.

I try, after all, to cook, eat, and serve in place, and in season. The result, ephemeral and memorable, is here a pie, there a soup, now a local apple, then a concoction of herbs from my garden to sauce homemade pasta. Foraging for mushrooms, blackberries, lily buds, ramps, and wild strawberries feeds a spiritual hunger, too. As the months pass and I concoct my recipes and my poems, I realize more and more how much my own time-fruit is necessarily local. It is unremarkable to the casual eye, and yet my grounding in this place is an essential feature in a way of living that hopes to make sense, and nourishment, of time, that human habitat and equivocal companion.

Northern Ohio, where I live, feels like nowhere in particular. It's part of the Great Lakes bioregion, and nobody quite knows whether it is the Middle West or the East or something in between. This part of the world is sometimes called America's North Coast, because of Lake Erie. It is also known as the Western Reserve, because Connecticut continued to claim it after other states had ceded their western lands. And this particular part of the Western Reserve is called the Firelands, because it was settled by Connecticut citizens who had been burned out of their farms and homes by the British during the Revolutionary War.

This region was thickly wooded and swampy before it was colonized and cleared by American settlers in the nineteenth century. Some of the land had been farmed by native populations long ago. They grew squash and maize and beans and had sizable settlements next to the lake and along the rivers and streams, but European diseases wiped them out in the sixteenth and seventeenth centuries. The forests they had cleared by extensive burning reclaimed this region. After that, malarial wetlands and a beech and maple climax forest prevailed until the middle of the nineteenth century. Native Americans still migrated through, hunting and fishing, following the animal herds and bird flocks and moving as the seasons moved, but they no longer had large settlements. That wouldn't happen again until the forests were cleared once more by European settlers and the wetlands drained for agriculture.

Glaciers have leveled the terrain until considerably south of here. My part of the world lacks the features of landscape—mountains, sea cliffs, waterfalls, deep forests, rugged outcrops, sweeping vistas—that we tend to associate with significant natural beauty and the inspiration of great poetry. Its climate can be harsh (grindingly cold in the winter, suffocatingly hot and humid in late summer), and its flatness has led many visitors to suggest that it's an unattractive location compared to almost anywhere else. A visiting British art historian, whom I picked up from the airport, watched the landscape pass for a few minutes and then commented succinctly, "Flat. Rather like Holland," and turned his attention to other things.

In a way, though, this uncelebrated part of the world is exactly right—for my own investigations of being and the being of the world around me, for my own efforts to write poetry, and for an enterprise like this book. I want to show that time and place can reward you in the quotidian, the everyday, that you need not go to any place other than the unremarkable place where you happen to be to find a daily, weekly, monthly beauty in your relation to time and the environment. That is why if someone demeans the nature that brims overwhelmingly in the fertile landscape around me, my instinct is to spring to its defense. In a late summer in the late sixties, a fellow faculty member's wife who had

just returned from a summer in France flopped down on somebody's
deck chair and announced, "Ohio is so ugly!" I understood instantly
why she said it, how the shift from Europe to middle America had
offended her eye, but I answered her by writing this poem:

OHIO

Looking across a field
at a stand of trees
more than a windbreak
less than a forest—
is pretty much all
the view we have

in summer it's lush
in winter it gets
down to two or
three tones   for
variety
there might be
an unpainted barn
water patches
a transmission tower

yet there's a lot
to see
          you could sit
all day on the rusty
seat of a harrow
with that view before you
and all the sorrows
this earth has seen
sees now   will see
could pass through
you like a long
mad bolt of lightning

> *leaving you drained*
> *and shaken*
> *still*
> *at dusk*
> *the field would be*
> *the same and the growing*
> *shadows of the trees*
> *would cross it toward you*
> *until you rose   your heart*
> *pounding with joy and walked*
> *gladly through the weeds*
> *and toward the trees*

I was trembling all over as I finished the sudden first draft of that poem. Much was at stake if you called Ohio ugly, if you forgot to avail yourself of your best connections with the intricate existence surrounding you, an existence amply represented by things like weeds, trees, fields, puddles, barns, transmission towers, and, above all and always, the ever changing light. Andrew Marvell speaks of the soul that "waves in its plumes the various light." Some people may like the light to be always about the same, as it is in the Mediterranean and southern California. More northerly climates, however, offer us enormous varieties of light, changing constantly with the days, weeks, months, and seasons.

Thus it was that, over thirty-three years in Ohio, developing as a poet, I began to be, without any deliberate program, a writer of place. A few years ago I received an award from the State of Ohio that described me as an Ohio writer and "a treasure of the state." Of course, I was pleased. I don't know about the treasure part, but it's right to say that I am an Ohio writer: born in Iowa, raised in Minnesota and Nebraska, educated in Minnesota and Connecticut, and then coming here to teach, I have become not just a Midwestern writer who happens to live in Ohio, but an Ohio writer.

Around the same time that this recognition arrived, my daughter, who is also a writer, became intensely interested in bioregionalism.

"That's what you do, you know," she told me, though I suspect she felt I didn't apply myself to it quite conscientiously enough. Again, it meant noticing what I had long taken for granted. I was in great part an environmental writer, and that meant, among other things, that I was deeply connected to, and cared about, my bioregion.

Poets trace their descent from shamans, who usually functioned as mediators between their communities and the larger creation around them, the mysterious web of being on which they depended and in which they located much of their sense of the sacred. They needed to know their community, its features and needs and forces, and they needed to know their natural environment, with an intimacy gained over a lifetime. That function, in my view, still pertains to a good working poet, though it is harder to establish in a world where we all move around so much.

The purpose of this book is partly to explore how my sense of place has grown so important to me. One meaning is surely related to the American literary imagination, as I have understood it and participated in it, to its need to resolve and clarify the relation of the self to the natural world in the peculiarly American terms of our own history and our own environment. I have also been responding to that crisis in Western thought that proposes a drastic need to reconceive, in our metaphysics and our ethics and in all of our cultural institutions, a better relation between human beings and their natural environment. My response has been imaginative, a making of poems, and it has been decidedly local, regional, and gradual.

This book makes no special claims for this region's natural beauty. The point is that any spot on the planet may afford the kind of harmony with time and nature we need to practice and incorporate into our lives.

"Incorporate" means "put into the body," and that is just what I do, through eyes, ears, touch, and mouth, using memory, imagination, and digestion, with the birds and trees I observe, the mushrooms and other edible plants I pick and grow in my garden, the food I cook, the poems I love, and the weather I live in. The process helps the inside match the outside, lets the consciousness synchronize itself with sun, moon, planet, and seasons. What could be more ordinary? And what could matter more?

If this is a book about place, it is also, as I have said, a book about time. How to deal with time, how to *abide* in it comfortably, is a problem all of us face. Because of the compound nature of human consciousness, which is in turn the source of our sense of self, we live in the present moment while also being aware, much of the time, of the past and the future, remembering the one and anticipating the other. This process grows more complex as we move forward in life. Sedimentary layers of experience accumulate in our memories, and they both burden us with recollections and make our sense of what is to come more elaborate and, often, more fearsome. How to balance selfhood and consciousness within the flow of time is a perennial human dilemma. If we dwell too much outside the present, obsessed with the past or with the future, it's as if we were not really alive at all. Buddhist teachers say we are dead when we live in the past or future, that we are alive only in the present.

While everyone has had wonderful experiences of centering completely in the moment, it's unrealistic to say, in our complex lives and in this present world, that we can simply enjoy, and dwell in, the present. I watched my mother gradually lose all her contact with the past and future as her Alzheimer's disease progressed. I know from that experience that to lose your hold on time, your understanding of yourself as living in it sequentially, is to lose your very identity. Even if we'd like to sometimes, we can't cut ourselves off from consequences our actions may have, and we cannot afford to ignore history, our own and everyone else's. Even a Buddhist master will probably oscillate between the ideal of total immersion in the present moment and the more practical reality of living with recollection and anticipation.

I have long had a hunch that our culture's dominant model of time as essentially linear is at the root of much unhappiness. Linear time appears to be irrevocable and is associated with tragedy and with death, with the recognition that what's done cannot be undone. It is also a powerful, if mostly unconscious, justification of our culture's excessive faith in the metaphor of human progress, as represented by technological development and growth. The whole history of the twentieth century challenges the belief in progress as a definitive model of time, yet that belief persists. Note that I say "definitive." Growth and prosperity and technological change have their merits, but our sense of their value needs to be tempered by a sense of continuities, eternal returns, essential rhythms of life that we abandon at our peril.

Undoubtedly, our experience confirms linear time as one important facet of being. We must face that and accept it. But surely our living in time, if we begin to open up to the activity of memory and the recurrence of the seasons, confirms aspects of the temporal that contradict and complicate simple linearity.

If you think about our units of time and their origins, you realize that the year and the day are products of our relationship with the sun, while the month stems from our relationship with the moon. The week is our own invention, and perhaps less valuable because more arbitrary, though a division of the moon's changes into four quarters feels natural, a binary based on new moon and full moon, divided again by the halfway points of each extreme. As for minutes and seconds, they are an arbitrary way of dividing time, but they gradually become natural to us as we live with them.

Taking the three most natural units of time, then, the year and the month and the day, I have tried to make them good and logical companions, congenial society whose movements I walk in step with, whose changes and recurrences I revel in. Thus it is that this book has acquired its structure. It is a partial record of my comradeship with time. It hopes to understand time in terms of place, and place in terms of time.

Because my enjoyment of the seasons does not separate the walks I take and the natural phenomena I observe from the poems I read or remember and the foods I find and cook, I have not excluded any of these things from my record of the seasons. Pleasure dislikes categories, and surely we do far too much compartmentalizing—now I'm at work, now I'm on vacation, now I am a consumer, now I am a worshiper, and so on, endlessly subdividing and categorizing our experience and dog-gedly playing our set roles. I have tried here to ignore some of the bor-ders and distinctions we normally live with. To me, it does not require a radical change of setting—going to live in the desert or even just at Walden Pond—to move toward a greater sense of unity: unity among possible interests and enjoyments, unity with the vast rhythms of sea-sonal change and planetary order, consummate unity with the patterns of life that occur all around us. Sometimes it just means ignoring the barriers we erect across our own lives.

What strange creatures we are when you come to think of it! We go inside special buildings to become conscious of what is all around us—churches to think of the creator and the creation, planetariums to think of the vast reaches of our universe, schoolrooms to become more sensitive to history, language, culture, and literature, laboratories to study the details of nature, computer rooms to "browse" among com-plex simulacra of reality. One consequence of this is that we miss things that surround us, the elements and the biosphere, the living things we share our brief time with. Our country is full of people who go outside as little as possible and then only to get from one place to another, one building to the next. Meanwhile, existence itself is a church, a plane-tarium, a classroom, a laboratory. Being is a momentous gift, greater than any web site. We worship when we cook and eat (or we should), we study the solar system when we notice the weather and the moon's phases and the seasonal shifts of constellations. We encounter the point of poetry when we take a walk in the snow.

Stressing these connections is the aim of this book. I want to collect together some of the favorite things—phenomena of language, cul-ture, and nature—that I take with me or encounter on my yearly jour-ney through the seasons, living in northern Ohio. Some have been with me most of my thirty-five years here; some are brand-new, part of a process of continual and inexhaustible discovery.

Lyric poems constitute a spiritual geography. They are one significant way we relate ourselves and our internal experience to the world around us. We do it by writing them ourselves, and we do it by appropriating and befriending the poems of others. In either case, we are often responding to the changing seasons and intent on the continuities we want to establish between the external and the internal. Readers should be warned that this text will swivel back and forth between prose and poetry. As I said, I think we live too much by categories. Having always wanted to find a book that comfortably mixes prose with poetry, alternating the lyric with the narrative and the discursive, I have finally tried to produce one myself. When I come to an insight or perception about the seasons, about place and time, that is already put well in a poem, mine or somebody else's, then I will weave it straight into the text and texture of my annual pilgrimage.

We are much given to distinguishing art from nature. A poem and a snowstorm, we think, must be two quite different things. But what if they aren't? What if I put them on an equivalent plane, if only to see how that feels? Readers open to such experimentation will, I hope, find rewards here for their temporary willingness to abandon categories.

Past and present pose a similar issue. Often I will go back, to earlier moments in my life and to people who are no longer with me. That isn't necessarily melancholy and it isn't necessarily a longing for the past. It's because the reality of memory seems to me as valid a part of the present as anything else. When, at sixty, I associate my life of the moment with other moments, some of them long gone, I am not "lost in the past" or "overwhelmed by memory." I am demonstrating actualities that are part of every human consciousness. Memory can be a great burden, of course; it means we take the bad with the good. But it is teacher, companion, album, and nest egg. The point is not to repudiate the present by means of nostalgia but to let memory inform what we see, do, taste, write, think, and, hopefully, understand.

Come with me and see if this feels liberating. Maybe our tidiness—this is poetry, this is prose; here is art, over there is nature; this is the present, that is the past; this is inner, that is outer; trees are physical, prayers are spiritual—is something we can cling to a little less tightly.

Recipes for each of the twelve months follow the chapters. There are something like sixty poems woven into this text, about five for each month. And because my own poems are such a significant part of my own spiritual history, I have not hesitated either to include them or to let them guide the discussion and set the tone. If they capture the seasonal truth or moment best, then by all means let them take over. The poems I discuss are the ones, mine and others', that came back to me as I thought about how I live with the seasons. They helped me think out what I was saying in the essays. The translations of poems from other languages are my own unless otherwise indicated.

In the essays that form the chapters of the book, I will run together all sorts of different things that I enjoy associating with this month, that season, things of place seen in time. *Things of place. Seen in time.* And I hope the result will not so much be specific advice on *how* to live in time as a simple reminder that most of us can live in time and in place more comfortably and happily than the culture presently around us seems to intend or encourage.

This book was mostly written over the course of 1995, then extensively revised in the two years that followed. It owes a great many of its improvements to valuable suggestions by my wife, Georgia Newman, who was especially good at helping streamline the manuscript, and to friendly readers who included:

> Tina Bennett,
> Stuart Friebert,
> Ruth Anne Green,
> Tom Van Nortwick,
> David Walker,
> Margaret Young.

To them, and especially to Georgia, I dedicate *Seasoning.*

Oberlin, January 1998

Seasoning

JANUARY

Cold and the Colors of Cold

· · · ·

I step outside on a January morning, into profound cold and emphatic silence. The air burns a little inside my nose, polar and alien. This world is still dark, though there's faint light showing through the trees in the southeast, a greenish-yellow glow, prefiguring sunrise. It's a little dispiriting to realize that the sun won't warm this world, can't yet revive it. January's sheer inhumanity is like the face of a glacier or a rocky cliff. One part of us wants to venture out, trying to make ourselves citizens of the cold; the other wants to hibernate, nest, be down among slumbering roots.

There's no snow right now. Breathing carefully, I pace across the backyard grass, enjoying the feel of its brittleness and the unyielding sensation of the frozen soil. So resolute is this cold that it seems a piece of luck just to be alive in it. The dark is gradually thinning out as light increases at the horizon, with peach tints starting now to the east and a kind of faint rosiness in the southern sky.

Then I hear the crow. It's way at the top of a tree down by the creek, some seventy yards away, ruffling and shaking itself like a balky umbrella. It must feel it owns this frozen landscape. Another crow answers from a half-mile off—sounds carry well in this frigid stillness—

· ·

and after a bit this one rises and flaps off down the creek. The crows strike me as totems of the winter. The harsh caw gathers and articulates winter's iron sovereignty, while the bird's behavior on the swaying topmost branch of the tree stakes its claim to be fully at home in the cold. The feathers contain the hues that are coming back into the world with the light: greens and blues of the sky, glossy hints of violet and brown like the winter woods.

One poem that always comes to my mind in deep winter, by Robert Francis, an underappreciated New Englander, is called "Cold." It begins this way:

> Cold and the colors of cold: mineral, shell,
> And burning blue. The sky is on fire with blue,
> And the wind keeps ringing, ringing the fire bell.

The consonants seem exactly right, along with the images and the subtle music of the various rhymings and repetitions. The very sound of *mineral* helps invoke the feel of winter. The stanza slips into the memory readily, to file away somewhere and bring back out every winter. It characterizes our paradoxical awareness of cold, the sense that it is also somehow fiery, like blue flame. We remember chapped lips, windburn, and frostbite.

Francis continues:

> I am caught up into a chill as high
> As creaking glaciers and powder-plumed peaks
> And the absolutes of interstellar sky.
>
> Abstract, impersonal, metaphysical, pure,
> This dazzling art derides me. How should warm breath
> Dare to exist—exist, exult, endure?

The answer to that question, if there is one, lies in the imagination, in its exultant response to otherness and mystery. It's a delighted skier and skater in the killer cold, continuous with its strange environment when all the other parts of us would run away or hibernate or freeze.

Even animals feel this sometimes, I think. My basset hound races around in newly fallen snow like a drinker on a binge.

Francis has invoked the vast reaches of space, and he does the same for time before circling the poem back round to his own winter situation:

> *Hums in my ear the old Ur-father of freeze*
> *And burn, that pre-post-Christian Fellow before*
> *And after all myths and demonologies.*
>
> *Under the glaring and sardonic sun,*
> *Behind the icicles and double glass*
> *I huddle, hoard, hold out, hold on, hold on.*

Fifteen lines that sum up a lot of what we feel and think in winter. The poem's way of inhabiting the cold even alters the sense of some words: sardonic means more to me when it's attached to the winter sun, so blinding that you have to squint in its presence, especially when there's snow cover. It's as though being sardonic weren't some human affectation but a godlike perspective, smiling past our petty concerns. In the face of it we huddle, we hold out, we hoard food and hoard words, like these from Robert Francis, and we hope to hold on. A crow doesn't breathe these ragged clouds of breath.

Our forays into the cold are brief, and when they end and we are back behind the double glass, hoarding and holding out, we like to cook food that feels especially nourishing. Root vegetables are my January favorites. They are, after all, what our ancestors stored up and then lived on through long winters. When I was a child, I didn't understand how people had had to survive on the root vegetables they could store through the winter, so I thought "root cellar" was an odd name for that place where the jars of preserved fruits and vegetables were stored— as if you went down there to view the roots of trees and bushes from underneath.

That meant potatoes, of course, baked or mashed or hashed or souped or pancaked, and it meant onions and carrots. It also meant beets, parsnips, rutabagas, yams, turnips, and leeks. Do they owe their current neglect to a collective memory of long winters, when after a while it seemed you would almost prefer starvation to eating one more turnip or rutabaga?

In fact it's a kind of touching base with our own history to cook the things that people cooked for their survival in leaner and harder times. Not to mention that these vegetables, in their varieties of texture and taste, grow to be fascinating. A rutabaga has a kind of reassuring substantiality, like a waxy prehistoric lamp, still preserving a dull yellow light if you cut into it. A leek is like some magical object from the mountains of Wales, a sorcerer's wand. Every time I peel a turnip I marvel at the subtle winter colorations, a planet with two purplish poles, one of which may have a skinny root twisting up from it, and vast tracts of lightly mottled desert. Under the skin is a surprisingly intense whiteness, like the middle of a blizzard.

On a bleak January afternoon, with the light draining fast from the world, I put potatoes, parsnips, and turnips in the roasting pan, cutting them into shapes like fingers or thin wedges, then halved leeks, a quartered yellow onion, and a couple of artichokes, trimmed a little and cut into wedges with their chokes removed. Later, at the table, the big platter of roasted vegetables accompanies a pasta dish, sauced with a ragù that's been simmering on the stove all afternoon. The allure of this meal lies in going back and forth: the ragù has fused the flavors of meat, wine, onion, carrot, celery, tomatoes, milk, nutmeg, salt, and pepper, and it bathes the pasta with a fragrant sauce. The root vegetables, meanwhile, are hard to stop eating. You keep spearing another one, deciding if it's a turnip or a parsnip, and then try some leek to shift the flavor. A good rough red wine belongs in this picture, too.

One still, gray afternoon I walk down to the creek with my basset hound, Ivy, and find that the ice is solid enough to support us. So we take the unfamiliar path the water normally takes, me walking gingerly, the dog skidding and sniffing, between banks where roots stick out, snow-covered, and along a surface that supports us when it shouldn't.

No signs of life except for raccoon, rabbit, possum, and deer tracks, winter hieroglyphics, inscriptions on the cold.

I wrote a poem more than twenty years ago, part of a sequence called "Water Diary," about walking on the same frozen creek; if it joked about the miracle of walking on water, it also called up the wonder that could go with that:

> *for several days the temperature stood so low*
> *that at last we could walk on water   and we did*
> *the creek creaked softly talking to itself*
> *along the banks through harmless fissures*
> *we brushed some snow aside and peered down through*
> *but could see nothing not water not even ourselves*
> *there was a strange sensation of wrinkles and darkness*
> *we knocked on the stuff   for entrance   for luck*
> *and an old man spoke from a book*
> *"why can't mind and matter*
> *be more like wind and water?"*
> *we looked up   snow was wobbling toward us*
> *through miles and miles and miles of soundless air*

What strikes me now is the sameness of the experience. The frozen creek I walk on is always a different one, according to Heraclitus. But experience is repeating itself. There is incessant change in the seasons and the patterns of growth and decay, birth and death, and there's constancy, a simultaneity of forces and presences that contradicts simpler notions of time.

This sense of incessant change as a constant, revealed in the midst of deep cold, turns up in a Chinese poem I recently translated, Du Mu's "Bian River Freezing Over":

> *For a hundred miles*
> *along this river*
> *the ice is closing*

harness jades
and jasper pendants
clink at the ragged edge

under the ice
water moves
the same way life does

racing away to the east
all day all night
nobody noticing.

As I wrap my scarf tighter and head back home, one other poem comes to mind, William Stafford's:

ASK ME

Some time when the river is ice ask me
mistakes I have made. Ask me whether
what I have done is my life. Others
have come in their slow way into
my thought, and some have tried to help
or to hurt: ask me what difference
their strongest love or hate has made.

I will listen to what you say.
You and I can turn and look
at the silent river and wait. We know
the current is there, hidden; and there
are comings and goings from miles away
that hold the stillness exactly before us.
What the river says, that is what I say.

Why ask these questions when the river is ice? The icy silence both withholds and contains all the questions and answers, the way the crow and snowman contain all the other colors. The hidden currents, out of sight and out of reach, make the river what it is and keep it moving even when it is silent and frozen. It's like "nothing that is not there, and the nothing that is," as Wallace Stevens notes in "The Snow Man," the austerities of winter forcing us to the limits of what we can know and understand.

For just a moment today, standing on a frozen creek, I feel closer to some of the answers. All of them partake of the deep winter silence, a presence and an absence, a sensing of a wholeness that comes, as Stafford suggests, from the poise, the held stillness.

Soups fortify the spirit against winter. Some of these same vegetables I've been roasting can be used in a *passato,* the Italian soup that puts cooked vegetables through a food mill to achieve a delicate purée. The one I've made most recently had cut-up chunks of onion, tomato, turnip, carrot, celery, and potato, along with some kale and beet tops and parsley. This same soup will be reheated and turned into a *zuppa,* served over a big chunk of toasted stale bread that's been rubbed with cut garlic and olive oil. So endearing are these soups you serve over stale bread—the variations are endless—that I've actually bought or baked good Italian bread and deliberately let it get stale. *Ribbolita* (reboiled) seems to be the other name for this combination of reheated soup and bread that is so nourishing and filling; Italians will make a vegetable soup and eat it in a fairly liquid form one day, then reheat it the next day and pour it over the toasted bread so that it ends up having a very thick texture. Then they'll argue about which way is better.

You can connect to existence by means of poems and meditations in the cold, about the cold, and you can connect to it by considering more fully what you eat in deep winter and why you eat it. I cook Italian food because it is harmonized with the changing seasons and because I think it is delicious. "Maybe vegetables are the secret of life," my wife remarked as we relished our *zuppa / ribbolita* version of that vegetable *passato.* Maybe they are. Their mystery is partly chthonic, wrapped up with our feelings about the earth and its mothering qualities. I wrote a poem that played with that idea:

ROOT VEGETABLE GHAZAL

The moon swings off in a bag like a market lettuce
And everyone gropes home by ant glint & beetle shine.

In the Hotel Potato, in waxy marble ballrooms,
The waltzers rustle to the croon of enzymes.

In the curved corridors of the onion palace,
The smell of mushrooms seeps from unlit closets.

Our city is littered with wormseed & forcemeat;
Mummies are hymning in our turnip-purple church.

Radishes cruise through the revenant storage warehouse.
The bones of a goose mark the way to an amphitheater.

Now we can scale the carrot, our tapering campanile,
To watch the platoons of gravel, the water-bead parade.

We with our thorn-wrapped hearts & ivory foreheads!
We with our mineral tunnels awash in mole-glow!

An ultimate journey into the earth, to a vegetable and mineral world, is one we all face. We spend our lives clutching a return ticket, and so it's natural to try to find some comfort and even entertainment in the fact that we come from the earth and will go back to it. That's not always easy. Darkness and strangeness await us. But the heart and skull are also root vegetables; they team up here to sing a duet that celebrates autochthony, our deep-rootedness and earth-dependence.

THE RECIPES

These recipes are organized, like the book, according to the months, though they need not, obviously, be exclusive to them. Some are mentioned in the essays, others arrive by association. If they have a very specific origin, I mention it. If they are more generic, arrived at by comparing cookbooks and experimenting at home, I claim them as mine, though of course no recipe was ever completely original. By the same token, nothing is ever cooked quite the same way twice, and my instructions will tend to reflect my consciousness of alternate possibilities, portions, and ingredients.

If you do not cook from time to time, you may want to skip the recipe sections. I never quite know what to say to people who don't enjoy cooking. They shouldn't do it, obviously, if it is of no pleasure to them. But I think my own relish of it goes back to my days as a graduate student. I loved food but was too poor to eat out. Moreover, after a day of intensive study in the library, cooking was a creative outlet. The good associations went on to compound themselves, and I would still rather, after a hard day of just about any kind of work—teaching, editing, translating, committee meetings, yard or garden work—put on some music, roll up my sleeves, and start puttering around in the kitchen making dinner. This part of my book comes by its credentials honestly, then; it's a confession of a lifelong pleasure.

It will be clear from the majority of these recipes that I am an Italophile when I get into the kitchen. It's a cuisine of endless variety, and the way it is closely tied to the seasons and the best use of food in season is part of the reason for my affinity with it. But I love Chinese food, too, for instance, and in summer I am drawn to Vietnamese and Thai recipes for hot-weather food. Recently, my greatest interest has been in the way peasant cultures—Mediterranean, Asian, Latin American—look at food and cooking. A friend has laughed at me: look at this middle-class, white, late twentieth-century American trying to emulate distant peasants. It does sound a little like wealthy women trying to dress like Native Americans or Mexican village girls. But I don't do it for appearance. My reasoning is that peasant cultures, which usually exist within a larger, dominant economy, know how to make the best use of what's available to them. They can't afford extravagant ingredients or exotic sauces, so they figure out how to work little miracles with ordinary things. And they live, by and large, close to the seasons and the rhythms I wish to inhabit.

It happens, too, that their cuisines are much healthier than those of most Americans. That, coupled with the fact that we live in a world where we desperately need to learn how to make more sensible use of our available resources, should be enough to make "peasantists" of all of us. I see this as an alternative to vegetarianism, and I see it as a very humanistic response to food. What's shaped by the genius of a people, a long communal interaction, has a value of its own. In the kitchen, the results speak for themselves.

These recipe sections will make interesting reading, I hope, and will connect readily to the meditations, anecdotes, and poems of the respective chapters. But I see them primarily as practical—a small cookbook for those who want some nourishment for the body that will go along with the nourishment of the spirit that I claim comes from a sensible and reverent response to time and place.

Unless otherwise indicated, all the recipes given here are portions for four people.

JANUARY RECIPES

Three Winter Pasta Dishes

No need to limit these to winter, but they are a wonderful antidote to cold weather. You'll note that they have fat in various forms—cream, bacon, cheese, eggs— and that means they have been subject to careful scrutiny by the "food police." Our appetite for fat probably rises in the winter, for perfectly natural reasons, and it seems sensible to respond to it without ruining your health. My wife, Georgia, a doctor, keeps careful track of how healthy or unhealthy our food seems to be, and lots of good-natured negotiating goes on in our house. As the assessments in the medical magazines change, so do some of our habits. Butter was banished for a while; now it's back. Red wine has had a dramatic rise of prestige. And so it goes.

The thing about pasta is that you can use a small amount of intensely flavored sauce to make a dish that's fundamentally very healthy. Thus the trade-off involved in some of these ingredients comes from the modest amounts used relative to the portions produced.

●

Spaghetti with Ragù

This recipe is for a double portion, in other words,
enough for 2 meals feeding 4 people and saucing a
pound of pasta each time. It's sensible to make a double
portion, since it's almost as easy as making one. You can
then keep the extra in the refrigerator for up to a week,
or freeze it, or give it away: an elderly person, living
alone, for example, can get 3 or 4 great meals out of the
second half of this sauce.

——⟨∞⟩——

    1 ½ pounds meat—ground beef or a
        mixture of beef, veal, chicken, or pork;
        you can also use chicken livers
    1 medium-sized onion, chopped
    6 tablespoons good olive oil
    ½ cup chopped celery
    ½ cup chopped carrot
    salt
    2 cups white wine
    1 cup milk

$^1/_2$ teaspoon nutmeg

2 14-ounce cans tomatoes (or 1 large, 28- or
   35-ounce), chopped, and their juice

You'll need a good-sized pot or casserole for this. Fry the onions in the olive oil for a few minutes, then add the chopped celery and carrot. After 4 minutes, add the meat. (Italian cooks, rather than using ground meat, often mince the hunks of meat by hand, or snip it up with scissors, preferring the resulting flavor and texture.)

When the meat has browned a little, salt it and add the wine. Boil the wine down until you have something about the consistency of syrup. Add the milk and the nutmeg, and repeat that reducing process. Add the tomatoes, and when the sauce has come to a boil, turn the heat way down, cooking the sauce, uncovered, all afternoon (3 hours minimum). Your entire home will smell terrific, a fragrant bonus. If the sauce gets too thick, add some hot broth or a little more wine. At mealtime, combine the sauce with freshly cooked spaghetti or other pasta, mix, add grated cheese, and serve.

Dried wild mushrooms can be put in this sauce, too. They should be soaked in hot water while you're frying the vegetables and meat, then added when the tomatoes go in. Their soaking water, strained, can also be added to the sauce if it needs liquid.

●

Penne with Vodka

This is such a family favorite that if I ask "What do you want for dinner?" I'm as likely as not to be answered with "Pasta with vodka." It's an extremely easy dish, especially given the pleasure it produces, and it can be featured as the main dish or served as an accompaniment to something else. If you want to be a gourmet about it,

use Polish or Russian vodka. If you're tempted to reduce the cholesterol factor by substitutes for the cream
or the cheese (notice I have allowed you to substitute
for the butter), don't. Make something else instead.
Or point out to yourself that it's meatless, after all, and
that pasta is always very good for us. This dish serves 4
as a main course, 6 as a side dish.

1 pound penne or similar pasta
1 stick butter or good margarine
1 cup vodka with $\frac{1}{2}$ to 1 teaspoon of hot
   pepper flakes added
1 cup heavy cream
1 cup canned tomatoes—if you prefer
   a smoother texture, drain and
   purée them
salt
1 cup grated Parmesan cheese

Cook the pasta in boiling water to which
you have added salt. You can make the
sauce while it's cooking.

Melt the butter in a pan big enough to
hold all the cooked pasta. Add the vodka
with the pepper flakes. Simmer a couple
of minutes. Now add the tomatoes and
cream and simmer about 5 minutes. Add
salt, anywhere from 1 teaspoon to 1 tablespoon.

Drain the pasta and add it to the pan.
On low heat, add the Parmesan. Mix and
serve.

●

Charcoal Burner's Pasta
(Carbonara)

This dish is so well known that I hesitated a little before
including it. It's such an easy and delightful pasta dish
for a winter evening's supper, though, that I couldn't
leave it out. I used to cook a version of this clipped out
of an article on the soprano Eileen Farrell. I've long
since lost the clipping, but I've run into many versions,
all quite similar, over the years. I think she used green
pepper in the dish, cut up and added with the onions—
or red peppers, which would brighten it all up.

This, again, is a main dish for 4 and a side dish for 6.
The bacon, egg, onion, and grated Parmesan seem to be
the essential ingredients. This version adds another cheese.

———

1 pound spaghetti, fettuccine, or other pasta
¼ pound bacon, preferably sliced thick
1 large onion, chopped
salt and pepper
½ cup chopped parsley (or less)
½ cup cubed cheese, preferably fontina
4 eggs, beaten
grated Parmesan cheese

Cut the bacon into squares of about an inch. Fry gently in a skillet and
remove to drain on paper towels when crisp. To the cooking fat (or to
olive oil, if you prefer) add the onions and, after a couple of minutes,
salt and pepper and parsley. Now add the cubed cheese, give it all a stir,
and cook it covered over low heat for a few minutes while you cook the
pasta. Return the bacon to the sauce.

Drain the pasta and put it in a bowl, still hot. Add the eggs and toss, letting the hot pasta cook the eggs. Now add the sauce from the pan, toss again, and serve, with grated Parmesan cheese on the side.

●

Roasted Roots

This is very much a "for example" recipe, since, as I indicated in the January chapter, the variations are infinite and inviting, depending on what you find available and what you feel like in the way of seasoning.

———

2 potatoes, quartered lengthwise
2 large onions, cut into wedges of 6 or 8
3 turnips or 1 large rutabaga, cut into fingers
2 carrots, in fingers
2–3 parsnips, also in fingers
2 leeks, quartered
$\frac{1}{4}$–$\frac{1}{2}$ cup olive oil, depending on the
    amount of vegetables
2–3 cloves garlic
sherry
soy sauce
2–3 tablespoons parsley

Heat oven to 400°. In a shallow baking dish spread out the vegetables in a single layer. Mince or slice the garlic and mix with the olive oil. Add a dash of sherry and a dash of soy sauce. Toss the vegetables in this mixture. Cover with foil and bake for 30 minutes. Remove foil, toss vegetables again, and brown for another 15 minutes. Add chopped parsley, and serve. Good with pasta dishes. Also very good served with rice pilaf (recipe follows), couscous, or barley.

●

Rice Pilaf

This is a Greek recipe, I think, and I now finish it in a
rice cooker, one of the wisest purchases I ever made.
Serves 6.

—◌◌◌—

  2 cups rice
  1 stick butter or margarine
  1 quart any good broth or stock, heated
  salt and pepper

Melt the butter in a skillet and sauté the rice, stirring, until it's lightly
browned. If you are finishing it in a rice cooker, add the rice, broth,
salt, and pepper, cover, and turn on the cooker. If you are finishing it in
the skillet, add the broth, salt, and pepper, cover the pan with a cloth
and then a lid, and simmer (no stirring!) until the rice has absorbed all
the broth.

●

Gaetano's Cauliflower

Gaetano Prampolini, Italian scholar and translator,
would laugh to think of having this dish named after
him. But since he introduced me to it, he deserves some
credit. Gaetano grew up in Spello, near Assisi, in Umbria. The dinner he cooked on a winter evening for
Charles Wright, me, and his mother was occasioned by
his bringing his mother back home to vote in the Italian
elections. She was a remarkable woman who had been
one of Italy's first woman doctors, and she had also been
mayor of Spello for a time. Gaetano's meal was simple:

fresh fish and local sausages, grilled over embers, were the main course. Simplest of all, and most memorable, was the cauliflower, dressed with the family's own olive oil and served with the family's own red wine.

—✺—

1 head cauliflower
crusty peasant-style bread
olive oil, as fresh and green as you can get it
garlic cloves, ½–1 per guest
salt and pepper

Boil or steam the cauliflower for about 10 minutes, or microwave it, covered, with a little water, for about 5 minutes. Test it then: it should be tender but not mushy. Meanwhile, slice the bread thickly and toast it lightly. Serve each guest a slice of bread and half a clove of cut garlic, and pass the cauliflower and olive oil around. Each diner can rub the bread with the garlic, then add cauliflower, olive oil, and salt and pepper to taste. This makes a great first course—it seems unspectacular but turns out to be delicious.

●

Sal Anthony's Chicken

My notes say that this came from a New York restaurant called Sal Anthony's and that its Italian name is *pollo alla frasatura*. It's easy and delicious, another winter favorite that goes well with things like roasted vegetables and rice pilaf.

—✺—

1 3-pound frying chicken, cut up
¾ cup olive oil
6 cloves of garlic, roughly chopped
juice of 1 lemon

1 cup chicken broth
20 black olives (cured in brine, e.g.,
    calamata), halved and pitted
12 bottled peperoncini, stems cut off
salt and pepper

Pat the chicken dry and season it with salt and pepper. Heat the oil in a large skillet and fry the chicken, turning occasionally, until it is golden brown, about 10 minutes. Add the garlic and fry until it starts to turn brown. Drain the oil from the pan, and then add the lemon juice, chicken broth, olives, and peperoncini. Cook this mixture over moderate heat for about 15 minutes. The liquid should reduce to the texture of a thin syrup. Serve the chicken on a platter with the sauce poured over it.

Three Winter Soups—Two Italian, One French

I pause here to give credit to Marcella Hazan, my goddess and mentor (through her books, I hasten to add;

I've never met her in person) with respect to Italian cooking. Except for one recipe that instructs me to boil a cauliflower for 30 minutes (which reduces it to a soggy mess), I can't remember her ever failing me. She's a great cook and a great teacher of cooking principles.

The first of the soups given here is in fact adapted from Giuliano Bugialli (*The Fine Art of Italian Cooking*), and I have many other sources in friends, magazines, and experiments with food first sampled in restaurants. Marcella Hazan, though, is still the cook whose books I turn to most often, and with the most gratitude. My family teases me about my devotion to her.

●

Blended Vegetable Soup (*Passato di verdura*)

I've never liked the word *purée*. It makes me think of baby food. Nothing could be less like baby food, at least the commercial variety, than this astonishing soup. Even though the vegetables are put through a food mill, they somehow retain their distinctive flavors, and the result is an incredible chord of culinary harmony.

⟳

> 1 large handful of kale or savoy cabbage
> 1 large or 2 small potatoes
> 1 medium-sized onion
> 1 carrot
> 2 celery stalks
> other greens as available, e.g., spinach, Swiss
>   chard, beet tops, in the same kind of ratio
>   as the cabbage, large handfuls
> 1 14-ounce can tomatoes, drained

6 tablespoons olive oil

1 quart broth or stock—chicken or beef

1 cup white wine

parsley, up to 6 tablespoons

$\frac{1}{2}$ cup cooked rice

salt and pepper

crostini, i.e., squares of bread fried in olive oil

grated Parmesan cheese

The vegetables all need to be trimmed and peeled, as necessary, then cut up into chunks the size of a thumb or finger. Bugialli always has you soak them in cold water for 30 minutes. Then you put them straight into a pot, without drying, add the olive oil and 2 teaspoons of salt, cover, and cook for about 25 minutes over low heat. Put them through a food mill into a bowl or right back into the stock pot.

Heat the broth and wine in a pan or in the microwave, put the puréed vegetables back in their pot, and add the warm broth and wine mixture. Simmer this for about 20 minutes.

Just before serving, add the rice, taste for salt, and add freshly ground pepper. Serve in bowls with the crostini floating on top and sprinkled with Parmesan. The flavor of the vegetables should be wonderfully immediate.

This soup is perhaps even more terrific reheated the next day. In that instance, we serve it over large hunks of toasted Italian bread that have been rubbed with cut garlic. (I have never tried puréeing the vegetables in a food processor, but I think it would work. You'd have a more fibrous, thicker soup, but you could increase the liquid accordingly.)

●

Tuscan Bean and Red Cabbage Soup

This is a classic, and it can be made as a mostly vegetarian dish, as in the recipe that follows, or you can add meat, including sausage, ham, or pork. When I make it meatless, I might round out the meal with a grilled lamb chop or pork chop, then salad and dessert. With meat included and thick slices of crusty peasant bread on the side, it becomes a 1-dish meal. Serves 4 to 6.

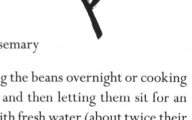

1 cup white beans (great northern or similar)
1 small red cabbage (about 1 pound) or ½ a
    bigger one, sliced and shredded
1 carrot
1 onion
1 celery stalk
4 garlic cloves
½ 14-ounce can tomatoes
1 quart stock or broth
salt and pepper
8 tablespoons olive oil
1 tablespoon chopped rosemary

You will have started by either soaking the beans overnight or cooking them in boiling water for 2 minutes and then letting them sit for an hour. Now drain them, cover them with fresh water (about twice their volume), and simmer for an hour and a half. Drain and set aside.

Mince the carrot, onion, celery, and 2 cloves of garlic (food processor is fine), and sauté them in 4 tablespoons of olive oil for 2 to 3 minutes. Now add the shredded cabbage and some salt and pepper. Cook this mixture, stirring frequently, for about 5 minutes. Add the tomatoes, cook a minute more, then add the broth. After about 20 minutes of simmering, covered, add the beans and give the whole thing another 20 minutes, covered, or, if you want to reduce it a little, uncovered.

Just before serving, heat the remaining 4 tablespoons of oil, flavoring the oil with 2 crushed cloves of garlic and the rosemary. Taste the soup for seasoning, serve in bowls, and add some of the rosemary- and garlic-flavored oil to each bowl.

If you've made enough to reheat, you can serve it the second day on toasted, garlic-rubbed bread for variety. You can also add fried sliced sausage if you have made it meatless and want some variety.

●

Winter Vegetable Soup of the Mountains (*La Potée à la montagnarde*)

This is from Roy Andries de Groot's 1973 classic, *The Auberge of the Flowering Hearth*. He writes about a mountain inn in the valley of the Grand Chartreuse and the two women who cooked there. His account of their year—I partly like the book because of its seasonal emphasis—and his collection of their recipes is a tribute to French country cooking. About this recipe he observes, "In virtually every mountain region of the world, there is at least one kind of 'rib-sticking' winter mixed-vegetable soup based on a rich meat bouillon. They are all completely flexible and can be made light or solid, according to the amount of potatoes involved. The ultimate test of solidarity is whether the ladle will stand up straight in the cooking pot!"

—◊◊◊—

> 1 small red cabbage, or ½ a larger one
> 1 onion, red or Spanish, minced
> 5 or 6 potatoes, sliced
> 1 parsnip, sliced
> 1 piece of bacon or other smoked
>   pork, ¾ pound or so, preferably
>   with rind on
> 6–8 tablespoons butter
> 2 quarts water

salt and pepper

1 cup or more red wine

croutons (optional)

Mince the cabbage and sauté it in 4 tablespoons of the butter in a large cooking pot. In a separate pan, sauté first the minced onion in about 2 tablespoons of butter, then, when you have added the onion to the cabbage, sauté the potato and parsnip slices in the rest of the butter. Add this mixture to the pot, then put the bacon piece on top, rind side up, add the water, salt, and pepper. Bring to a boil, then simmer, covered, for about 3 hours.

Remove the bacon piece and set it aside. Cool the soup a little and skim off the fat. Drain the vegetables, saving the broth, and purée them, either in a food mill or a food processor. Return the broth and vegetables to the pan and put the bacon back in.

Half an hour before serving, reheat the soup. Add the wine about 15 minutes before serving. If you want a thick soup, making it a sort of main course, the way we like to, then you need to make sure you use a lot of potatoes. You can also reduce the amount of broth. The recipe here makes a moderately thick soup if the potatoes are medium-sized to small.

De Groot says that the French way of serving the bacon is to put it on a hot platter, bring it to the table, and slice it, putting slices in each soup bowl before ladling in the soup. The pork you use can be anything you want, from hog jowls to pig's feet to ham, and you may want to add croutons, as he suggests, when you serve the soup.

FEBRUARY

All My Other Lives

* * * *

Last night I fell on the ice in my own driveway, landing heavily on my arm, which is sore and tender today. This morning I broke the coffee-pot. I feel a heaviness settling into me that doesn't seem to be alleviated by majestic icicles or the distant sound of a woodpecker, hammering in the woods.

It must be February.

I doubt that my response to the month, a spreading moroseness, a ponderous anger and obstinacy, is everyone's. My gloom is personal and comes partly from particular losses that mark the month when it swings round again: my wife ten years ago, her father nine years ago, and my mother last year.

It seems to me I've been staring out the window for about an hour. A slight thaw is in progress, so an erratic spattering of drops, too com-plicated to form a pleasant rhythm, falls from the roof onto the stones by the screened porch. There's a downy woodpecker working at the suet cage I've hung from the spruce tree outside my window.

My love of birds comes from my mother. She fed them, identified them, studied them. Her joy in them never diminished, over all her eighty-eight years. Some of my earliest memories involve her pointing out birds and then telling me their names. I still associate the thrill of sighting the creature, a pulse and flash of quick nervous life, and connecting a marvelous name to it: brown thrasher, rose-breasted grosbeak, Baltimore oriole. Once more a poem by Robert Francis comes to mind:

THE SEED EATERS

The seed eaters, the vegetarian birds,
Redpolls, grosbeaks, crossbills, finches, siskins,
Fly south to winter in our north, so making
A sort of Florida of our best blizzards.

Weed seeds and seeds of pinecones are their pillage,
Alder and birch catkins, such vegetable
Odds and ends as the winged keys of maple
As well as roadside sumac, red-plush-seeded.

Hi! With a bounce in snowflake flocks come juncos
As if a hand had flipped them and tree sparrows,
Now nip and tuck and playing tag, now squatting
All weatherproofed and feather-fluffed on snow.

Hard fare, full feast, I'll say, deep cold, high spirits.
Here's Christmas to Candlemas on a bunting's budget.
From this old seed eater with his beans, his soybeans,
Cracked corn, cracked wheat, peanuts and split peas, hail!

There was something birdlike about my mother. When Alzheimer's had destroyed her ability to name and distinguish the birds, she still enjoyed watching them. My father kept adding bird feeders, and the local seedeaters—chickadees, juncos, purple finches, goldfinches, occasionally a redpoll or a siskin—made their back porch a crowded convocation.

I know her death was a mercy and her life long and complete, but I want her back. I want her to share these woodpeckers with me.

Grief is labyrinthine. It weaves itself into everything else so that you encounter it everywhere you go, a soreness and a heaviness. Grief's geography is bleak, a tundra or a steppe. It's a river that gradually cuts a deep gorge, altering the inner landscape permanently.

Like a woodpecker worrying at a tree trunk, I'm drilling back to the day of my mother's death, just one year ago. My wife has called in the morning to alert us that she is "actively dying," a phrase doctors routinely use without irony. My father and I spend the day taking turns sitting by her bed—there is only room for one of us at a time—in the nursing home.

Unconscious, her strength spent from two hip operations, from Alzheimer's and osteoporosis, from eighty-eight years of staying alive, she is breathing more and more shallowly as her life and strength ebb away. We don't have her hooked up to any contraptions or measuring devices, unnecessarily prolonging her life. We can see that "actively dying" means a steady decline in vital signs. It is at least going to be a peaceful end.

The hours crawl by, mixing certainty and uncertainty. It takes us a lifetime to die. Then it just takes a winter day. Here we all are, at a great mysterious border, we pawky living creatures on one side, ashamed and humiliated, and some other reality, unknown to us, on the other.

Sitting by my mother's side, wishing she could hear me, I start talking quietly. Just a few phrases of affection and consolation. I recall a poem I wrote about her, for her, fairly recently:

MARY YOUNG AT EIGHTY-EIGHT

My mother, shrunken like an old sweet apple
out of a half-forgotten orchard,
her mind as hollow as an apple seed,
greets me now, her middle child,
without the least idea of who I am.

Her eyes glitter. Nothing behind them.

Or has she simply journeyed to a prairie?
No houses, no towns, no roads—clear sky
a few clouds riding aimlessly across it,
and a bird or two, meadowlarks probably,
tossing around in its depths.

I look at my hands, moved and bored. I hold my breath; I try breathing in unison with her, a slow, subsiding rasp.

Then it is over. The border shifts away, the living rearrange themselves. A compassionate glance from the local accountant as he crosses the lobby and climbs the stairs. Hugs and pats. People are kindly, hushed, concerned. Arrangements begin. The tundra stretches ahead.

Part of me assents very readily. A life has ended gracefully. An institution neglected in our time—the deathbed vigil—has shown me its human value. Part of me resists, stubborn and resentful. My concern shifts to my father. I know already how hard it is to lose a mate. All through the months ahead, his loss will implode inside him, again and again. He will wake in the night, thinking she is next to him in the bed, and then will come the shattering recollection of her absence.

Surviving will be precarious, tricky. Depression will fall and fall, like rain and sleet and snow. Like tears. The river will form and begin to carve its gorge.

⌒

Around here the streams and rivers flow north, into Lake Erie. They make the one significant variation in our glacier-flattened landscape by eroding the shale and creating dramatic valleys with steep cliffs and thickly wooded bottomland.

Today I watch the swollen Vermilion River, a churning commotion of icy gray water, as I walk around the huge river bend called Mill Hollow. The shale cliffs are hung everywhere with huge icicles, frozen seepings from the myriad springs they harbor. At another time these icicles, some of them larger than people, might be resplendent to contemplate, but today the wind is so knifelike, the whole scene, with its rock-hard duck ponds and coldly boiling river, so perverse and uninviting, that it reminds me how much such features form crucial parts of Dante's deepest hell. I came here hoping to cheer myself up, but miscalculated the effect of that cold river, this cutting wind.

Eating and grief have a relationship that we don't always glimpse. I remember a back, upstairs room in my grandmother's house—my mother's mother—that had an uncommon fragrance: colder than the rest of the house all winter, curtainless and well-lit, it was full of drying corn, kernels spread out all over the floor on what must have been sheets of plywood. This air-dried corn could be rehydrated and then creamed or stewed for corn puddings, succotash, or hominy. It could, of course, be ground into meal and flour for corn bread, cornmeal mush, and corn pancakes. Some people had to grind their corn at home if they were far from any settlement, but it's a hard task, and if you had the option you would take it to a miller, who would ask you how coarse or fine you wanted it.

This, after all, was another way people got through the long winters, along with their animals. The hogs and horses and cows and chickens lived partly on ears of field corn, dried first in shocks and then stored in cribs. The humans ate the kernels from ears of sweet corn, put up in jars or dried. You could dry the corn on the ear and shuck it later, or you could shuck it first and then spread the kernels out for drying.

Corn in the Western Hemisphere helped foster alternatives to Old

World culture, first with the American Indians, from as far north as there's a decent growing season to the tip of South America, and then among the European settlers. Corn cultures, we're told, tend to be more fluid, less hierarchic. Controlling wheat production and distribution was an important feature of feudalism. Corn is more adaptable. As John Thorne reminds us, raising corn doesn't even require cultivated fields. You can plant it around and among stumps, on land you're still in the process of clearing.

Corn is, after all, the major New World grain. One of the best ears of corn I ever tasted was sold as a snack on the little train from Cuzco to the foot of Machu Picchu. It was white, and the kernels were extraordinarily plump, sweet, and juicy. But my winter cooking with corn tends to follow an Old World precedent, using the corn flour Italians call polenta.

The Italians didn't know the trick of New World corn users: you have to treat the grain with lime or with some kind of sodium source to achieve the right nutritional balance. A handful of ashes in the pot— a sprinkle of grief?—wasn't just superstition or flavoring for North and South American Indians, it was essential nutrition. Thus, Italian peasants who depended too much on maize (or *granoturco,* as they called it, lumping anything foreign under the general heading of "Turkish") suffered pellagra, while the tortilla makers of Mexico and the hoecake makers of North America escaped it, partly by using the ash trick and partly by growing corn and beans together, the two plants providing each other with necessary soil nutrients and their enzymes complementing each other to fill human nutritional needs.

Still, polenta returns to us now, in fancy restaurants and, increasingly, in North American home cooking, to marry back into the culture that thrived on things like johnnycake (for *journey cake?* Or *Shawnee cake?*), Indian pudding, corn pone, spider cake, and, for that matter, moonshine whiskey.

I once served polenta, thinking I was producing a real treat—I cook it enthusiastically and with confidence—to Charles Simic, a poet and good friend who was visiting our college. He took one look and exclaimed: "Polenta! I swore I'd never eat it again!" Simic was born in

Yugoslavia and lived through the Second World War there before im-
migrating to the United States. Polenta was what kept his family from
starving when they had nothing else to eat. The incident drove home

the lesson of cultural and historical relativity. This delicacy, which
greatly interests us now, is of course poor people's food, part of a starvation diet in some times and places.

To balance the Simic recollection, I'll add that I remember eating
polenta with two other poets, Charles Wright and Mark Strand, in an
ancient villa they and their families had rented in Italy one summer.
One of the best dishes at a festive evening meal was a platter of cold polenta, sliced in the traditional Italian way with a thread. We had it with
grilled squab and a special bottle of red wine Mark had brought along.
It felt as though Petrarch might walk into the room at any moment.

Polenta, or cornmeal mush if you prefer, is solid and filling. Because
its taste is fairly neutral, it combines admirably with lots of other
foods. The advent of the microwave has enormously simplified the process of preparing it, and I often make a batch at lunchtime, if I'm home,
or before I leave in the morning, set it to chill, and then reheat it by
grilling or frying it for the evening meal. It takes to highly flavored
foods as accompaniment, and the Italians like it with meat sauces, with
salted fish, cod or herring, with cooked greens, and with Gorgonzola.
It can certainly be treated as a pasta substitute, and one of the tastiest
preparations has you alternating layers of polenta with meat sauce and
grated cheese to bake like a lasagna.

My research puzzles the family sometimes. When I made a corn
bread in an iron skillet on top of the stove and defended its burned bottom by suggesting that that was exactly how it would have been for the
pioneers, Tom, our eleven year old, quite logically asked why, when we
had a modern kitchen and good ways of preparing things, we would
want to duplicate something primitive. He had a point. It's hard to explain how food nostalgia works, how the curiosity about other times,
as well as other cultures, can absorb a cook's interest. But his question
helped me realize that deeper connection between eating and grief.
My imagination began to move from the recent grief for my mother—
I had probably been trying in a way to connect with her as a cook, and

with her family traditions, through my corn bread and Indian pudding—to an older and even more painful loss: my wife's death from
cancer ten years ago this same month.

The last months of Chloe's life vie with the empty months that followed for the title of most appalling. Both before and after her death, I
often asked myself whether, and how, I could go on. Through December of 1984 and January of 1985, into February, the month of her
death, she declined steadily from a combination of cancer's progress
and the toll that chemotherapy exacts. When her heart stopped during
a transfusion for anemia, they managed to start it again, but she never
recovered consciousness. Her death soon after was a release from her
quiet, patient suffering and therefore, in one way, a relief. But it left
me bereft and adrift in the middle of winter, and I know now, looking
back, what perilous shape I was in for many months.

My reason for existing had been focused on her care. Now I felt use-
less. I wrestled day and night, numbly, with the silent, muscular angel of depression. I quarreled mildly with friends and colleagues and
students, living in a haze of grief and loss, feeling like a sort of sham-
bling monster. I showed up late for appointments and rehearsals, or
forgot them altogether. At home alone, I played music, my one real so-
lace sometimes—Sibelius, Monteverdi—and drank too much. I was
grimly fixated on just getting through this time somehow. I taught my
classes and served on my committees. I kept repeating to myself what
the characters in Chekhov say when they experience irreparable loss:
"We must work!"

No one could comfort me; nothing could reach me or touch me.
And only gradually, as the world turned slowly into spring and summer, did I regain a sensible hold on life. It is a rhythm I relive every February. This tenth time around, I at least know what I am going through,
but there are moments when the grief is as fresh and raw as ever.

During her last month of life, Chloe had practically no appetite. I
could see that that was part of the reason for her decline, and I was des-

perate to find things she would eat. We had already been through the brown rice and macrobiotic regimen some cancer patients explore, without success. The food seemed both foreign and uninteresting to her. Then I suddenly discovered, as January groaned toward February, that what appealed to Chloe most was the bland, middle-class, middle-American food that her mother had cooked when she was growing up. Comfort food, we sometimes call it, comforting *because* it is bland. When she expressed a desire for things like tuna-noodle casserole, and more to the point, when she managed to eat them, I dutifully began ferreting out such recipes and making them.

I was filled with a terrible foreboding, one I had lived with for a year and a half, since the cancer was first diagnosed as having metastasized, but I could stave it off a little if I could find something that helped revive Chloe's fading appetite. Never mind if it was made with packaged onion soup or topped with crumbled Cornflakes and Velveeta cheese!

I realize now, as I try to connect with my mother by thinking about what she cooked as a young wife and what she ate as a young girl, that Chloe was doing the same thing. Her mother had died of cancer almost seventeen years earlier. It had happened when we were living in England, so that she never got home to say good-bye or take her leave at a funeral. That distance from the death compounded her grief in the years that followed, and I see now that she was forming a bond, in that last month of her life, with her own mother, through her dying and through her memory of her childhood's kitchen and the dishes it produced.

Food's meanings run deep in our lives, and the reasons we have for eating what we eat can be profound and complicated. If you've ever had food poisoning, your body will remember it ever afterward, and you will be apt to refuse the food permanently. If you associate certain foods with certain pleasures and reassurances, you will seek them out when you are feeling especially needy. One man's madeleine is another man's poison? Our eating is a conversation with our own history and thus, inevitably, with those we have lost, our dead.

A dialogue with the dead is not a bad thing, however. It's essential to our health, mental and physical, and if the dead can only answer back obliquely, through things like recipes and memories, we listen all the harder. We sit down at their table.

The temperature plunges and the month grows colder and colder. "The world's whole sap is sunk," as Donne says. Even broad daylight does nothing to warm the world up, as though the sun has lost its heating function and only retained, grotesquely, its ability to light a cold, raw world. The wind across the lake out of Canada, the one we sometimes call the Siberian Express, blows steadily, day after day, driving life before it into burrows and nests and dens. Existence seems to grow more and more precarious as we move toward the middle of the month and the full moon that the Indians called Hunger Moon.

I'm still stalled here, "behind the icicles and double glass." It seems to me I've been staring out at this frozen landscape much of the month. The birds at the feeder are about the only thing that seems to distract me. Again I call to mind a cherished poem by Robert Francis, this one about waxwings in February, feeding on the berries of a bush like the one that borders my lot. I've seen them there, treating the bush like their personal restaurant:

WAXWINGS

Four Tao philosophers as cedar waxwings
chat on a February berrybush
in sun, and I am one.

Such merriment and such sobriety—
the small wild fruit on the tall stalk—
was this not always my true style?

Above an elegance of snow, beneath
a silk-blue sky a brotherhood of four
birds. Can you mistake us?

To sun, to feast, and to converse
and all together—for this I have abandoned
all my other lives.

35

The kind of reincarnation Francis is imagining would certainly solve
some problems, I think to myself.

And now comes a most potent memory. In the last week of Chloe's
life there was a blizzard that lasted most of the afternoon. She was reading and resting in the living room, and called out to me to come see
something. There, just visible in the swirling snow, about twenty feet
from our large windows, a hawk was killing and eating a mourning
dove.

I wrote a poem about this event, and it concluded the second part of
a long meditation on process and motion as integral parts of existence
and perception:

And yesterday a red-tailed hawk
killed and ate a mourning dove
in the middle of a snowstorm
in our own backyard. For five minutes
that made a violent, bobbing center
for everything else in sight:
the swirl of flakes, the pine boughs humped with snow,
the smaller birds who fled,
our curious eyes and breath.
And then the center shifted.

Any still point we choose
is relative to observation;
the planet rolled ahead, dragging
its dead and gorgeous moon,
great storms shot up on the sun,
whole galaxies stood by and gleamed
and maybe an owl in a hollow tree

two hundred yards away from us
swiveled his head and blinked
hearing the little death.
The hawk rose up, his tail a flare of rust,
and a sprinkle of torn feathers
began to blow across the snow
till we could see no more.

I will also, of course, forever associate the event with Chloe's illness and death. There, just two days before she herself was taken away, was a vivid illustration of how nature works and why death and life are in-terpenetrating realities.

Before any of the three February losses I have mentioned, more than twenty years ago, I was trying to work out my sense of the strangeness of February. In a poem composed in 1971, sketching impressionisti-cally, I picked as an image the snowplow that comes at you, lights on, behind the foaming cascade of snow it is making. An Ohio snapshot, or a haiku.

FEBRUARY

1

The plow comes on.
Two lights inside a huge
white wave of snow.

The closing stanza of that same poem now gives me shivers because of the way it foretells my Februaries of the future:

5

Double sunlight. A child
trots in a circle in the snow.
One cardinal, bright as a wound,
sails from a spruce to a bush.

> *Even when happiness*
> *rises through your body*
> *terrible sorrows*
> *are an inch from either cheek.*
> *Can you go on? Listen:*
> *this book the earth*
> *is turning a page.*

If my future losses are predicted there, there is also a suggestion of how to get through February's evils. Happiness rises in the body as sap does in the trees. Life asserts itself. That does not erase sorrows that are always close at hand, but it helps counterbalance them. The cardinal is like a wound, but it's also a bit of life, preparing to mate and nest.

On an early morning past the middle of the month, I step outside, over creaking snow, into a world that is a little lighter at this time each day. As I glance toward the creek, a large owl takes off from the wild cherry tree near the back of my yard and flies noiselessly off through the pines. My heart soars with the bird—owls are rare enough that it always thrills me to glimpse one and be able to watch it a moment in flight. The owl's flight is utterly silent, and that is what makes it so ghostly to us and so deadly to its prey.

In our imaginations the owl has stood for wisdom and for death. Why do I take it now for a good omen? Maybe *because* it represents death and night, and in a form we can admire and partly understand. We cannot reverse the engines of mortality we live among, so we must try to make imaginative use of them, turning them into stories and images we can live with. I'll take the owl to stand for my trying to acquiesce in what I cannot alter.

We all listen closely. The earth is a text we often read with our eyes. But sometimes we make do with what we hear, the sound of a giant page, the almost imperceptible whisper of the owl's wing in the sly light, turning, turning a page, the movement on to the next part of the story of the year.

FEBRUARY RECIPES

I decided I had invented the perfect February meal one
night when I served grilled game hen, fried polenta
squares, and broccoli rabe. The combination of flavors,
matched with a bottle of zinfandel, would be good in
any month, but its February appeal must partly have
been based on the warming and filling character of the
corn dish and the greens, along with the promise of
summer in the grilled food. I do my winter grilling in
the fireplace, on a simple contraption called a Tuscan
grill. There are lots of electric indoor grills on the market now, too, so that devotees of grilling can pursue
their enthusiasm all year long. For me, though, the cast-
iron grill above the embers remains the best possible
way to cook chicken, game hen, steak, or chops. The
wood fire imparts a special flavor, and the activity of
building and tending the fire gives you a bonus for the
rest of a winter evening.

Basic Polenta

I make this in the microwave, which saves the time and energy of stirring the pot. It might also work in a regular oven. My recipe is adapted from Barbara Kafka's *The Microwave Gourmet,* which would be worth having just for its adaptations of polenta and risotto to this simpler and almost foolproof method of preparation. (I'm aware of the slight irony of my fixing polenta in a microwave while puttering with a wood fire to do grilling. We all make our own choices about which corners we want to cut and which we want to restore.) The recipe below serves 4, but it makes some sense to double it, since leftover polenta is so tasty and versatile.

1 cup cornmeal
3 cups water
2 teaspoons salt
freshly ground pepper
3 tablespoons butter
grated cheese (optional)

Stir the water and cornmeal together and add the salt. Put the dish uncovered in the microwave for 6 minutes, stir, and cook for 6 more minutes. Add butter (up to 3 tablespoons) or margarine or olive oil. If you wish you can add grated cheese. This is also the time to add chopped anchovies or any other flavoring agent. Pour the mixture into a greased loaf pan and let it chill. Later you can slice it and grill or fry the slices.

My ratio of 3 to 1 yields an even more solid polenta than what Barbara Kafka recommends for a "firmer" polenta. I like something really solid for reheating. Be advised that you can serve polenta straight from the dish, like a porridge, and that the chilling stage is more typically used in summer or for the leftover portion. I just like the way it firms up when it chills and then presents itself for slicing, so I almost always make it that way.

●

Polenta with Ragù

Using the ragù recipe from the January section, you can create a fine combination in one of two ways. Either serve the polenta with ragù sauce on top, or make this concoction that is very much loved in Italy, a sort of lasagna treatment.

———

1 "loaf" polenta (see above)
1 ½ cups ragù (see p. 12; this is ½ of that double recipe)
1 ½ cups grated cheese (Parmesan or fontina)

The polenta can be porridge-style, though I prefer thin slices. Alternate layers of polenta, ragù, and cheese until you have filled your baking dish. Some recipes include a béchamel sauce as the other layering agent, and that is certainly good but not, in my view, indispensable. Bake in a 400° oven for 15 to 20 minutes.

Pork Tasting like Game

This delicious concoction is from Marcella Hazan, who says it reminds her "of the great game and polenta feasts we used to have on the Lago di Garda when I was in my teens." That's good enough for me. I associate that lake with Catullus, Tennyson, Ezra Pound, Charles Wright, and a wonderful lunch involving a trout.

Certainly the method of cooking with wild mushrooms, bay leaves, and juniper berries turns pork into something that reminds Italians of boar, a dish they greatly love. My point here is how well its flavor marries with the polenta.

1 ounce dried wild mushrooms

1 small onion

6 tablespoons olive oil

1 ½ pounds cubed pork (what butchers call "city chicken" works well)

½ cup white wine

3 tablespoons vinegar

3 anchovy fillets, chopped

2 bay leaves

2 dozen juniper berries, crushed

salt and pepper

You'll have soaked the mushrooms in hot water for half an hour, and you can save and filter their soaking water for inclusion in the sauce.

In a casserole, warm the olive oil and sauté the onion for a few minutes. Add the pork and brown on all sides. Add the wine and vinegar and boil them down a little. Now add the mushrooms, their liquid, the anchovies, and the bay leaves and juniper berries. Add salt and freshly ground pepper, turn the heat down, cover the casserole, and let the dish simmer for an hour and a half.

Just before serving, boil the sauce down a little, to reduce it to the consistency you like. If there's fat, you can skim it at this time. At the table, you can serve this on top of a platter of hot polenta, or on the side, letting each guest serve the meat sauce next to, or on top of, a helping of polenta.

●

Polenta with Sausages and Tomatoes

Again, the marriage of pork and polenta is a delightful one. This uses tomatoes to complete the picture. And, once more, one excellent version of this is to be found —where else?—in Marcella Hazan's first volume of *The Classic Italian Cook Book.* (The first was from volume 2.)

—◦◦◦—

1 carrot
1 celery stalk
1 small onion
1 thick slice bacon, or 2 thin slices
3–4 tablespoons olive oil or butter
1 pound Italian sausage
1 14-ounce can tomatoes

I peel, cut up, and put in the food processor the carrot, celery, onion, and bacon. After chopping it fine, I cook it in the olive oil or butter for 4 minutes. Then I add the sausage, cut into 1-inch chunks, and cook that for about 8 minutes. Finally, I add the tomatoes and cook the whole lot at a simmer for at least half an hour.

The same serving suggestions apply as above: you can pour everything over a platter of polenta and bring it to the table, or you can serve them separately.

All these polenta and meat sauce dishes are robust, healthy winter food, prime examples of what I call "peasantism." They can be served with assertive, fruity red wines like Barolo, Rosso di Montalcino, zinfandel, and Rhône reds like Hermitage, Gigondas, and Châteauneuf-du-Pape.

The pork dishes would also sit well with a big white wine—one of those blockbuster California chardonnays with lots of oak and pineapple overtones. In my opinion those wines do better with savory foods than they do with cream sauces or dishes that have sweet elements.

●

Polenta with Rapini or Other Greens

You could make this dish with spinach or turnip tops, and probably with kale or collard greens, but we prefer the slightly bitter, slightly buttery flavor of the greens that Italians are able to grow in February, variously called "rapini," "rape," and "broccoli rabe." It seems to come in 1-pound bunches in the store, and its cost seems to fluctuate during the winter, so the thing to do is watch for it and check to see if the price is down a little. Even if it isn't, you may end up buying, for while rapini is perhaps an acquired taste, it doesn't take long to be addictive.

If I have vegetarians at my table, as is often the case (my daughter and stepdaughter), or vegetableholics (which might describe my wife), I will serve this as an alternative to the meat sauces given above, often doubling the recipe.

1 bunch (about 1 pound) broccoli rabe
3 cloves garlic, smashed and peeled
5 tablespoons olive oil
salt and pepper
lemon juice (optional)

Wash the greens well. (You may need to discard some tough stem ends and some wilted leaves.) Cook them for 5 minutes in a pot of boiling salted water. Drain them and, when cool, chop them into 1-inch lengths. In the warmed olive oil, gently sauté the 3 garlic cloves until they are well cooked but not burned. Remove them, turn up the heat, and add the greens (they do not need to be dry). Stir and cook in the oil for 5 minutes. Season with salt and pepper and, if you like it, some lemon juice. Some cooks add a few tablespoons of butter at this point, just before serving.

●

Grilled Game Hens

Thaw and split 2 game hens (this is for 4 people; half a hen per person). Marinate them (1 to 4 hours) in a mixture of olive oil, lemon juice, salt, pepper, and rosemary. Over embers in a fireplace, if you have a fireplace grill, or using an electric grill or oven broiler, cook for about 35 minutes, turning occasionally. Serve with sliced, fried polenta and broccoli rabe. The polenta slices don't need much attention. I sometimes fry them lightly in the same olive oil I'll use to cook the greens (i.e., very garlicky) and then keep them warm on the side. They can also be quickly heated in a broiler, but I wouldn't recommend putting them on the fireplace grill; they are a little too wobbly for that kind of treatment.

●

Other Polenta Uses

I'll conclude this cornmeal/polenta riff by mentioning that the fried or broiled polenta slices are of course good with sweet things. You could have them with maple syrup, a February product, or with fruit sauces like raspberry or strawberry.

Polenta goes well with salty fish, like dishes made from dried cod and herring. As I've mentioned, you can stir things you like right in after you have cooked it and before you set it, including olives, anchovies, herbs, and nuts.

The slices make an excellent appetizer, too, usually grilled and then spread with something like Gorgonzola cheese, and maybe chopped toasted walnuts.

Most of the uses I've described are Italian, but they are quite close to what Americans have long done with sliced cornmeal mush—recognizing how well it goes with pork sausages, with tomatoes, with cheese, with syrup, and with chicken. To me, corn bread and fried chicken are as classic a combination (maybe with some fresh cooked black-eyed peas thrown in) as polenta and grilled chicken, and I think the way African Americans have traditionally cooked greens with smoked pork and then eaten them with corn bread—soul food—is part of the same set of discoveries.

My recipes are by way of polenta because that's the route by which I discovered, or rediscovered, the virtue of cooked corn, food of my own ancestors. The main point is that this winter food, a basic porridge or pudding made from ground corn, is about as versatile as one can imagine. I haven't even mentioned the tortilla or the tamale!

●

Provençal Daube

This is a dish I've been making in cold weather for a long time. I've lost my source recipe, Elizabeth David's *French Provincial Cooking,* but not my sense of gratitude to that book. This is a recipe that can be done in a microwave (Barbara Kafka has a version in *The Microwave Gourmet*), but then you'd miss out on the bonus of having your whole house filled with this gratifying smell for an entire winter afternoon. Make it on a Sunday and enjoy the anticipation it creates. Elizabeth David quotes a French writer who says, "Oh, the daubes of my childhood!" referring to the smell of the stews simmering most of the day on the stove. I hope my own children say that someday!

—◈◈◈—

3 tablespoons olive oil
4 diced carrots
1 diced onion (large or medium)
6 cloves garlic, smashed and peeled

some orange zest

1 bay leaf

3 pounds beef, rump or chuck, sliced
    in pieces $\frac{1}{2}$-inch thick and about
    the size and shape of playing cards

2 tablespoons salt

1 cup red wine

1 cup stock—chicken or beef,
    canned or homemade

pieces of bacon and/or bacon rind

$\frac{1}{4}$ cup brandy or cognac

Put the ingredients into a 2-quart casserole in the order listed: first the olive oil, then the vegetables and seasonings, then the meat, the salt, and the liquids. You can save some of the smashed garlic to tuck around among the meat pieces, which is what you'll also do with the bacon and bacon rind. I used 2 slices of bacon and a 10-inch by 5-inch piece of bacon rind, cut into smaller sections, the last time I made this. Heat the wine and pour it over the whole thing, then the stock, then add the brandy. Some people flame the wine and the brandy; it's optional.

Bring the liquid in the casserole to a boil, then take it off the heat, cover it with both a sheet of aluminum foil and a lid, and set it over a very low fire to cook for 3 to 4 hours. You could also put it in a very low oven. A daube is always better cooled and reheated, or "mellowed." If you have time, then, cool it the same day for reheating before serving or make it the day before and plan to serve it the next day. The problem with this, of course, is that if you've been smelling it all afternoon, you'll want to dine on it come supper time.

Daube is good served with cooked noodles, rice, potatoes, and, yes, polenta. You can also serve it over toasted bread or fried croutons. The sauce is so rich and savory that you want something to soak it up.

Sometimes, just before serving, French cooks add a little more seasoning in the form of a *persillade,* a little mixture of chopped garlic, parsley, and anchovies, maybe some capers. Whether you do this is up to you. It might depend on the subtlety or coarseness of the red wine you are serving. If your daube is well seasoned and your wine is restrained, a Beaujolais or a Bordeaux, you may not need it. On the other hand, it really makes your palate sit up and take notice, and it goes well with Rhône reds, zinfandels, and big Italian red wines like Barolo or Brunello.

We could never quite remember the name for *persillade,* so we'd say when the time to serve it came close, "Do you think this needs a *persiflage?*" I don't suppose a Frenchman would find that funny.

MARCH

The Farmer in Deep Thought

· · · ·

The day is gray and somewhere between chilly and mild. The sun is around somewhere, but not out, and it's hard to tell whether it's morning or afternoon. The world feels stripped and inert, featureless. Walking by myself, I come to the edge of an empty field. It's not clear whether it's a vacant lot, a patch of untilled ground, or a stretch by the side of the road.

This field is not empty. It contains, on this windy and nondescript March day, the following things: many varieties of brown weeds, some purplish berry canes, a few leafless bushes like sumac, and some young saplings, like buckthorn; some insects and other small creatures, field mice and shrews, birds coming and going, small lives preserving and perpetuating life; the hidden energy, masked and stored, that will bring new growth and vitality back into the world as the season advances. And for me, at least, as I step out into it, it harbors the spirit of William Carlos Williams.

The weeds are part of our cultural baggage, both literally and figuratively. Most of them arrived with settlers from the Old World, either as stowaways or because someone thought them useful for flavorings or medicines. Weeds need cleared land, which we give them, for their aggressive colonizing, which reflects ours.

The way weeds get their seeds distributed is a fascinating study in ingenuity and determination, part of the story of their vitality and universality. There are the burrs of burdock and the little toothed seeds, beggar ticks that animals pick up in their coats (and clothes) as they pass by. Their folk names range from the poetic, "Spanish needles," to the pithily descriptive, "sticktights."

The single most impressive flower head that has survived the winter in this weedy field is the teasel. It is a thorny, bristly contraption shaped like a small bomb and ornamented by four flaring spikes. They surround the bristled cone like elaborate handles. Seeds are lodged behind the bristles, and the wind must shake them out—I don't think birds can get into them to feed—but even at the far end of winter the heads and seeds are remarkably intact, looking indestructible. I know that the plant's name comes from its usefulness to weavers. Apparently you can use the flower heads like brushes, to card or tease wool.

The cattails that line the edge of the pond or the wet ditches by the side of the road have tops that look like corn dogs in the fall, when they are new. By spring they are like pieces of ragged old upholstered furniture, losing their stuffing. Sometimes the brown case has disappeared altogether by this time of year, and the top of the stalk is just a ragged mass of fluff. Thousands and thousands of seeds are being released with this stuffing, carried away on the wind or across the water. And the fluff gets used, too, by mice for winter nests and by birds for spring ones. Muskrats, meanwhile, dine on the roots and use the stalks to build their burrows.

It's the same story with milkweed. Late in the summer their blossoms are the food plant for the monarch butterflies that migrate through on the immense journey that will take them, over several generations, from Canada to Mexico. Then the pods of the milkweed dry out in the fall, split open, and gradually, a few at a time, release their parachutist seeds. This simple process has inspired any number of poets as a metaphor for spiritual transformation and release.

Poets and weeds make, I think, an alliance of eccentricity and vitality. Each weed, looked at a little more closely, begins to seem rather exotic. Their variety and differences emerge. It's partly the poetry of the very names—*joe-pye weed, motherwort, tansy, yarrow, heal-all, peppergrass*—partly their reproductive features and their interaction with other plants, animals, and insects, and partly the mysterious healing properties attributed to some of them. This "empty" field or "vacant" lot inevitably quickens with interest and life when you start to scrutinize it a little. It's a banquet for the birds and both food source and cover for the little rodents that inhabit it.

William Carlos Williams is the American poet who did the most to enlarge our vocabulary of poetic appreciation to include places like this weedy lot and times of year like this gray March day. His New Jersey was enough like my Ohio to give me a thrill of recognition every time I read poems like the following:

> *By the road to the contagious hospital*
> *under the surge of the blue*
> *mottled clouds driven from the*
> *northeast—a cold wind. Beyond, the*
> *waste of broad, muddy fields*
> *brown with dried weeds, standing and fallen*
> *patches of standing water*
> *the scattering of tall trees*
>
> *All along the road the reddish*
> *purplish, forked, upstanding, twiggy*
> *stuff of bushes and small trees*
> *with dead, brown leaves under them*
> *leafless vines—*
>
> *Lifeless in appearance, sluggish*
> *dazed spring approaches—*
>
> *They enter the new world naked,*
> *cold, uncertain of all*

save that they enter. All about them
the cold, familiar wind—

Now the grass, tomorrow
the stiff curl of wildcarrot leaf
One by one objects are defined—
It quickens: clarity, outline of leaf

But now the stark dignity of
entrance—Still, the profound change
has come upon them: rooted, they
grip down and begin to awaken

What the poem offers is the promise that a sustained act of attention, looking more and more closely at what seems at first merely a "waste of broad, muddy fields" filled only with "dried weeds," will reward the world and the reader with spring, with renewal. The gradual change of seasons matches an expansion of knowledge about the environment and a shift in the standard definitions of beauty and pleasure.

The reader gradually begins to realize that there are more colors in this scene, red and purple (sumac? berry canes?) along with the brown leaves and blue mottled clouds, and there are wild lines of direction, not just standing and fallen, vertical and horizontal, but "forked, up-standing, twiggy / stuff," sinuous if leafless vines, "stiff curls," and, just beginning to unfold, outlines of leaf.

All this apparent lifelessness contains a drama of birth and creation that is profoundly exciting. Suddenly we are in touch with the season through particularities—the first signs of life and green in the humble grass, the fernlike wild carrot leaf. And as the world begins to awaken, we awaken into it, into a better and closer knowledge that makes little distinction, for example, between art and science, so often set at odds as forms of knowledge and perception, a knowledge that does not disdain the interest and beauty of lowly weeds like wild carrot, also known as Queen Anne's lace.

Williams the doctor, who watched scenes like this pass as he drove to the quarantine hospital, and who delivered babies all his life, needed no categories for what he saw. He wanted to help create a new art, a modern art, for America. He could say, "They enter the new world naked," and in doing so deliberately align birth, newness, and spring with the new beginnings of art in the twentieth century in a place like New Jersey.

To an eye trained even on European modernist presentations of natural beauty—Van Gogh, Cézanne, Matisse—Williams's drab fields are at first startling. They seem "Lifeless . . . sluggish / dazed. . . . " But that cold wind *is* familiar, and the "one by one" defining of objects is a distinct pleasure, akin to natural history's naming and identifying and to photography's apparently unmediated exploration through close-ups. There's a "stark dignity" here, the dignity of beginnings and entrances, an opting for simplicity and naturalness, an American sensibility that is better placed in New Jersey than, say, in Zurich or London or Paris. I can't imagine any European poet composing something like the following, succinct and defiantly plain, another from the great 1923 collection *Spring and All:*

> *The farmer in deep thought*
> *is pacing through the rain*
> *among his blank fields, with*
> *hands in pockets,*
> *in his head*
> *the harvest already planted.*
> *A cold wind ruffles the water*
> *among the browned weeds.*
> *On all sides*
> *the world rolls coldly away:*
> *black orchards*
> *darkened by the March clouds—*
> *leaving room for thought.*
> *Down past the brushwood*
> *bristling by*

the rainsluiced wagonroad
looms the artist figure of
the farmer—composing
antagonist

A fisherman might walk through this late winter field looking for the dried stalks of goldenrod. On stalk after stalk he would find ball-shaped swellings called galls, two-thirds of the way up. They started the winter brown but have weathered by now to a wonderful shade of tarnished silver. These galls come from the egg-laying habits of a fly that deposits, along with the egg, a chemical that makes the plant form a tumorous growth around it. The idea is that when the egg hatches, the grub eats the surrounding plant material and has a snug winter home for itself.

I say "idea" because the fisherman, who will obviously have in mind using these grubs as bait for fishing, will be disappointed to find, again and again, a small hole bored in the galls. A bird has been there ahead of him, perhaps a woodpecker, making a winter feast of it. The goldenrod galls are mostly empty.

Poets and naturalists share a love of finding beauty in the unlikely, turning over rocks, scrutinizing weeds, uncovering more meaning and vitality than first meet the eye. Someone watching me examine goldenrod galls in a brown weedy field might conclude that I was wasting valuable time. At some earlier point in my life, I must have been similarly engrossed in studying puddles, as the following section of "Water Diary" testifies:

walking the tracks in early March
thinking where would I store a handcar
we ponder the fast clouds my son and I
and stare at winter's house   look down:
smashed grass gravel in a pool rainrings
wet rust on the tracks the creek rushing

no trains today no setting out arriving
the wind bucketing off through the trees
and sunset a skin of ice on each red puddle

Poets can seem loony in their preoccupations. When Hopkins squatted down to study the look of rainwater on a gravel path, his fellow priests thought he must be "touched." I'm sure Williams experienced that reaction, both about his poems and his interest in "lifeless" March fields. Perhaps we poets are simply more at home in March, with its variable weather, its unpredictable vitalities, and its legendary tendency to make people and creatures a little crazy. The month's associations with madness have many sources, including the behavior of animals like hares, but they also resonate with the weather. Spring will seem to arrive suddenly and dramatically, then just as dramatically disappear, replaced by raw, wintry wind and snowflakes like swarms of white gnats. We admire crocuses poking up even as we button our coats against thick sleet. The proverbial lion and lamb do their quick-change act all month. And the unpredictability makes people a little edgy, a little goofy.

Still, March has constants. One is the wind. Another, at least in this part of Ohio, is the chorus of tree frogs, the spring peepers. A few warm days are enough to encourage them, and then the nights, even though they get quite cold, are wallpapered with their chirping, a sound that has been compared to jingling bells and is often mistaken for crickets.

We almost never see the peeper frogs, since they emerge at night to join their chorus, but I remember noticing one once, against a tree trunk, marked across the back with a ragged *X* (explaining its scientific name, *pseudacris crucifer*), looking lithe and chipper as frogs go, and surprisingly small—about an inch long—for something that contributes to such a wall of noise all night.

It strikes me that they must be long-standing residents of this area. When it was mostly wetland and swamp, infested all summer with malarial mosquitoes, it must have had its nightly March choruses of tree-

frog song. This is an old sound I'm hearing, not a product of human settlement like the weeds, but ancient and enduring, independent of our
presence. Walking around outside last night, watching the full moon
in a mackerel-scale sky, it occurred to me that this distinctive sound
of spring has been one of its earliest and most predictable features in
the time I have lived here, some thirty-odd years. I used to watch for
daffodils and forsythia to appear, and for certain migratory birds, like
the grackle. Spring's arrival has been a matter of noticing more each
year. And all along, I realize, I could have noticed, as we learn to notice
weeds, those peepers and their nightly choruses, a sure and early sign
of spring.

Across the pond at the wildlife preserve, on this day of weak March
sunshine, an elderly couple have set up lawn chairs in the cold daylight
and are fishing with floats and bobbers. They know the fish are getting
active, too. Do they know how to cut open the milkweed galls to get
bait? I'm too shy to ask them. Besides, their pleasure seems perfectly
complete and self-contained. They may take home some bluegills or
crappies for their supper, but whether the fish bite or not, they're obviously just enjoying the chance to be out by the water in the first moments of the new season.

Time to eat some fish! I mentally flip through possible recipes. My
associations with March and fish eating probably have a lot to do with
Lent. It's a time when the stores make sure they stock seafood for their
Roman Catholic customers; the rest of us line up to take advantage.
But I think the association of March and fish also has to do with notions
of the water's warming up and boats being launched. Around here
people wait for the big lake to open up as a sign that the weather's improving. Some of them get their boats out of winter storage and start
thinking about the taste of fresh walleye. Fish goes with March and its
other signs of life, intimations of change in temperature and weather.

In the kitchen, absorbed with thoughts about March's variations and variegations, I also find myself cooking some of the vegetables that arrive this time of year. There are club-sized leeks, there is curved and feathery fennel, there are big green globe artichokes. Leeks should open the month, really, since the Welsh national day, St. David's Day, is March 1. I'm partial to the name of the saint, as well as to things Welsh. I find leeks, which the Welsh wear as a national symbol on March first, very appetizing. They require long cooking and are another food that has benefited from the advent of the microwave; braising them till they practically melt is an easy matter now. Artichokes cook well in the microwave, too, since they basically steam themselves there, retaining moisture but not getting saturated the way they do when you boil them. As for fennel, I tend not to cook that but to eat it raw, dressed simply with olive oil, salt, and freshly ground pepper. Its mildly licorice taste comes through nicely.

March weather means you can begin to do a bit of foraging for wild edibles, too. A walk in the woods while they still seem mostly brown and dormant turns up no wild flowers yet, but there is wild onion, wild chives, and the very pungent leaf called garlic mustard. My daughter showed me the other day how good the dandelions are this early in the year. Later on they'll be too bitter, but right now their white crowns just above the root and young green leaves are delicious. We tried a dandelion salad, concocting a warm dressing, and were surprised at the absence of bitterness in these young greens. People think of them as a tonic for the blood in the spring, and whether it's psychological or physiological or some of both, I can recommend the picking and eating of March dandelions, a sleight-of-hand whereby—as in Williams— despised weeds are transformed in interest and value.

In the midst of all these meteorological, culinary, and emotional variegations, in a month that resembles the *X*-marked peepers and leopard frogs, I stoop to admire the brown and green dappled leaves of the trout lily, not yet in bloom. Dappling, both the word itself and the

58

concept, always brings to mind Gerard Manley Hopkins, poet and priest and naturalist, who, like Williams, helped me learn to notice and love the world, to take in what he called piedness, the variegating tendency that runs through the natural world as well as through experience, memory, and emotion:

PIED BEAUTY

Glory be to God for dappled things—
 For skies of couple-colour as a brinded cow;
  For rose-moles all in stipple upon trout that swim;
Fresh-firecoal chestnut-falls; finches' wings;
 Landscape plotted and pieced—fold, fallow and slough;
  And all trades, their gear and tackle and trim.

All things counter, original, spare, strange;
 Whatever is fickle, freckled (who knows how?)
  With swift, slow; sweet, sour; adazzle, dim;
He fathers-forth whose beauty is past change:
   Praise him.

Hopkins struggled to reconcile his orthodox, hierarchical Christianity with his pagan, pantheist love of nature, and the strange results give his life and personality a dappled meaning, one that distresses you if you are looking for consistency and uniformity, one that delights you if you accept existence's contradictions. Such delight will not be without consciousness of the poet's painful struggles.

March also brings back thoughts of James Wright, the poet from Ohio who died in 1980 of throat cancer in New York City, far from the home state with which he had such a love-hate relationship. Wright's troubled life sometimes made his relations with others problematic. His poems, too, are variegated, frequently spotted and blotched by sentimental gestures. We love them and we wince at them. I heard him read twice in his lifetime, and was struck by the power and beauty of his voice as he recited his poems. Alcoholism and smoking produce the kind of cancer he suffered from, but it seemed a particularly appalling thing that he should lose that commanding voice in the process of los-

ing his abbreviated life. After he died I found myself imagining that he
would now be able to return to this place, to the subtle and haunting
early Ohio spring:

ELEGY IN THE FORM OF AN INVITATION
James Wright, b. 1927, Martin's Ferry, Ohio;
d. 1980, New York City

Early spring in Ohio. Lines
Of thunderstorms, quiet flares
On the southern horizon.
A doctor stares at his hands.
His friend the schoolmaster
plays helplessly with a thread.

I know you have put your voice aside
and entered something else.

I like to think you could come back here now
like a man returning to his body
after a long dream of pain and terror.

It wouldn't all be easy:
sometimes the wind blows birds
right off their wires and branches,
chemical wastes smolder on weedy sidings,
codgers and crones still starve in shacks
in the hills above Portsmouth and Welfare . . .
hobo, cathouse, slagheap, old mines
that never exhaust their veins—
it is all the way you said.

But there is this fierce green
and bean shoots poking through potting soil
and in a month or so the bees
will move like sparks among the roses.

And I like to think
the things that hurt won't hurt you any more

and that you will come back
in the spring, for the quiet,
the dark shine of grackles,
raccoon tracks by the river,
the moon's ghost in the afternoon,
and the black earth behind the plowing.

I try to accept the deaths and losses that streak and fleck the lives and renewals, and I try to connect them with this tango of two seasons, winter and spring advancing and retreating, cheek to cheek, all through this mottled month.

I take as my emblems for March the most splendid "pied" things I know, the great sycamore trees of our area. We have them, I think, because they love rich soil and water, and where we haven't totally cleared the land, along the little creeks and larger rivers, the sycamores rise up in imposing fashion, their branches outflung in stately amazement. I put one in a poem once, in a March section. The poem is "In My Own Back Yard," and the sycamore featured stands on the other side of the creek that runs behind our house:

Hunting for duck eggs at the end of March
I watch three mallards and a speckled female make
a tight flotilla on the swollen creek.

The dog barks at her counterpart
on the other bank. Nothing is green
the way these mallards' heads are green.

Empty-handed, I turn back to the house.
Small waterlights
play on the underbranches of the ash. High up
the sycamore lifts its light-peeled limbs
against a turning sky.

These trees are a little like King Lear himself, gone native and blending majesty with a kind of rugged craziness. They seem to be lit from within. The older and larger they are, the more their white underbark is exposed, so that they catch all the light, especially on a drab March day among a lot of brownish, blackish, purplish, reddish trees and bushes.

To see a sycamore at the other end of one of those broad muddy fields Williams mentions, as if regarding from its vantage point the same scene you are regarding—the dried weeds, standing and fallen, the patches of water—is to be taught how piedness can be transcendent. The sycamores belong to that brown and muddy, drab, and apparently lifeless world, and they rise up from it, towering grandly toward the wild and pied March sky.

The sycamores flash and sing as I pass them in the car or wander beneath them in the commonplace March woods. They teach me, as Williams does, and Wright and Hopkins do, to love the world by looking closer, the world in its piedness, the variegation of seasons, of love and loss, of sunshine and tornado, throat cancer and song.

MARCH RECIPES

Fish Soup, Italian Style

There are so many names for this that it's hard to know
what to call it. Marcella Hazan's version is called *il brodo
de papa,* because she got the recipe from her father. *Cac-
ciucco* is the Tuscan name for it, from the area around
Livorno or Leghorn, and that is what Giuliano Bugialli
calls it in *The Fine Art of Italian Cooking.* If you want to
use the American name, call it *cioppino.* And if you're or-
dering it in an Italian restaurant, you might find it under
the traditional title of *zuppa di pesce,* which translates as
the above, "fish soup," and which implies it will have a
piece of bread in it.

———✦———

an assortment of seafood—e.g., 1 pound
   monkfish or cod, 1 pound catfish fillets,
   1 pound shrimp in the shell, 1 pound squid,
   1 dozen littleneck clams, 1 dozen mussels
some fish heads and bones if they are available
Bermuda onion
1 large bunch of Italian flat-leaf parsley
3–6 cloves garlic
½ cup olive oil

½ cup white wine
1 large can Italian tomatoes
2–3 tablespoons tomato paste
¼ cup red wine vinegar
red pepper flakes
salt and pepper
6–8 cups broth or stock (homemade meat stock
    is best here)

For the broth, heat the olive oil and add the onion, parsley, and garlic, chopped finely (I use a food processor). Fry for a few minutes, then add the wine and let it cook down for 5 minutes. Then add the tomatoes, the vinegar, the tomato paste, the red pepper flakes (to taste, maybe between a teaspoon and a tablespoon?), the salt and pepper. When this has all simmered for about 10 minutes, you can add the fish heads and bones, if you have them. If not, throw in a fish bouillon cube and/or one of those little bottles of clam juice you can usually find in the store. Now you can add your broth or stock, making sure you have quite a bit if you are hoping for some leftover broth that makes a great risotto.

This broth can simmer on the stove for a couple of hours (another nose bonus around the house the afternoon you make it). If there are fish heads and bones in it, you will need to strain it and purée the contents through a food mill back into the pot. If not, you can leave it pretty much alone. It will be ready to cook your seafood, a process you'll start about 45 minutes before you want to sit down to eat.

Meanwhile, clean the squid, cut off the tentacles, and chop the cleaned-out bodies into rings. If you have clams or mussels, steam them in separate pots until they open, then either set them aside if you like to serve them in their shells or take them out of the shells if you intend to add just the edible parts to the stew. (You can also cook them in the microwave, in a dish with pierced plastic wrap over it, about 3 minutes for clams and 2 minutes for mussels.) Cut up your fish fillets into bite-sized chunks. Don't use fish like sole or orange roughy here—they will tend to dissolve and disappear; firm-fleshed fish like cod, monkfish, and of course salmon or swordfish are called for, though I have also used catfish successfully, wondering what Italian cooks would think of my sneaking a freshwater fish into this saltwater dish. I beg you not to omit the squid; they are easy to get because they freeze well and are kind of fun to clean once you've figured out how they are put together. And the shrimp seem essential, too. They add to the look and taste of the dish immeasurably.

The order of cooking reflects the length of time things take. The squid go in first; they need 20 minutes to half an hour. The fish chunks take about 10 minutes. Then the shrimp and the clams or mussels can go in for the last 5 minutes or so.

In individual bowls I put the shellfish if I have left them in their shells, along with a chunk of Italian country bread, toasted and rubbed with garlic. Then I ladle the soup over, making sure a variety of seafood pieces is included and that there's plenty of broth to soak into the bread. A little chopped parsley over the top if you have saved some out, and it goes to the table. People generally go politely nuts over this dish, and it isn't as time-consuming as it sounds, once you have the hang of it.

●

Risotto di mare

I put this in next because it is so good made with the left-over broth from the fish soup. Like polenta, risotto has benefited from the advent of the microwave, so I will give 2 versions here, the traditional and a microwave adaptation. I don't think anyone could tell them apart.

1 medium-sized onion (red or yellow), chopped
2 tablespoons olive oil
2 tablespoons butter

1½ cups Arborio rice (regular rice works, but it's not as good)

salt and pepper only if necessary (the broth is usually spicy enough)

3–4 cups broth (left over from the fish soup and supplemented if necessary with fish stock, chicken stock, etc.), depending on how liquid you wish the result to be—3 cups produces a very thick risotto

If you do this in a casserole, heat the olive oil and butter together, then sauté the onion until it's golden. The broth should be heating in a separate pan. Add the rice to the onion and sauté it until it starts to turn golden brown. Now begin adding the hot broth, about ½ cup at a time, stirring constantly. When the rice has incorporated the liquid, add another ½ cup. When all the hot broth has been absorbed, the rice will be pretty well cooked, especially if you like it al dente. It should take about 20 minutes at the most. When it's done, take it off the heat; some cooks add another tablespoon of butter at this point, to make the risotto a little creamier. Mix and serve.

The same thing can be done in the microwave. Heat the butter and oil for 2 minutes with a piece of waxed paper over it to avoid splattering. Then add the onion and do 2 minutes more. Then the rice and another 3 minutes. Now add all the broth (you don't have to have heated it previously). Cook it uncovered for 9 minutes. Stir well, then cook for another 8 minutes. This will

produce an al dente risotto, and you can add a couple of minutes to the cooking time if you like it softer.

If you have leftover pieces of seafood from your fish soup, you can add them shortly before serving, during the last couple of minutes, just long enough to heat through.

●

Tuna with Onion Confit and Roasted Peppers

You can put the peppers in the oven to roast and then start the onion confit, which cooks slowly and takes about half an hour. The peppers need to be "sweated" before they are peeled and cut up into strips. Then things go quickly: the tuna takes 10 minutes total and the peppers just need a quick sautéing (I use the pan I sear the tuna in) before you assemble the dishes for the table.

—◦◦◦—

2 medium-sized onions
6 tablespoons olive oil
2 tablespoons crème de cassis
4 sweet red peppers
4 tuna steaks
salt and pepper

Slice the onions thinly, or dice them, depending on your preference. Sauté them in 4 tablespoons of the olive oil over a low heat, stirring often, for about 10 minutes. Now add the cassis and cook over a very low flame for another 20 minutes.

Roast the peppers in a very hot oven for 15 to 20 minutes, or broil them until their skins are charred all over. Remove them from the oven and put them in a paper bag for 5 to 10 minutes. When they are cool enough to handle, peel them, seed them, cut them in strips, and set aside.

Heat the other 2 tablespoons of olive oil until almost smoking. Add the tuna steaks and cook them for no more than 2 minutes on each side. Put them into a pan or dish and set them in a slow oven until they are cooked through to your liking. I prefer them a little rare in the center and so I don't usually give them more than 5 to 10 minutes in the oven, depending on their thickness.

When the tuna is ready to serve, fry the red pepper strips quickly in the same pan you used to sear the fish. Put the tuna steaks on plates and put the onion confit on one side and the red pepper strips on the other. Salt and pepper the tuna and the pepper strips, and serve.

●

Grilled Red Snapper with Cumin

This treatment would work with rock cod, ocean perch, or any similar fish. The article I got it from said that it is done with sea bream at La Cagouille.

—◊◊◊—

4 small snappers or 2 large ones,
   cleaned but with the heads left on
cumin seeds
vegetable oil
olive oil
sea salt or kosher salt

When the fish are ready to grill, make little cuts all over on both sides and insert cumin seeds, 4 to 6 per side for small fish, 8 to 12 per side for large fish. If the weather's warm, you can do this on an outdoor grill; if cold, use a fireplace grill. The grill should be thoroughly oiled with vegetable oil just before you put the fish on. The fish should be rubbed generously with olive oil.

Grill the fish quickly over the hot coals, 2 to 3 minutes a side—enough to put grill marks on the skin—using an oiled spatula to turn and remove the fish. When they've had their grilling, put them in an oven pan, cover them with foil, and put them in a 300° oven for 10 minutes or so, 15 if they are large. You check to see how done the fish is by sticking a knife behind the head and pulling the cut open: if the meat is opaque, the fish is ready to eat.

To serve, put some warmed olive oil on each plate and set a fish on it, or half a fish if you are dividing large ones; you can also pour the oil over, about a tablespoon per serving. A strip of coarse salt goes on the plate, next to the fish. The result is spectacularly good and laudably simple, just the grilled fresh fish, the cumin flavoring, the oil, and the salt.

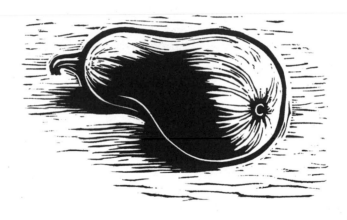

Fish Steaks with Ginger Beurre Blanc

I usually use this with fish steaks, but it would work with fillets as well. The recipe came from a newspaper article that noted its origin as *An Ocean of Flavor: The Japanese Way with Fish and Seafood* by Elizabeth Andoh.

———◆◆◆———

4 fish steaks
4 tablespoons ginger juice (grate ginger
    on cheesecloth and squeeze juice
    out, or put ginger pieces through a
    garlic press)
¾ cup sake or dry sherry
4 tablespoons chopped shallots
4 tablespoons finely minced ginger
4 tablespoons rice wine vinegar
1 stick unsalted butter
salt

Marinate the fish steaks or fillets in the ginger juice and ½ cup of the sake for an hour or, if refrigerated, for an afternoon. To make the beurre blanc, combine the shallots, minced ginger, ¼ cup of sake, and vinegar in a pan. Reduce to about half the original volume. Off heat, whisk in the butter, 2 tablespoons at a time. When the butter is integrated and the sauce is thickened, you can keep it warm in a pan of hot water.

Pat the fish dry, salt it lightly, and sear it in a nonstick pan or in a pan with a little oil in it. Sear on both sides, and the fish should be ready to eat, a little rare in the center. Serve on heated plates with the sauce poured over and pickled ginger on the side or as a garnish.

●

Italian Swordfish Tidbits

Another gem adapted from Marcella Hazan's second volume, *More Classic Italian Cooking.*

———◆◆◆———

4 swordfish steaks
salt and pepper
½ cup olive oil

3 tablespoons chopped parsley
¼ cup lemon juice
2 eggs
vegetable oil for frying
flour
lemon wedges

Cut the swordfish into chunks, a size that would take about 2 bites to eat. Marinate them in the oil, parsley, and lemon juice, along with a generous amount of salt and freshly ground pepper, for an hour at room temperature or an afternoon in the refrigerator, turning them from time to time.

When you are ready to cook, have your oil hot and ready. Pat the fish pieces dry with paper towels, dip them in beaten egg, one at a time, then in the flour, then put them gently into the oil. (Hazan suggests enough oil to come up ¼ inch on the side of the pan.) The fish pieces will form a golden crust on one side. Turn them as the crust forms, and when the second side is done, transfer them to paper towels or to a cooling rack. When they are all cooked, sprinkle them with salt and serve accompanied by lemon wedges.

●

Halibut Steaks to Eat with California Chardonnay

The reason for this recipe's title is that it stems from an article in a short-lived but intriguing magazine I used to get called *Wine and Food Companion*. The editors explored the best possible combinations of food and wine, and one article, "Big Fat Mamas Can't Dance . . . Or Can They?," argued convincingly that the big, rich, fat chardonnays from California need to be matched not with big, rich, fat creamy dishes but with dishes that balance against the wine's tendencies. Chardonnays can overwhelm delicate food, but they can also taste hot, harsh, or coarse when matched with dishes that are too rich, too salty, or too creamy. The ideal fish dish with chardonnay, the editors argued, was something like the following:

———⟨ɘ/ɘ⟩———

4 halibut steaks, or 2 that are large
    enough to serve 2 people each
1 sweet red pepper
1 mango or 1 papaya, not very ripe
1 bunch cilantro
1 clove garlic
3 tablespoons olive oil

You're going to grill or broil the fish, and you can use the technique mentioned above, finishing it briefly in a moderate oven to keep it from drying out. On it you'll spread a salsa made from combining in a food processor the pepper (which you can roast first and peel), the papaya or mango, the cilantro, and the garlic, with the olive oil added to blend and bind. Notice there is no salt in the recipe thus far. You can add it at the table, but be careful: very much will destroy the balance to create the right contrast with the wine. And the chardonnay to go with this delectable seafood treat? My own favorite is Kistler, a wine so huge it sometimes seems like 2 or 3 wines at once; but there are so many, some of them quite reasonable, like Beringer and Fetzer Sundial, that you can experiment with your own choices and develop your own preferences. Good chardonnays are coming out of Australia and Chile, too.

Homemade Gnocchi

This came from the magazine *Cook's Illustrated,* which happened to arrive in March. An article by Jack Bishop described his experiments with gnocchi and his elimination of unsuccessful ingredients and techniques to arrive at a light, succulent *gnoccho,* tasting potatoey, a little pillow of delectability.

2 pounds russet or baking potatoes
1 ½ cups flour
2 teaspoons salt

You start by baking the potatoes, 45 minutes to an hour, in a 400° oven. Peel them while they are still warm, and then put them through a potato ricer. (If you don't have one of these, it's worth getting one; they are about $10 new, or you can probably find one in a flea market.) After the riced potatoes have cooled, hand mix them with the flour and salt. The dough should not be sticky; if it is, add flour. Quarter the dough and roll out one quarter with your hands into a ropelike shape, about ¾ of an inch thick. Cut the rope into ¾-inch sections and roll each section across the back of a fork so that the tines leave ridges in the dumpling. Put the ridged dumplings onto a cookie sheet as you work. Repeat with each of the three quarters. You should get about a hundred gnocchi, which you can refrigerate until you are ready to cook them. You cook them in batches in boiling salted water. They are done when they float to the top, and you can remove them with a slotted spoon and transfer them to a warmed serving bowl. When they're all cooked, add your sauce and serve. You can pass grating cheese around at the table.

The sauce I made for these is extremely simple: Halve 2 pounds of plum tomatoes and cook them for 10 minutes, covered, in a saucepan.

Put them through a food mill and return to the pan with some salt and pepper, a pinch of sugar, 4 or 5 tablespoons of butter, and a bunch of fresh mint leaves. Simmer this sauce for half an hour, and it will be ready to pour over the gnocchi. If you have some fresh basil on hand (or basil leaves preserved in salt, the best way to keep them), you can add them instead of the mint, toward the very end of the cooking.

Does this recipe sound like a lot of work? It isn't. The gnocchi take a little time to roll out and cut up and ridge, but the process is rather fun, and the superior results, over the kind you buy already made, frozen, are well worth the small extra trouble. This is a great combination of two great foods, the potato and pasta. And in the summer you will want to have it with pesto made from your own garden basil. Nothing is much better!

Braised Leeks

I overcooked this the last time I made it because I love the way the leeks sort of caramelize if they are cooked long enough, and for once I overdid it. I recommend keeping an eye on them in the second stage of cooking.

4 large leeks, or 6 smaller ones
$\frac{1}{2}$ cup chicken broth
salt and pepper
butter

I usually cut the leeks in half, after removing the whiskers at one end and the green part at the other. This gives me a chance to look for dirt, which often shows up in the outer layers, and to wash them off if they need it. Then put the leeks in a glass bowl, microwave-safe, laying them next to and on top of each other like fireplace logs. Pour the chicken broth over, then sprinkle with salt and pepper and dot with butter. Cover with microwave wrap and cook at full power for 15 minutes. Take the leeks out, remove the wrap (carefully!), and turn them over a little in their juice. Put the wrap back on and give them another 10 minutes at full power, checking in the last few minutes to make sure you aren't overcooking them. If you like them caramelized and that hasn't happened, you can always extend the cooking time by a minute or 2 at the end.

This is so good, and so easy, that I make it practically every time I find good leeks at the store.

●

Dandelion Salad

It's common in Europe, and especially around the Mediterranean, to gather "weeds" in early spring for salads. They are seen as herbs, of course, rather than as weeds, and are considered beneficial to health as well as tasty. Bitterness is valued, so there's a cultivated taste there that we may not share, but I have found, as I indicated, that early dandelions are really not that bitter.

I quote Patience Gray, whose *Honey from a Weed: Fasting and Feasting in Tuscany, Catalonia, the Cyclades, and*

Apulia has to be considered a classic of what I've been calling peasantism: "Gather young dandelions by cutting a stub of milky root together with its head of leaves, or take the plant whole when small. Wash under the tap, pare the root, leave in water for one hour, then drain, shake dry, and serve with a vinaigrette dressing, or add to a well dressed beetroot salad." I'll just add that I think a warm dressing goes best with this. That means you've heated your olive oil, sautéed some shallots or maybe some of those wild onions in it, and added your vinegar—we used balsamic—and salt and pepper at the last minute, before pouring it over the greens. This wilts them a little and seems to bring out their flavor and slightly reduce their bitterness.

APRIL

Black with Possibility

· · · ·

April is troubling. It makes us restless and hungry. The rank smell in the air, especially after a recent rain, is unsettling, a little sinister. Small expeditions, even if just to the local woods to inspect the early wildflowers, grow more urgent and attractive. Surely Chaucer understood this restless impulse, opening his *Canterbury Tales* with a catalog of life and activity in April, matched with the human response. He mentions the rain and the wind, the new growth, the stronger sun and the birdsong. Then he turns to people, longing to go on pilgrimages, partly because of a spiritual hunger and partly because of the simple desire to be outdoors, moving around. Eliot's morose speaker in *The Waste Land* doesn't want the world to come back to life, but Chaucer's notes, more shrewdly, that we don't have much to say about it. A paradoxical sense that the earth knows how to renew itself, while we inevitably grow older, gives a bittersweet feel to successive springtimes.

Tolstoy spoke of this in a letter that James Wright quoted in a *Paris Review* interview in 1975:

> *Tolstoy worried about this question. He was asked in a letter by a pacifist group if he could give them a definition of religion. . . . Tolstoy worried*

· ·

78

about this letter and then, as I recall it, he said, "I can only go back to myself: I look around me and I see every year that, no matter what people do to themselves and to one another, the spring constantly renews itself. This is a physical fact, not a metaphysical theory. I look at every spring and I respond to it very strongly. But I also notice every year that spring is the same new spring and every year I am one year older. I have to ask the question: what is the relation between my brief and tragic life and this force in the universe that perpetually renews itself? I further believe that every human being asks this question. He cannot avoid asking it—it is forced upon him. And his answer to that question is his religion."

The many ways in which Tolstoy's insight plays itself out in our lives help to demonstrate its centrality. James Wright was certainly perceptive in relating it both to lyric poetry in general and to Williams (whose obsession with spring and the imagination he was praising at the time) in particular. But the manifestations of our "religion" permeate every corner of our lives, and they are sometimes very subtle.

Each spring is a little more detailed and interesting to me. I have gradually accumulated a sense of what unfolds in March, April, and May, which things belong to which month. The storehouse of detail fills out my experience a little more each year. If there is, as Tolstoy notes, a melancholy difference between our own aging and nature's dependable renewal, a compensatory pleasure may lie in our more and more acute awareness of the season's meaning and the humanity/nature paradox. Wang Wei stresses this in one of the first Chinese poems I ever translated: his speaker is watching the activities around him on a farm and is overwhelmed for a moment by his particular memories of loss. His glass of wine sits untouched before him. The emotional pattern might be said to combine Eliot and Chaucer.

A SPRING DAY AT THE FARM

Pigeons coo in the eaves
apricot orchards
bloom white at the edge of town

the farmers are out with axes
pruning the mulberry trees
hoeing watercourses

swallows hunt up old nests
old men sit in the sun
almanacs on their laps

I have forgotten my glass of wine
thinking of lost friends,

> *dead friends,*

in a blaze of old pain.

Maybe when we're young we're such a part of the season that we don't need to notice it. We *are* the spring. Then, starting to age and remember, we begin to sense and appreciate the differences, and with them, the details. Wallace Stevens's speaker in "Le Monocle de mon oncle" says: "I am a man of fortune greeting heirs; / For it has come that thus I greet the spring. / These choirs of welcome choir for me farewell." Spread out before us as we grow older are two simultaneous maps: the difference between our own youth and age, and the difference between all human life and the great wheel of the seasons.

The first spring I really took in, the one in which I first began to study the advance of the season, was in my early twenties, when I was a graduate student in New Haven. I had been solitary and scholarly all through the winter, and now, as I emerged from the library and walked the streets and campus in the freshening light and air, like a monk who has come out of his cell, I was surrounded by forsythia, then magnolia and wisteria, by crocuses, then jonquils and daffodils, then hyacinths and tulips. I was seeing these things as if for the first time, and I was abashed at what I had failed to notice when I was younger. Wasn't all my "learning" and all my attempt to be a poet by poring over the work of other poets a kind of misplaced studiousness? What about the book of the world, unfolding majestically around me?

Of course, the book of the world, in this case, was a human production, a city in which certain bulbs and shrubs had been carefully planted and nurtured in order to make the season flamboyant and pleasurable. I didn't understand that at that time, but because I was in Connecticut, not very far from where Wallace Stevens had lived, I connected my newly discovered spring pleasure with his. The deep and significant connection between place and poetry was beginning to make itself felt to me, outside my library and classroom learning. I imagined Stevens as a character named Mr. Marblearch, a portly business executive. I praised and teased my favorite poet as both slightly comical and yet hugely perspicacious:

PUTTING IT MILDLY

Into the uproar of April emerged Mr. Marblearch,
Ready again to be well aware of the weather,
For a normal informal part in the burgeoning season's
Annual matters of magnitude.

Like a cat encountering cream he encountered the colors
And tapped his cigar so as not to endanger the flowers;
He paused in thought by a solemn and wild forsythia,
Fancies assailing his head.

"This sun," Mr. Marblearch said, "is enlarged
Like the oldest idea enjoying its newest form
In an epochal fashion. Ahem. It is like a sublime
Balloon that will never burst.

"Furthermore," he went on, beneath a magnolia,
"To have a sky in one's head, a bush in the breast,
Is to partake of the pattern, the bee and the tree
Being in season."

Marblearch colored in the season's din
With the whole magnolia, alive on the grass
In the role of forsythia, feeling the morning sun's
Ideas hot on his face.

Now, many years later, I feel sometimes as though I have become Mr. Marblearch, taking a pleasure in the inventory of April that is both richer and more melancholy.

I remember walking into the local supermarket a couple of years ago and seeing a number of people clustered around something in the produce department. When I got closer, I saw that it was a big display of locally grown green asparagus. The people who were responding with interest and excitement were in their fifties and sixties and seventies. Hardly anyone in their twenties or thirties was as likely to find the first big crop of asparagus an exciting event. Their enjoyment was clearly a welcoming of a particular phenomenon of a particular season.

I join the crowd around the asparagus, too, now, and I look for new ways to prepare it. I roast it with olive oil and salt, serving it with a lemon wedge. I steam and then bake it briefly with grated cheese sprinkled over it. Years ago, in a magazine, I saw a recipe for asparagus with a raspberry sauce, a dish that offered visual delight along with an intriguing combination of flavors. I've long since lost the recipe and my memory of the exact ingredients, so the other day I tried reconstructing it, figuring that the raspberry sauce had to be a kind of *coulis*—fresh or, more likely, frozen raspberries combined in a blender with some oil and vinegar—to be poured over boiled or steamed asparagus cooled to room temperature. I found myself using balsamic vinegar and adding some cassis (blackcurrant liqueur), along with the olive oil and a dash of soy sauce. The results were a recipe reborn, perhaps even improved.

Asparagus goes well with cheese, with eggs, with butter, and I have a Chinese recipe that flavors it with black beans. It tends to sweeten the taste of wine, so the drier the wine you drink it with, the better. The stalks I like best range in thickness from pencils to fingers. Their bud heads should be firm and intact, and they should be straight and crisp. My mother always snapped off the bottoms of asparagus stalks, but that's a matter of taste: what you get in the store may be edible almost all the way down.

Strange, sweet April! On the fiftieth anniversary of the liberation of Buchenwald, survivors journeyed to that awful place to remember things like the commandant's wife who inspected prisoners' skins and tattoos to select material for her lamp shades, and who used mummified human thumbs for light switches. Unimaginable horrors, freshly recollected in the green lap of the new-come spring. A man who is now a rabbi in Israel tells a story of being picked up in the camp, eight years old, by one of the U.S. soldiers who liberated it. "How old are you?" asked the soldier. "Older than you," the child replied.

Turbulent, menacing April! A pickup truck sits in a tree, deposited there by a tornado. Daffodils line a lakeshore. A child is an old man. Red maples shine in the rain. A thumb is a light switch. We think we cannot go on, but the world does and we are taken with it, by it. It makes itself new to remind us how ancient it is. Each day the goldfinches that come to my feeder are a brighter shade of lemon-yellow, more vivid even than the daffodils or forsythia, their winter plumage, a kind of drab yellow-brown, changing to something almost gaudy. Every day the tint of the grass is a trifle greener. The world seems filled with raucous cries and whispered secrets. Night brings strange dreams we only half remember.

People long to go on pilgrimages—driven by memory, in some cases, driven by spring, longing to synchronize human existence with these forces of renewal. Poets prowl the landscape, too, realizing, as James Wright put it in praising Williams, that there is something in the human imagination that is like the spring. Here is Rilke, in the *Sonnets to Orpheus*:

> Listen. You can hear harrows at work,
> the first ones. Again, the human rhythms
> in the hanging stillness of the rank
> early-spring earth. What's coming seems
>
> untasted, completely new. What
> came to you so often seems now to
> come the first time. You always expected it,
> but you never took it. It took you.

Even leaves that hung on the oaks all winter
seem, in the evening, to be a future brown.
Sometimes the winds pass a signal around.

The thickets are black. But heaps of manure
are an even darker black in the pastures.
Every hour that goes by is younger.

That insight—"you never took it. It took you"—is the same one Chaucer was articulating. As for "Every hour that goes by is younger," that leaves me speechless.

Is the imagination the part of us that is more than human, or the part that connects the human with the nonhuman? There's no true either/ or in that question. It puts the same idea two different ways.

April brings Easter, a disorderly mixture of pagan and Christian associations. Rabbits and eggs help us revive old ceremonies of fertility, ones in which the hare, symbol of increase and lechery, laid eggs, symbols of sacrifice, purity, fertility, and resurrection. In some parts of the world, they slaughter and roast the new lambs, eating them with the new greens. The lamb becomes the Lamb of God, his blood the blood we are supposed to be washed and baptized in. Hot cross buns carry an icing cross of Christian symbolism on a sacred pagan object, some early Christian bishop's solution to a custom that his converted populations were unwilling to forgo. Is Christianity the icing on the ancient bun of reverence for the superior forces of nature?

A shiny little shrew runs out from its burrow among the pine needles to grab some bird seeds below the feeder I'm watching. A waxwing lands nearby. The shrew runs back. A white-crowned sparrow, which seems to be wearing a black-and-white-striped helmet, replaces the waxwing. Cold clouds pass overhead. Glistening, purposeful, driven by one of the biggest appetites and highest metabolisms in the animal world, the shrew returns again and again.

Our yearning to be part of nature is a yearning to have nature's unfathomable powers of renewal. Whether we imagine it in terms of godhead or of natural fertility symbols, there is a wistfulness about all our spring and Easter celebrations. They presumably had the power of myth at some earlier stage, but maybe we have always half-realized how much they also represent happy, hopeless wishing.

I wrote an "Easter Ghazal" after a powerful dream in which Chloe, my dead wife, had returned to life. In the dream our emotions of meeting were gentle and pleasurable, a radiant, breathless moment. I had dreamed her alive before, but the previous instances were always problematic, fraught with anxiety. In the history of my grief, the first April after her death marked a kind of turning point, a sheltering of my loss in the larger context of renewal. By the second and third Aprils, this surfacing through grief at Easter was tangled into the presence of a new family—three stepchildren hunting for Easter eggs and enjoying the boisterous sense of the new season. We had a pet rabbit, and we cavorted in the yard on a warm Easter Sunday, spraying each other with the hose:

EASTER GHAZAL

Dreaming the dead back to life: pleasure & gentleness.
Grateful for this miracle, this bubble of reunion.

Harps bounce & hum there in the firmament.
The fundament. Coining likenesses. Did you say something?

Bricks crumb, bones powder: this helps make potting soil.
Clay reproduces! Ploughs heal the fields they wound.

Today we trim the rabbit's nails upside the hutch,
Nail up the bat-house, baptize each other with the hose.

I'm flame. A flag going up a flagpole. I'm
the beetle dropped by the mother bird, picked up again.

The heart's a tomato with lips. Woodpeckers tap hosannas.
Sleepy blips & explosions fleck love's radar screen.

Something rises. Something drops. Elastic days!
Tonight this window's black with possibility.

My dream was ironic in the light of day, but it gave me new energy any-way. Suddenly Easter, with all its paradoxes of loss, fertility, suffering, contradiction, and joy, made more sense than it had ever made before.

The stone is rolled aside, and godhead steps out, then vanishes. People buy new hats—are they trying to be blossoming plants?—and wear new outfits in Easter parades. Red flowers open and open. Old and new emotions buffet us. Ants show up, busy and hungry, in our kitchens. Life surges around us, beyond all our control and under-standing, and we submit. These forces are not quite the same as us, as our lives. Sometimes we submit to them reluctantly, sometimes gladly.

Magical changes are taking place in the silent woods. My favorite per-son to go foraging with is my daughter, Margaret. She is enthusias-tic, knowledgeable, and curious, a born naturalist and forager, and an adventurous cook. On Easter Sunday, when the preparations for our dinner are well along, we have an hour and a half to explore a nearby woods. I am cooking ham and my asparagus with raspberry sauce. Mar-garet is making mashed potatoes with chopped-up greens that have been simmered in milk, what the Irish call "champ." She'll use the dandelions and chives and wild onions she has been gathering outside. My sister, Ruth, who is visiting, is constructing a salad that includes Gorgonzola, pears, and walnuts. Our dessert will be an Italian short-cake with pastry cream and strawberries.

With all this to look forward to and an appetite to work up, we turn pilgrims for a time and visit a muddy tract of river-bottom woods to look for new wildflowers. The afternoon is gray and mild, like so many days of this month. The morning rain has not left the woods as mucky as we feared they'd be, and our progress is easy and meandering. We quickly identify a number of current wildflowers. There is spring beauty, a member of the purslane family, white flowers rising between long leaves. I show Margaret hepatica, which comes in two varieties, with round-lobed and sharp-lobed leaves. Margaret shows me cut-leaved toothwort, a member of the mustard family that is also known as pepper root because of its pungent tubers. Another white flower we find is the rue anemone, with small, delicate leaves and a blossom that resembles a more petite version of the hepatica's. Our favorite wildflower of this trip may well be squirrel corn, with its fernlike leaves. The blossom does indeed resemble a corn kernel, though the name is actually said to be based on the resemblance of the roots or tubers to grains of corn. This plant belongs to the fumitory family, like Dutchman's breeches and earth smoke.

I like the lore associated with wildflowers and the different names and uses that have been attached to them over the course of time. A recent book, *The History and Folklore of North American Wildflowers,* by Timothy Coffey, accompanies us on this foray. I learn from it that spring beauties have also been known as "fairy spuds"; that the Cherokee gave concoctions of hepatica to people troubled by dreams of snakes; and that squirrel corn was called "ghost corn" by the Onondaga, who thought it food for spirits, while Ohio settlers called it "Indian potatoes." Since it was also known as "colic weed," it must have been thought to help babies deal with the fretfulness of colic. Another of its names, "stagger weed," suggests quite other possibilities.

The woods are peaceful and dreamy. An early butterfly floats past, one I don't recognize. Coltsfoot is out, skunk cabbages are quite plentiful, trout lilies and mayapples are just coming, but I want to show Margaret a plant I found the other day, not yet in bloom, that I couldn't identify. The bright green leaves, looking like something in the lily family, are in clusters and clumps all through these woods. I bring Margaret, who has been pulling wild onions, chives, and cress for her potato champ, a leaf, asking her if its odd, oniony smell will help identify it. One sniff and her face lights up with excitement. "Ramps!" she exclaims. "You've found ramps! I didn't know those grew around here!"

Our enthusiasm probably puzzles my sister, who is from California by way of Connecticut. People in this area have heard of ramps because our neighboring state of West Virginia makes such a fuss about them. It's as if every little town in that state has some kind of spring festival or celebration devoted to the picking and eating of ramps in conjunction with other seasonal dishes, such as lamb. Like fiddlehead ferns and mo-

rel mushrooms, this is a celebrated seasonal delicacy. And it's practically growing in our backyard!

The ramps need a good deal of washing, but their freshness and fragrance is delightful. I make two dishes with them, a frittata (an Italian-
style omelet) and some oily scallion cakes, a Chinese specialty my family delights in. In the one case they are standing in for fresh, early garlic
of the kind Italians love to cook in April. In the other, they are playing
the role of green onions. I eat one raw, just to see how much they bite
back. I find they taste like leeks but are more tender, and while their
odor is strong, the flavor is quite mild. I find myself wondering how
long their season will last.

The finding and harvesting of the ramps will now become an annual
April event for me. Customs can be long-held, customs can disappear
and reappear, customs can be created on the spot. Ramps for Easter
dinner sounds like a tradition worth founding. Next time I harvest
ramps I think I will try stewing them in butter and stock, maybe as
part of a soup. I have a hunch they would help make a distinguished
vichyssoise.

⌒

Easter echoes and reverberates all through the rest of the month. It is,
after all, named for the pre-Christian goddess Eostre, also spelled Eas-
tre or Ostara. She was the pagan goddess of the dawn (her name may be
cognate with Aurora), and the entire month of April was once known
as Eostur-Monath, the dawn month. We can compress the meaning of
it all into one story, Christ's Passion, or one symbol, the egg or the rabbit, but we can also live with it all month, mulling over the question
Tolstoy's letter poses. I often think of George Herbert, another favorite
poet, during the month of April, mostly because his lyric "Virtue"
comes so readily to mind on a fine spring day:

> Sweet day, so cool, so calm, so bright,
> The bridal of the earth and sky,
> The dew shall weep thy fall tonight:
>> For thou must die.

Sweet rose, whose hue, angry and brave,
Bids the rash gazer wipe his eye:
Thy root is ever in its grave,
*   And thou must die.*

Sweet spring, full of sweet days and roses,
A box where sweets compacted lie:
My music shows ye have your closes,
*   And all must die.*

Only a sweet and virtuous soul,
Like seasoned timber, never gives;
But though the whole world turns to coal,
*   Then chiefly lives.*

Herbert is trying to solve the Tolstoy problem by turning the tables on nature here, making it the ephemeral presence and the human soul the permanent one. It's as compact a presentation of Christian belief's answer to the humanity/nature paradox as one can find. And perhaps Herbert is right, who knows? Until its last stanza his poem simply calls up the brevity and change that belong to the months of spring. Each of the first three stanzas might be thought to respond to April, May, and June, respectively. The final one, which must of course resort to nature (and art, since seasoning and building with timber are a human use of natural material) for its metanatural message, has an apocalyptic ring to it; if the soul *lives* like seasoned timber in a conflagration, it is burning, too, burning well. Perhaps it is meant to be a kind of phoenix, rising from its own flames and ashes.

It was late April in 1983 when Chloe got the results of her breast biopsy and was told she must have a partial mastectomy. We held hands as the doctor explained the results. The news was a powerful blow. Her mother's death had begun this way, and we had consulted the statistics that calculated her odds. Yet there was a good chance of fighting the illness off, holding it at arm's length for some time. We could be brave with each other, and hopeful to our family and friends. The day we told the children—both were in high school then—and some of our family, we felt a sudden need to be out of the house, alone together, away from all the sympathy and concern. We drove east and south to the local reservoir and then walked down a country road, West Road, hand in hand, savoring the twilight of a mild April day.

Hardly one word was said. Too many things were obvious. The world was almost unimaginably beautiful, made up simply of late sunlight, some cows grazing, a few birds singing in the trees, the whole burgeoning spring landscape. And we were facing death, not knowing how close or far off it was, but unquestionably facing it.

Later, trying to recall that moment, it seemed to me that one of us had actually made the banal but necessary observation that the world was very beautiful, but I could not for the life of me remember which one it was. That at least bespoke our closeness in that moment. Our emotions, twined round the fear of death and loss, responding with aching love to each other and the world around us, were almost exactly the same. There would be another spring for her, one more, and many more for me, though my springs would from now on be colored by this moment and this sense of loss, and my time would come as well. As in the relation between my Easter dream four years later and the day that followed it, all this was and is well beyond the simple relationships of irony. When we get beyond irony, and get far enough, we encounter mystery. And language will not serve us there, though it may help bring us to the threshold.

The dawn month was filled with loud lamentations in the old religions. The death of Adonis was widely mourned and wailed. His images were carried by loudly weeping women and cast into the sea. There were flutes and drums, sobbing and keening and breast-beating. All this in hope that the god would rise again and the months of darkness yield to months of light.

The customs still make sense to me. I don't suppose our decorous society could persuade people to lament and wail in Easter parades, but if they did it would express a necessary meaning of the month and our relation to it. Tolstoy and Herbert lead my parade. They walk arm in arm, weeping and smiling. Pilgrims, first and last, driven by spiritual hunger and the good cheer of improving weather. They disagree, but secretly they agree. They wear ramps in their hats and wildflowers, picked in the woods, pinned to their lapels. Grackles prance and flutter beside them, shining darkly. Rilke follows behind, a shrew perched on his shoulder. The drums are beating more and more ferociously, the flutes are wailing a piercing wail.

APRIL RECIPES

Six Ways to Cook Asparagus

Asparagus and Peppers with Penne

This combines the great spring flavor of asparagus with roasted peppers and pasta. The pasta finishes its cooking with the sauce, a feature suggested in the Union Square Cafe's version of this recipe.

1 pound fresh asparagus (preferably thin stalks)
2 sweet red peppers
2 sweet yellow peppers
3 tablespoons butter
1 large clove garlic, minced
1 pound penne
2 cups chicken stock
1 cup grated Parmesan or similar cheese
2 tablespoons salt
freshly ground black pepper
slivered almonds, toasted (optional)

Wash the asparagus, snap off the tough bottoms, peel any lower stalks where the skin seems too thick, and cut into pieces about the length of your thumb. Meanwhile, roast the peppers under a broiler or over a flame until black all over, cool in a paper bag, peel, and cut into small strips.

Melt the butter in a large frying pan (you'll eventually want it to hold all the pasta), and sauté the asparagus pieces for about 5 minutes. Don't do more than brown them lightly. Now add the peppers and garlic and continue cooking and stirring for another couple of minutes. Add the chicken stock.

The pasta should be about three-quarters cooked in boiling salted water. After you drain it, you can add it to the sauce once the chicken stock has come to a boil. Cook until the pasta is just ready, add half the cheese and salt and pepper. When the mixture has been transferred to a bowl or serving dish, put the rest of the cheese on top, sprinkle with the toasted almonds (they enhance the nutlike flavor of the fried asparagus), and serve.

●

Asparagus with Fried Eggs, Italian Style

Just as spinach goes well with eggs, so does asparagus, and the combination of these two April foods is a delightful light supper that cheers you up without filling you up. I serve this with a salad and a light white wine and follow it up with a sweet dessert (ice cream or crème brulée or sherbet). It would obviously also make a lively, fancy lunch for guests.

—⟨∅∅∅⟩—

1 pound asparagus, trimmed and
    bundled
6 tablespoons butter
4 eggs, room temperature
½ cup grated Parmesan or similar cheese
salt and pepper

I usually cook the bundled asparagus in an asparagus cooker. Since I prefer the thin asparagus, this only takes about 5 minutes. Cooking time should depend on the thickness of the stalks and your own preference about how done or limp they should be.

Melt the butter in a large frying pan and cook the asparagus gently until it is just lightly browned. Sprinkle on the cheese, add salt and pepper, and as soon as the cheese melts, remove the asparagus to a warm serving platter. Now fry the eggs in the remaining butter until they are just set. Giuliano Bugialli suggests the following method, which is tricky but satisfying: crack the egg and keep the yolk in one side of the shell while you pour the white into the frying pan; do that for all the eggs, then put the yolks carefully on the top and center of each white. The result is nice looking and needs only 3 minutes in a covered pan to set. The number of eggs should be determined by the rest of your meal. If this is to be the main course, I like to have 2 eggs per person; if it's part of a larger meal, 1 egg per person will be plenty.

To serve, simply set the eggs carefully on top of the asparagus on the platter, sprinkle with salt and pepper, and bring to the table. As with so much Italian food, it's partly the sheer simplicity of this dish that makes it attractive. If you have fresh local asparagus and have gone to the extra trouble of buying your eggs locally to insure their freshness and the better flavor you get when they come from a farm rather than a factory, you will be rewarded accordingly by the flavors you produce!

●

Roasted Asparagus

The simplest of these recipes, but no less tasty for being
so easy.

———❧———

1 ½ pounds asparagus, washed and trimmed
3 tablespoons extra virgin olive oil
salt
1 lemon

Brush the asparagus with oil, salt it, and roast in a 400° oven for 10 to
12 minutes. Serve with lemon wedges.

●

Asparagus with Raspberry Sauce

The sauce is wonderful to look at and complements the
flavor of the asparagus beautifully.

———❧———

1 ½ pounds asparagus, washed and trimmed
½ cup fresh or frozen raspberries
3 tablespoons olive oil
2 teaspoons balsamic vinegar
1 tablespoon soy sauce
1 tablespoon sugar
1 tablespoon crème de cassis (optional)

Steam the asparagus until it is tender, about 5 minutes for pencil-thick
spears, 7 to 10 for thicker asparagus. Spread the cooked asparagus on a
platter to cool. Tilt the platter slightly so the juices run down to one
end. You can drain them off after 15 or 20 minutes. Meanwhile, put
the raspberries in a blender or food processor, along with the olive oil,

vinegar, soy sauce, sugar, and cassis (if the raspberries are frozen and already sweetened, you may not need the sugar), and blend. Pour the sauce attractively over the asparagus on the platter and serve.

●

Asparagus with Parmesan Cheese

In this recipe, you boil or steam the asparagus, then finish it in a hot oven with the cheese.

—◗◗◗◗—

1 ½ pounds asparagus, washed and trimmed
½ cup freshly grated Parmesan cheese
salt and pepper
butter

Boil or steam the asparagus in your usual fashion. (You will certainly want to acquire an asparagus cooker if you really get to enjoy this vegetable.) Keep the cooking time short. Arrange the cooked asparagus in a baking dish. If you can get it in one layer, sprinkle the cheese, along with salt and pepper to taste, on top. Dot with butter. If there are layers, alternate them with layers of cheese and bits of butter, and salt and pepper. Bake in a hot (450°) oven for about 10 minutes, or until the cheese forms a light brown crust.

●

Asparagus with Black Bean Sauce

This is a Chinese recipe, so I will follow it with 2 dishes that complement it nicely and make up a complete oriental meal.

—◗◗◗◗—

1 ½ pounds asparagus, washed and trimmed,
steamed 10 minutes

1 tablespoon salted black beans

2 cloves garlic

2 tablespoons peanut oil

1 cup chicken or vegetable stock

1 teaspoon sugar

2 tablespoons rice wine or sherry

1 tablespoon soy sauce

1 tablespoon cornstarch

1 tablespoon sesame oil

Fermented salted black beans are available in Asian groceries and keep well. Most people rinse them before cooking. In this case, chop them with the garlic after you have rinsed them, and fry this mixture briefly in the peanut oil (you can use butter if you prefer). Add stock, sugar, rice wine or sherry, and soy sauce. Boil the sauce until it's reduced by about a third. Turn the heat down, add cornstarch mixed with 2 tablespoons of water. When the sauce has thickened, add the sesame oil. Keep the sauce warm until you are ready to pour it over the warm asparagus.

●

Pork Fried like Fish

The title of this dish also translates as something like "in the style of fish," a common but not very poetic way of describing the method. It could be called "hot and sweet and sour pork," but the flavorings are subtle and far from the "sweet and sour pork" of third-rate Chinese restaurants.

—◦◦◦—

4 pork chops (1 pound or more of meat)

6 scallions

1 tablespoon fish sauce or soy sauce

1 tablespoon sesame oil
pinch of ground roasted red pepper
    (Szechuan peppercorns, preferably)
3–4 tablespoons minced ginger
4 cloves minced garlic
4 tablespoons peanut oil
2–3 tablespoons chili paste
1 tablespoon sugar
1 cup crunchy vegetable (sunchokes,
    water chestnuts, or potatoes)
1 tablespoon cornstarch mixed with
    1 tablespoon water
1 tablespoon vinegar

The pork should be slivered or shredded for stir-frying; sometimes you can buy it that way, and you certainly don't have to use pork chops—any lean pork will do. The scallions should be cut up the same way, and then the pork and scallions marinated in the fish sauce, sesame oil, and pepper for at least half an hour.

Stir-fry the finely minced ginger and garlic for a minute in the hot oil. Then add the chili paste, the vegetable (use sunchokes if you can find them), the pork and scallions, and the sugar. You stir-fry this mixture vigorously for about 5 minutes or until the pork is quite thoroughly cooked. Then add the cornstarch mixture and, after it has thickened, the vinegar. The result should balance the hot, sour, and salty aspects, with a touch of sweetness. Taste it before serving and add any of those elements you think may need intensifying.

Oily Scallion Cakes

This dish comes (as does the previous one, more or less) from another 4-star cookbook, Ellen Schrecker's *Mrs. Chiang's Szechwan Cookbook*. It is messy to make and incredibly tasty. We have a family joke that if all else fails, we can make a living selling these onion cakes at fairs or on the street. Nobody can resist them!

—✍—

3 cups flour
1 cup water
10 to 15 scallions
sesame oil
peanut oil
salt

There are basically 4 steps involved here. Make a dough with the flour and water, and let it sit for half an hour. Chop the scallions into tiny pieces, aiming to get about 1½ cups. I do the dough in my dough mixer and the scallions in my food processor, saving a little time and work and losing no flavor.

Divide the dough in half and roll out half on a surface you have sprinkled with sesame oil. You want a rectangle about the size of a regulation piece of typewriter paper. Spread the rectangle with peanut oil, about 1½ tablespoons, and sprinkle it with a teaspoon of salt. Now sprinkle half the chopped scallions all over it. Roll it up like a jelly roll and divide the roll into 3 sections. Pinch the ends to try to hold the scallions inside, but you won't completely succeed. You now have 3 objects about the size of tennis balls, and when you repeat the process with the other half of the dough, oil, salt, and chopped scallions, you'll have 6.

Keeping your working surface oily, you are going to flatten each of these balls into a round cake about 8 inches in diameter. Be cheerful and disorderly. You want most of the scallions to stay inside, but they are going to get out, and the cakes are going to split open. It's okay. Your work space will get messy, but the end result is well worth it.

Fry the cakes one at a time in hot peanut oil and drain them. It's best to flatten them out only as you are ready to cook them, so you can be flattening the next one as you are frying the first, etc. After you've finished, you can sprinkle the cakes with salt and cut them into wedges for serving. I guarantee they will disappear rapidly, and people may even fight over the last wedges. If I had to name the 10 most delicious things to eat I know of, these scallion cakes would undoubtedly be on the list.

As mentioned above, we made these very successfully with fresh-picked ramps, too.

●

Frittata with Ramps

Cooking with eggs in April seems to be customary in many cuisines. This Italian omelet that I made with the ramps I found in the woods is described in a wonderful book called *The Tuscan Year.* This book, by an English writer, Elizabeth Romer, details the customs and cuisine of an Italian rural family through the seasons— especially those of the wife, Silvana, who makes cheese, harvests olives, visits her neighbors and relatives with special dishes, and lives a year close to the seasons and to what the land provides. It is a routine that has character, nobility, and antiquity, so if it is "peasantism," it exemplifies the best characteristics of that life: the use of fresh ingredients, simple preparations that bring out the character of good food, a close knowledge of what the seasons mean and make possible.

In April Silvana gives the house a thorough cleaning and then invites the local priest round to sprinkle holy water in every room and to bless a dish of eggs. She then invites him back for a lunch that includes a spread of hard-boiled eggs mixed with pickled vegetables and mayonnaise on her *crostini*. Eating the eggs is as important as blessing them. One does not want to waste good food. Another dish Silvana makes in April combines the frittata—the flat, cakelike, and well-done type of omelet Italians favor—with young garlic, *aglio fresco*. Romer recommends young leeks as a substitute for the fresh garlic bulb and stalk. I found that our local ramps were an ideal stand-in for *aglio fresco,* but I believe this dish can also be made with a combination of spring onions, leeks, and garlic.

—◁∾▷—

> 1 large bunch of ramps
>   (or substitute spring onions,
>   leek, and / or garlic)
> 4 large fresh eggs
> salt and pepper
> 3 tablespoons olive oil

How much ramp you use is a matter of taste. I would think you would want to end up with about 2 tablespoons of chopped ramp per egg. The ramps need thorough washing, and you can use the white bulb, the red stem, and a bit of the green leaf. Slice the bulbs in rounds, chop the stems and leaves, and set aside. Beat the eggs and season them liberally with salt and pepper. Heat the oil and, when it is hot, fry the ramps over a fairly low flame until they soften and the white parts turn golden. Add the eggs and turn up the flame. Let the eggs cook until they are fairly firm, then slide the frittata onto a plate. Turn it over with a spatula (or with a second plate if you are in danger of breaking the frittata) and slide it back into the pan so that the top side can brown to match the bottom. To serve, cut into wedges. Frittatas are often served at room temperature.

Margaret's Champ with April Greens

To give a recipe here would be making an informal
thing too formal. The point is that the Irish way of serving mashed potatoes with chopped fresh greens in them
provides inspiration for an effective way of using the
chives—both wild and domestic—wild onions, dandelions, and ramps one finds in April. To her mashed potatoes, which she had combined with some goat cheese
and buttermilk, Margaret simply added a cup or so of assorted chopped greens, making a ratio of about 6 to 1.

Spring Rolls

This, too, is intended to take advantage of the sudden appearance of fresh chives. They grow so well in April and
into May that anyone who loves true spring rolls, as opposed to the rather appalling version, usually called egg
rolls, served in most Chinese restaurants, will find it
hard to resist making them at this time of year.

20 spring roll wrappers
½ pound ground pork (or turkey or veal)
½ cup chopped shrimp (fresh or dried)
1 tablespoon cornstarch
1 tablespoon soy sauce
1 tablespoon sherry or rice wine
2 tablespoons peanut oil
6 dried black mushrooms (or tree ears),

soaked in hot water 30 minutes and
cut in shreds
½ cup shredded crisp vegetable (water
chestnut, Jerusalem artichoke,
jicama, or Chinese cabbage)
½ pound fresh bean sprouts
½ cup stock (chicken or the mushroom
soaking liquid)
2 cups chopped chives (or ramp leaves)
1 egg

The ground meat and shrimp can be tossed with some cornstarch and a little liquid—soy sauce for the meat and rice wine or sherry for the shrimp. Dried shrimp should be soaked for 13 to 30 minutes first. Heat the peanut oil in a wok, then add the pork mixture. After a couple of minutes add the mushrooms or tree ears, the shredded vegetable, and the bean sprouts. Add half the stock and cook for a minute or 2. Add the shrimp mixture, then the rest of the stock, including more cornstarch if it seems to need thickening. Remove the wok from the heat and, when the mixture has cooled, add the chives.

When you are ready to fry the spring rolls, fill the skins as you heat oil in a deep fryer or wok. Have a beaten egg at hand for sealing the rolls. Take a spring roll skin and spread it out diamond-fashion. Put 2 to 3 tablespoons of filling in the lower half. Fold the bottom over the filling. Fold again, just past the halfway point. Bring each corner over to make an envelope, sealing the flaps with beaten egg. Roll up the envelope and seal. Fry the egg rolls a few at a time until golden brown, drain on paper towels and newspaper, and serve with the following sauce:

4 cloves garlic
1 tablespoon vinegar (rice wine or other white vinegar)
1 tablespoon chili paste (or less—this makes a fairly hot dip)
1 tablespoon sesame oil
3 tablespoons fish sauce or soy sauce

You can put everything in a blender or food processor. Adjust amounts and ingredients to your preference (a jalapeño pepper, for example, is an interesting variation for the chili paste, lime juice can replace the vinegar, coriander is a useful addition, etc.). Serve in individual bowls for dipping.

A meatless version of this dish can be had by substituting a flat, well-cooked omelet, cut in shreds, for the ground meat. Or you can simply include other vegetables, though I suggest avoiding celery and egg-plant. The idea is that the inside filling should be crunchy, with an interesting variety of flavors, the fried skin should be light and also crunchy, and the dip should be a real wake-up call to the mouth. If you hate raw garlic and hot pepper (or have trouble digesting them), it's easy to tame down the dipping sauce.

Two other points about spring rolls: They make good party food, sliced in half or thirds, and they can be very hot inside if you serve them right after frying them. Don't burn your mouth!

MAY

I Once More Smell the Dew and Rain

. . . .

As May moves forward, words like *froth* and *spray* keep coming to mind. Some trees are blossoming, some are leafing out, and the woods seem to fill slowly with white froth and green foam. Around town, forsythia add a buttery effervescence. As the crab apples and redbuds join in, magentas, fuchsias, and purples lather and spume everywhere you look. There's something about a fully blooming dogwood that seems to dazzle and to sizzle. Ebullience, fizziness, is everywhere in the air, an electricity that seems to affect even the earthworms you turn up as you till the soil for the garden. The worms change length and thickness restlessly, contracting, expanding, coiling, and uncoiling, always the same volume but never the same shape.

And the mushrooms, as the season begins with the morels, are like hardened foam, too. Pushing up unexpectedly and unpredictably from the earth, morels have an especially bizarre and gothic quality, with their spongelike conical caps and phallic impudence. Hollow and smoky, wrinkled and intricate, they are absolutely delicious to eat. Finding them, for a mushroom hunter, easily matches the better-known bliss of the trout fisherman, and they have the advantage, unlike trout, that if you can't eat your whole catch fresh, you can dry them and their flavor will be, if anything, even more intense when you reconstitute them.

My idea of a perfect spring episode is finding a half dozen morels and making them into a risotto or a sauce for pasta. It combines a number of pleasures: food that you would have to pay very steep prices for if you bought your mushrooms from a specialty grocer or, even more, if you ordered them in a gourmet restaurant; the old ritual of heading to the woods, going out into nature to reaffirm our connection to it, as when people in England gathered and brought back home the white blossoming branches of the hawthorn that they called "may"; and the excitement of the hunt and the thrill of successful foraging, as if to remind us of our hunting and gathering origins.

Our first stay of any length in Italy, in 1979, furthered our interest, as our sense of what wild mushrooms meant to Italian cuisine grew. One day, in the little town of Arcidosso in Tuscany, a weather-beaten old man came up to us in great excitement. He had one arm, having lost the other in World War I. Under this one arm was a basket, and in that basket was one of the biggest mushrooms I have ever seen, a huge porcino he had found somewhere up on the mountain, along with two smaller ones. We all admired his find. "From these mushrooms," he told us, "our cook will make a pasta sauce, enough to feed half the village. And they will be here tonight to eat it. Word will get around!"

I also remember a lecture that Gary Snyder gave at Oberlin College, where I teach. Discussing the climax forest as an example of how nature recycles materials and as a lesson human communities ought to emulate, he talked about fungi as a metaphor for poetry, breaking down and remaking dead matter, turning decay to humus, to something useful. We turn to poetry to express our deepest and most difficult feelings. It will make use of events and terrors nothing else can manage to deal with. Wasn't a poem, Snyder asked in an aside, really a kind of mushroom?

Somebody once said that if it were not for fungi, the whole planet would be covered by huge piles of dead wood. Not having leaves and roots, unable to manufacture food by means of chlorophyll, fungi are a special kind of "plant" that needs organic matter to exist. The decay of logs, branches, and roots is their very means to life. They feed on the flesh of animals, plants, and even other fungi, recycling life and death as they go.

How could I resist something that simultaneously resonates of good food, human community, ancestral foraging, mystery and darkness and dream, and finally metaphor itself, the language within the language, that source of creativity that I hunt, cherish, and treasure?

Some years back, I set to work systematically, learning how to find and identify mushrooms. All through the summer and fall I prowled the fields and woods for specimens, learning the major groups and their defining characteristics, taking the spore prints, differentiating among the similar kinds. After a year and a half, I felt sufficiently confident to begin cooking with mushrooms, drying them when they lent themselves to that means of preservation, and rejoicing in new discoveries, edible or not.

Morels are the elusive little spring treasures that initiate the mushroom hunter's season, fitfully but sometimes spectacularly. They are among the most prized and most elusive of the edibles, and no one has yet been able to grow them regularly in "captivity."

I remember very well the first time I went hunting specifically for morels. I knew from the books that they appeared early—"when oak leaves are mouse ears" is the folk wisdom on when to stalk them—and that they liked abandoned apple orchards. I knew of a very overgrown and desolate apple orchard in walking distance, and I searched it thoroughly one Sunday afternoon without finding a thing. Maybe it was *too* abandoned.

Returning home, a little dejected, I crossed a neighbor's backyard and suddenly found at my feet, as astonishing compensation for my search, some ten or eleven morels, buff-colored stalks with brown caps, ranging in height from three to six inches, in the thick grass behind our neighbor's garden. I split the find with the owner and had four or five good-sized morels to bear home in triumph.

A pile of fresh morels has an odor that makes you think someone just walked by smoking a first-rate Cuban cigar. I think that first time we simply cooked them in a little butter and ate them fresh, savoring the smoky, woodsy flavor. We promised ourselves an annual hunt for this particular example of nature's bounty. The experiments with pasta sauces and with risotto would come later.

The next year I found the old apple orchard in which I hunt regularly every year. The orchard covers about an acre and is so overgrown that just getting around in it takes time and effort. You move along slowly, eyes on the ground, pushing the twigs of little saplings and the prickly blackberry canes aside, watching for the smooth stalks and spongy wrinkled caps of morels. Here and there you encounter large ant-hills, and sometimes a morel will be growing next to one. Sometimes you find one mushroom by itself, sometimes a group of three or four. Some years you come away empty-handed, some years you are well rewarded. The best year was a May when, by my count, we took about thirty-five morels from that one acre over the course of the month.

More than twenty-five years ago I wrote a poem about May called "Homing." At the time it seemed to me that political events—Nixon's invasion of Cambodia, the Kent State and Jackson State shootings —had inspired the poem. And it is true that they insisted on weaving themselves into it. But the poem is really a dismissing of history and politics as overwhelming forces and facts. It counterposes life and family and spring and the enduring powers of nature to the dark and troubling events that had happened, for once, to fall in that playful, unfolding month. It shows me, or my persona, feeling morose and homeless because so deeply troubled, both by the political events and by the weird comedy of a poet-friend who took the political calamities so much to heart that they became an excuse for a terrific bender. But it also shows spring moving inexorably forward, majestic and indifferent, a counterpoint to our follies and miseries. The crows, the smoke bush, the vision of my farmer uncle, the clouds and trees and the gold-finch—most of all, perhaps, the innocent and devastating tulip—signal reassuringly to me that I have a home if I will just take note of it. It includes death, to be sure, mine and all others', but it is larger than any historical concern, no matter how troubling.

The poem was an attempt to process the events of that May in order to be able to go on. I say "process" rather than "understand" or even "order" because I do not think a poem needs to claim full comprehension of experience or make sense of what is fundamentally senseless. It is a mushroom forming in the duff of reality and chaos, a mycelial network of associations that suddenly gives rise to some organization, a fruiting. It simply tries to counter what Stevens called "the pressure of reality." In this case, there's an appeal, from within linear time, the nightmare of current history, to the larger meanings and rhythms that tend to subsume human misery and error.

HOMING

1

"Attacks are being launched
to clean out enemy sanctuaries . . ."

Watching the president's features
I'm childlike
homesick.

For what?
A warm basement in Des Moines
a den in a thicket
the dense invisible pulsar
in the huge Crab Nebula . . .

2

The visiting poet
has been on the bottle
all over Ohio. Come back

to the state he was born in,
missing his wife and New York apartment,
he rolls his big flushed
baby's head and whispers
"I want my mother."

Unwilling to be left alone
unwilling to talk to us
he recites for awhile like a bright child
and goes to bed hugging his misery.
Next morning he grabs a bus south.
I wave good-bye in the exhaust.
Everything's shaking.

3

The jackrabbit flushed by the car
is scared. In stiff
zigzag bounds he cuts
along the highway, then swerves suddenly
across an open field. Eighty yards to trees.
An easy shot.

But he knows
where he's going.

4

Pedaling home I glimpse
a sea-green boxcar
drifting along the tracks
by itself
and my uncle Bert, the best
farmer in the family,
dressed in fresh overalls
clinging to the ladder
is he waving me off
or beckoning?

At dusk
a half dozen crows come
slowly over
the factory, the dairy
heading back
to their roost in the swamp
too far in
for hunters to follow.

In the yard
the smoke bush sings:
You have
nowhere to turn to
now.

5
Heavy and calm
summer rolls in
grass rises around us
like mother love
clouds build
in great treeshapes
yellow, peach, violet
disperse or crash in storms
and the trees, cloudlike
boil up in the wind
jittery, blazing green.

A black and yellow bird
whose name escapes me—
startles me into pleasure
as I walk near the quarry
thinking of war, of the steady
state theory, of my children and
my parents, standing together

at Stonehenge
that Easter Sunday
my wife's mother
died of cancer.

Goldfinch! He flies up, wings
beating, is he in
my family, are we
home?

6

Sometimes I have to remember
to notice my children. Today
my daughter brought me a tulip
waxy and white, its petals
about to scatter——
hugging her I caught
in the fragrance of her hair
a smell of kinship.

Later we all
drove to the country
to see the green
sprouts in the long
plowed fields
the lambs, chickens, earthworms
who live so surely
on and in their earth, and when
we were tired
I glanced at the stacking clouds
and said
"Let's go home."

And we went
together, down the paved road
and not

as each of us would go
sometime, alone
rushing
across the black fields
toward the moon
that old bone
floating
out beyond evening.

My poem begins with Nixon, as the month began, and it ends with the Ohio fields and the moonrise. I couldn't seem to leave James Wright out of it, despite the problematic "gossip factor." And I think I found a home, after all, among the seasons, on and in the earth.

A twenty-five-year-old poem can seem like it was written by some- one else. But I put so much of what mattered to me, and still matters to me, into "Homing" that it feels oddly close and recent. What baffles me is that I am about the same distance in time from that poem as I was from the end of World War II when I wrote it. Does the fact that the second quarter-century feels closer than the first mean it has gone faster? I think rather that it shows how the second half of a life has more detail because mature awareness gives us a more capable and reliable memory. We can move around adroitly among many experiences. It may be that we idealize our childhoods because we really can't remem- ber them very fully, and even our adolescence and youth don't have the texture, retrospectively, that characterizes our memories of our thir- ties and forties and fifties. Memory is a faculty that has to come of age, and it may almost be the last part of us to mature and develop its fullest powers. So that terrible and wonderful May, and all its details, James Wright and the tulip and the goldfinch, feel remarkably close and recent.

⌒

Our frost date in this area is around the middle of May. Some put it even later, at the end of the month. Most of the peat pots I started in April are showing sprouts now, and I can begin putting them in where I have weeded and tilled a little: some spinach plants, some arugula shoots, some deer-tongue lettuce, and some kale. Coriander, a key herb for several great cuisines, gets a special new place, where we have taken out a scraggly bush.

Wrestling that bush out of the soil, chopping at its roots with a hatchet, I feel a surge of empathy with the pioneers who cleared this land with crude tools, cutting and tugging and sweating all day long. We second-guess them now for their insensitivity to native American cultures, but surely they earned some sense of ownership through the sheer physical exhaustion they experienced trying to clear and drain land for cultivation. We ought to be more grateful to them.

A good hard rain helps the little plants settle in. More planting is ahead, but I take some time off to go hunting for morels, unsuccessful so far but enjoying my walks in the spring woods, sometimes with the ecstatic dog as companion. At the wildlife preserve, the swallows swoop and skim the pond steadily, gathering insects for their newly hatched chicks. All this parenting activity has a measured and reassuring quality to it, the world going on with its business of regenerating itself.

The human spirit must flower. That sentence insisted, despite my initial resistance, on being set down. It sounds too obvious, too banal. But it is part of a truth that people bypass, and in bypassing it they deprive themselves of meaning and beauty. And then they die. The trope of the flower is finally even more crucial and essential than the trope of the mushroom.

Mushrooms are our ghosts, our dark side, our miraculous imaginative somersaults from rot to fruit. But flowers, simply, are what we are. We want to open to the light, to spread and blossom spiritually, to have an existence that feels adequate to our emotional needs and longings. Blooms-R-Us. We need to reconnect with that fact often, unembarrassed, just as we need to connect with the seasons, with spring and fall, with birth and mortality.

This morning I drove to the mall on an errand. The flowering trees and bushes were in full bloom everywhere, and I was listening to a tape of opera arias by Puccini—great full-throated, big-hearted singing, full of agony, inspiration, and celebration. Human passion, grandly flowering. I think about the idea that we are flowers. So many poets have written about the human spirit in these terms that you would think the metaphor couldn't retain its hold on us. But the great tropes seem to have infinite resources of renewal because they stem from our senses and the physical world we live in. They outlast the malls, even the mighty civilizations. Tu Fu understood this:

SPRING SCENE

The state goes to ruin
mountains and rivers survive

spring in the city
thick leaves   deep grass

in times like these
the flowers seem to weep

birds, as if they too
hated separation
flutter close by
startle the heart

for three months
the beacon fires
have been burning

a letter from home
is worth a fortune

this white hair
is getting so sparse
from scratching
pretty soon
it will be too thin
to hold a hatpin!

Human sorrow is real and complex here, but it is framed and contained by the larger reality of nature's ongoing vitality, which is fundamentally indifferent—the flowers only seem to weep—but nonetheless reassuring in its continuity.

Of course the continued use of the flower/spirit comparison means that poets are going to be self-conscious about it, aware of the precedents and sensitive to the gaps in the trope, the ways in which it doesn't quite fit us. Thus it was that in the eighth century that same great poet, Tu Fu, could tease himself, in "Seven for the Flowers Near the River," about his intoxication with spring and his shaky identification with the flowers. Thus it was that in the seventeenth century George Herbert could write honestly and recklessly of the joy of his recovered health and creativity:

THE FLOWER

How fresh, O Lord, how sweet and clean
Are thy returns! Even as the flowers in spring:
To which, besides their own demean,
The late-past frosts tributes of pleasures bring;
Grief melts away
Like snow in May,
As if there were no such cold thing.

Who would have thought my shriveled heart
Could have recovered greenness? It was gone
Quite under ground; as flowers depart
To see their mother-root, when they have blown;
Where they together
All the hard weather
Dead to the world, keep house unknown.

These are thy wonders, Lord of power,
Killing and quickening, bringing down to hell
And up to heaven in an hour;
Making a chiming of a passing-bell.
We say amiss

This or that is:
Thy word is all, if we could spell.

116

O that I once past changing were,
Fast in thy Paradise, where no flowers can wither!
Many a spring I shoot up fair,
Offering at heaven, growing and groaning thither;
Nor doth my flower
Want a spring shower,
My sins and I joining together.

But while I grow in a straight line,
Still upwards bent, as if heaven were mine own,
Thy anger comes, and I decline.
What frost to that? What pole is not the zone
Where all things burn,
When thou dost turn,
And the least frown of thine is shown?

And now in age I bud again,
After so many deaths I live and write;
I once more smell the dew and rain,
And relish versing. O my only light,
It cannot be
That I am he
On whom thy tempests fell all night.

These are thy wonders, Lord of love,
To make us see we are but flowers that glide:
Which when we once can find and prove,
Thou has a garden for us, where to bide.
Who would be more,
Swelling through store,
Forfeit their Paradise by their pride.

I have been memorizing this Herbert poem this month. The lines of the
second and sixth stanzas seem to have a special pertinence to my life

and its renewal after grief, and I love to repeat them to myself as I walk around outside or putter in the kitchen.

The flower trope seems to have great integrity and longevity. I think of Rilke, early in this century, in one of the *Sonnets to Orpheus,* critiquing our human ways by reminding us that flowers have openness, receptivity, and a kind of legerity that we long for:

> *Look at the flowers, loyal to the earth—*
> *we lend them fate from fate's border, but*
> *who knows if they regret the way they wither?*
> *Maybe it's we who are their real regret.*

> *All things want to float. And we go around like burdens,*
> *settling ourselves on everything, ravished by weight;*
> *what deadly teachers we are, when things in fact*
> *have the gift of forever being children.*

> *If someone took them into inmost sleep and slept*
> *soundly with things—how lightly he might rise*
> *changed, to changed days, from that communal depth.*

> *Or maybe he'd stay; and they'd blossom and praise*
> *him, the convert, now one with those brothers and sisters*
> *all still in the midst of the winds and the meadows.*

Rilke suggests that finally to merge with the flowers would be to accept our mortality, an enchanted sleep with the natural world for company.

The smells of May are vivid, intoxicating. The sounds are sometimes strange: a chain saw, a flock of crows so distressed they seem to be announcing the end of the world. Around me are the killdeer: birds in the plover family that have adapted perfectly to this current environment. They nest on the ground, around plowed fields and pastures, even around malls and cinemaplexes and megastores, wherever there is some open space and enough grass or weeds. They are quite happy nesting on this flat, sometimes featureless world of ours.

Their cries—their name comes from the fact that the repeated sound is like "kill-deeeeer"—sound both plaintive and sweet, and they scurry around in front of me as I jog on the fitness trail, trying to lure me away from where their nests and hatchlings are hidden in the high grass. This is a song I can translate, I think, this sweet, forlorn song of theirs. I tried it once:

HOMAGE TO
WILLIAM CARLOS WILLIAMS

Where I park
the grass today
is lit with pink

magnolia petals
same as the black
Chevy Impala

dotted with green
bud husks from
a maple &

in clear puddles
on the black
asphalt the gray

spring sky is
strangely mirrored:
a song that gives

the world right
back to itself
or the continuous

cries the killdeer
cry around us
here——cries

neither sad nor
happy, cries
violent & sweet

as spring itself
wild with
wanting to live.

The American Indians named the months around the moons they featured. They called May the month of the Planting Moon and the month of the Song Moon. One pictograph combined the two concepts by showing a singing bird perched on the handle of a planting stick. That song is a flowering. It can be the weird shrill call of the killdeer, it can be an aria by Puccini. It will begin, at least, to sum up the designs and meanings of May.

MAY RECIPES

Wild Mushroom Risotto

This is my favorite morel recipe, but I have named it
to remind myself and my readers that you can use any
edible mushroom here, any time of the year. If you go
morel hunting in May and come back empty-handed,
temper your disappointment by buying some shiitakes
in the supermarket or soaking some dried porcini in
hot water. That way you at least get to taste something
that rewards you for your interest. I think the single
best mushroom risotto I ever had was made not from
morels but from porcini, probably dried ones given the
time of year (early June). It was on the part of the Italian Ligurian coast called the Cinque Terre, in a little
town called Monterosso, where the poet Montale spent
his summers from childhood on.

4 ounces wild mushrooms,
    cleaned and sliced
2 tablespoons unsalted butter
2 tablespoons olive oil
1 medium-sized onion, minced
1 cup Arborio rice

3 cups stock—beef broth, mushroom
   soaking liquid, and white wine
2 teaspoons salt
freshly ground black pepper
Parmesan cheese

Most mushroom hunters like to clean mushrooms by brushing off dirt and debris rather than washing them. Morels need to be sliced because you sometimes find bugs inside them. Washing is okay if it makes you feel better about them.

To prepare this in the microwave, melt the butter and oil first in a serving dish, for example, a quiche dish, with waxed paper over the dish to avoid splattering. Give them 1½ minutes at full power. Then add the onions (waxed paper again) and microwave another 1½ minutes at full. Now add the mushrooms and go another 1½ minutes. Then stir in the rice and cook for 2½ minutes. Stir in the 3 cups of stock. The richer the stock, the better. If you have homemade broth, you'll get the best risotto, and you'll find that white wine makes a good supplement, as does the liquid in which you've soaked the mushrooms if you are using dried ones.

You can abandon the waxed paper now. Cook for 9 minutes, stir the dish, then cook for 9 minutes more. The risotto should stand for a few minutes after coming out of the oven, and then you can season it: salt and pepper stirred in, then cheese if you feel it will supplement the flavors. But taste it first: if the mushrooms are good, you may want to let their flavor dominate, leaving cheese out.

If you make this without a microwave, simply follow the same order at the stove: sauté the onions in the butter and oil, add the mushrooms, then the rice, then the stock, a little at a time from a pan where you are keeping it hot. As the stock is absorbed by the rice, you can add more until it's all gone. This will take about 20 minutes. Some people dump all the stock in the pot, cover it, and stir it after 20 or 30 minutes. You can test the rice to see if it's done by tasting a grain; it should still be a little chewy or crunchy. If you haven't used all the broth, stop. If you've added it all, you can drain the rice. If the rice doesn't seem done, put some more liquid in until it is. I honestly don't know whether a stove-top risotto, lovingly attended and stirred, is markedly better than a microwave version. I do know the microwave makes it really easy, allowing you to work on other dishes, so I nearly always go that way.

You can use just about any mushroom for this dish, but I wouldn't recommend substituting the rice. Arborio rice is definitely worth looking and paying a little extra for.

●

Wild Mushroom Soup

This is based on a recipe in Margaret Leibenstein's *The Edible Mushroom*. Again, it is a morel recipe that you can adapt for other available mushrooms if you don't get lucky in your hunting. You can also use dried morels, reconstituting them in hot water and saving (and straining) the soaking water to add to the soup.

8 ounces fresh morels (or other
    mushroom, 4 ounces if dried)
3 tablespoons butter
1 chopped shallot
1 bay leaf
1 tablespoon flour
4 cups stock—chicken, veal, or beef
1 egg yolk
1 cup sour cream
4 tablespoons chopped fresh tarragon

Slice the morels (you want to make sure the stalks are hollow, for one thing; if not, they're false morels, which are slightly poisonous; also, they occasionally have little beetles or grubs living inside the stems) and clean them off. Melt the butter in a pot you can cover, add the shallot (you should have at least a tablespoon), and sauté for a couple of minutes. Add the mushrooms, stir to coat, put the bay leaf in, and cover the pot. You are "sweating" the mushrooms at this point, and you'll need low heat and 3 or 4 minutes to accomplish that. Remove the lid and sprinkle the mushrooms with flour. Stir well. Add the stock, a little at a time, stirring continuously, then cover the pan and let the soup simmer for half an hour at the most.

Whisk the egg yolk and sour cream together and add them slowly to the soup, stirring continuously. Serve the soup in bowls with chopped tarragon sprinkled over the top. Some variations: Add a little Madeira before the stock goes in. Use crème fraîche in place of sour cream.

●

Fresh Oregano Sauce for Gnocchi

Make the homemade gnocchi recipe described in the March chapter (p. 72). (I find I get hungry for gnocchi at least once a month, and that I get a lot of satisfaction out of baking the potatoes, combining their riced flesh with the flour, and rolling out, cutting, and shaping the gnocchi; seeing good-looking baking potatoes in the market often sets off my gnocchi urge.)

6 tablespoons unsalted butter
1 cup fresh oregano leaves
¾ cup grated Parmesan cheese

Melt the butter in a frying pan. When the butter foams, add the oregano and remove it from the heat. Take a moment to savor the fragrance
released by the contact of fresh herb and hot butter! As you cook the
gnocchi, pour some of this sauce and a sprinkling of cheese over each
batch. Toss at the end and serve, with additional grated cheese available
at the table.

This is an adaptation of a classic that is usually made with fresh sage
leaves. If you have those, you can substitute, cutting them into strips.
You won't need a full cup's worth, more like half to two-thirds.

●

Mango, Sweet Pepper, and Sorrel Salsa
for Grilled Fish Steaks

This is a version of a recipe from the March chapter.
The salsa will go well with salmon, halibut, or swordfish steaks. They should be simply grilled, brushed be-
forehand with a little olive oil to help keep them from
sticking. If you're using the outdoor grill, you can give
them about 2 minutes to a side and then finish them in
a slow oven for 10 minutes or so if they are thick and
their centers are still too raw for you. This is a matter
of taste, and I would rather undercook the fish—you
can always zap an underdone steak for a minute in the
microwave—than risk making it dry and dull.

———◦◦◦———

1 sweet red pepper
1 mango (need not be very ripe)

1 cup sorrel leaves, cut in strips
1 clove garlic (optional)
$\frac{1}{2}$ cup olive oil
salt and pepper

You can chop the ingredients by hand or you can put them into a food processor. Add the olive oil last, as a binder. Add just a very small amount of salt and pepper. Great with chardonnay!

●

Tarragon Spread for Bruschetta

If you are grilling, toast your thick slices of country bread right on the grill, rubbing them with a cut clove of garlic after you take them off. Spread the egg and tarragon mixture on and serve either as an appetizer or as accompaniment to a meal of grilled meat and salad.

2 hard-boiled eggs, chopped
$\frac{1}{2}$ cup fresh tarragon leaves, chopped
2 tablespoons capers
$\frac{1}{4}$ cup olive oil
salt

Combine the eggs, tarragon, and capers, then add the olive oil and whisk gently. Add a pinch of salt. Spread on freshly toasted bread slices or let your guests do that from a bowl.

●

Tarragon and Parsley Sauce

Mostly we associate tarragon with French cooking, but
it is much loved and much used around Siena, where,
as *dragoncello,* it is used for sauces like the following:

———

1 large slice stale bread, soaked in
    water and squeezed out
$\frac{1}{4}$ cup fresh tarragon leaves, chopped
$\frac{1}{4}$ cup fresh Italian parsley, chopped
1 clove garlic, chopped
$\frac{1}{2}$ cup olive oil
salt and pepper
1 tablespoon wine vinegar or
    balsamic vinegar

Put the bread, garlic, tarragon, and parsley in a food processor. Pulse
to blend. Add olive oil gradually. Remove from food processor to a
small bowl, and season to taste with salt and pepper. Stir in vinegar.

For a quick main course in May, microwave or poach four skinless
boneless chicken breasts, slice them, put them on a small platter, and
add this sauce.

●

Garmugia

This is a soup from around Lucca, in Tuscany. I make it
in May because I can get fresh fava beans and fresh peas,
as well as asparagus and artichoke. It is a vegetable-
lover's delight.

———

4 tablespoons olive oil
4 scallions, chopped

4–5 slices of prosciutto, chopped
1 pound fresh fava beans, shelled
1 pound garden peas, shelled
$\frac{1}{2}$ pound asparagus, cut in 1-inch
    pieces
4 artichokes, quartered and trimmed
$1\frac{1}{2}$ quarts stock—chicken, veal, or
    vegetable
salt and pepper
5 tablespoons chopped parsley
slices of country bread toasted and
    cut into strips

Fry the scallions and prosciutto lightly for 5 minutes in the olive oil. Add the beans, peas, asparagus, and artichokes (which you will have trimmed of their chokes and inedible portions of the leaves), and sauté for 5 minutes or so. Add the stock and bring the soup to a simmer. It will need about 15 minutes of gentle cooking to be ready. Season with salt and pepper, add the parsley, and pour over the toasted bread strips in individual bowls.

This soup is tricky because it depends on the freshness of the vegetables and on cooking them just to the point of readiness. They should not be crunchy or chewy but should still project their freshness. Ground meat—beef or veal—is sometimes added in the first stage, but I don't find that it really improves the soup, and in fact if you want to be totally vegetarian you can omit the prosciutto, use vegetable stock, and still have excellent results. Be careful not to overseason or overcook, and don't be discouraged if the first batch is not perfect. This soup grows on you and requires patient trial and error, along with some experimentation. Basil and fennel are sometimes added to the parsley.

Pasta Sauce Puccini

The idea of naming this dish for Puccini, my May composer, isn't entirely arbitrary, since he came from Lucca (home of the soup described above), and this pasta sauce has versions that are ascribed to that city as well. It is a cousin of the famous *pappardelle con lepre,* pasta with hare sauce. Giuliano Bugialli gives a rabbit version, which he traces to Lucca in his *Foods of Tuscany.* The duck version came from a *New York Times Magazine* piece by Nancy Harmon Jenkins.

Duck and rabbit may sound like very different meats, but the basic method of cooking the whole carcass in a sauce of vegetables, wine, and tomatoes, then stripping the meat and returning it to the sauce works very well with either animal. The result has a knockout flavor, a dish that looks like just another pasta dish but turns out to be rich, filling, and deeply memorable. I would tend to want to make it with rabbit in the spring and duck in the fall.

If you want a dish that really smacks of Lucca, make big pasta ribbons (e.g., with the lasagna attachment of your pasta maker) and cut them into 2-inch squares. Or buy or make broad ribbon noodles, *pappardelle.*

—⟨∾∾⟩—

1 pound fresh pasta, squares or broad ribbons
1 duck (about 2 ½ pounds) or 1 rabbit
    (about 2–3 pounds)
1 large onion, red or yellow, chopped
2 small carrots, scraped
2 celery stalks, chopped
3–4 ounces prosciutto, pancetta, or bacon,
    diced

1 large clove garlic
4 large sage leaves
1 handful of rosemary leaves
$\frac{1}{4}$–$\frac{1}{2}$ cup olive oil (less with the duck,
    more with the rabbit)
2 cups wine (you can use white or red, but it
    should be dry)
1–2 cups chicken stock
2 pounds fresh tomatoes or 1 large can Italian
    tomatoes
salt and pepper
3–4 tablespoons chopped parsley
grated Parmesan cheese

If the duck or rabbit has been frozen, you will have thawed it and cut it into quarters or into 6 pieces. If you have time and are inclined, you can marinate it overnight with the wine and coarsely chopped vegetables and herbs. Drain, saving the wine, and dry off the vegetables.

In a food processor create a paste made up of the celery, carrot, onion, garlic, sage, rosemary, and prosciutto. Sauté the paste in the olive oil in a large frying pan that has a lid, or in a casserole. When the mixture is softened and fragrant, add the duck or rabbit pieces and brown them, turning frequently. Now add the wine and let it cook down. Add the stock and do the same. This may take 15 to 20 minutes total. Put the tomatoes through a food mill, whether they are fresh or canned, and add them. Fresh tomatoes don't always cooperate with the food mill, so give them 3 minutes in the microwave if you want them to go through easily. Season with salt and pepper. Add the parsley.

Cook this mixture covered for an hour, adding water or stock or wine if the mixture seems to be getting too dry. Take the lid off and cook an additional 15 minutes, again adding stock if you need to. Remove carcass pieces and set them out on a board to cool. Remove the meat from the bones and chop it roughly, then put it back in the casserole and let it cook a few minutes more. Skim fat from the sauce if you have been cooking duck. Adjust seasonings. The sauce is ready for the pasta.

Cook the pasta briefly in boiling salted water and add it to the sauce if you have room. Mix thoroughly. Turn the whole thing into a serving dish and send to the table. Portions at the table should be sprinkled with grated Parmesan and ground black pepper. This whole thing tastes as good as a Puccini aria sounds.

JUNE

With Barnaby the Bright

. . . .

Memorial Day and the college's commencement always coincide in my life, and they mark an emphatic turn from spring to summer. Finishing up grades, saying good-bye to students, stepping away from a hectic schedule, I am grateful once more for the three-month summer break. I once suggested that a teacher is a kind of vegetation god, torn apart during the year and reassembled over the summer. I was only partly joking.

Certainly it is agreeable to approach the cool green tunnel of the summer with a different pace—an amble rather than a scurry. Even the small town I live in changes appreciably, reverting to a sleepy community where hardly anything seems to happen. The traffic lights are reset to blinking red and amber. Huge deciduous trees, loaded with foliage, loom quietly over somnolent green streets. Now and then a bicyclist passes. Summer rains, ranging from the barest sprinkles to fierce thunderstorms, cross our emerald world. We seem a little lost: to history, to geopolitics, to issues of scope and moment. The summer can feel timeless, as though it were all summers at once, stretching back over innumerable small-town years—shirt-sleeve and ice-cream and softball years.

I once tried to characterize this as a sense of being submerged:

. .

> There is so much green in summer
> That the town sinks through water,
> A mottled Atlantis, where you might stroll
> On a brick street some leaky evening
> And see above you a black whale
> Nosing and browsing
> Among the caverns of the trees.

Space becomes relative, somehow, as though the normal differences and distances no longer pertain. Something similar happens to time. Every past moment is copresent with every other and with the present instant.

Perhaps there is something *too* dreamlike and suspended about the summer. By the time August rolls to a close and the students return, we will be glad enough to have them back. For now, though, it's a stretching and luxurious welcome to summer that colors the consciousness and seeps through long days and gentle nights.

In 1980, George McGovern spoke at our commencement. He made us all more aware of, and more worried about, the nuclear arms race. Soon after, I finished a journal poem called "In My Own Back Yard," whose last section, a May-June transition, partly reflects his emphasis on fear of a nuclear Armageddon, a fear my whole generation grew up with. Here again, though, as in "Homing," note how the political issues tend to be comprehended by the larger sense of an existence that surrounds and outlasts them:

> Late May. Summer coming on again. I think
> Li Po may not be back. Worried about
> the world's end, as, I realize,
> I have been most of my life,
> I take my work outside
> and sit on the deck, distracted.
> It was a day like this, I think,
> in Hiroshima.
> Distracted.

J U N E

There must be something in the pine-cones
that the chickadees—there's another one.
What's this that's snowing down? Husks, pollen,
freckle-sized petals from our wild-cherry trees!

We sneeze and plant tomatoes. Ultimatums. The world
comes close and goes away
in rhythms that our years
help us begin to understand.

We haven't long to live.
And the world? Surely the world . . .
A deep breath. Sunshine.
Mosquitoes, bird calls, petal hail.

To be human, as I grew up, was to be aware that we might destroy ourselves and a good deal of the world we lived in at any moment. Even in my own backyard. I couldn't plant a tomato or watch a chickadee in a way that was entirely free of a fearful, almost inconceivable possibility. But the poem balances on the edge of a recognition that our destruction might not be the world's, that it is even egotistical of us to imagine we can destroy existence. The poem dozes with its unanswered questions in the summer sunshine, acknowledging the limits of political understanding and the limitlessness of being in that dreamy, hammock-slung summer sense of timelessness, ripeness, benevolent sunshine.

As June transforms spring into summer, the days move majestically into long twilights and then deep night, then back again. Thunderstorms approach like armadas, ships of the line, firing off lightning. Around town, as the month opens, the azaleas and rhododendrons bloom profusely, irises and peonies make flamboyant appearances, and honeysuckle and wisteria are prodigious both in their look and in their heady fragrances. But it is the trees that dominate. Their height and lavish greenery made the world seem submerged to me when I wrote that poem. They enter the summer at their peak—oaks, copper beeches, maples, sweet gums, a few surviving elms—standing resplendently full in summer sunshine upon their firmly outlined shadows.

One tree that blossoms spectacularly in late May and early June is the horse chestnut. Suddenly, horse chestnuts are covered with sensational white flower clusters, as bedecked and festive as a Christmas tree. The flowers are described as "bell-shaped" in the tree books, but they could also be called conical: they look like miniature white spruce trees. For a week or so they transform the tall horse chestnuts with stunning displays of white bloom, and then, just as suddenly, they are gone.

Our native buckeyes, meanwhile, are more apt to get planted for the attractiveness of their fall foliage, if at all. Their flowers are a greenish yellow, and not nearly as impressive. Their large seeds, like those of the horse chestnut, are known as "buckeyes" because of their resemblance to a large deer's eye, a rather poetic naming. The seeds were thought to help ward off rheumatism; settlers carried a seed in their pocket for this purpose. In fact, its seeds, bark, and foliage are all toxic in various ways, ways that have sometimes been considered medicinal (in the case of the bark, especially) but that have also been used, for example, to poison fish. The wood has served for furniture, musical instruments, floorboards, and boxes, so that this rather strange and oddly serviceable tree, while it doesn't bloom with the flamboyance

of its Eurasian cousin, was eventually adopted by my state as an effica-
cious symbol.

The fitness trail where I exercise every other day in summer provides a variety of majestic trees. First comes a group of evergreens, all
fragrant at this time of year, some pollinating heavily with a greenish
dust. Then I pass a row of Russian olive trees on one side and a row of
American elms on the other. Beyond the elms is a honey locust that
matches their three-story size, and a little farther down a great big bur
oak, more like four stories.

The dog goes with me, zigzagging. The killdeer scurry past or fly up
a little and settle back down, folding their elegant gull wings, showing
their neat bands of black and white against their brown bodies. But our
activities feel dwarfed and a little pointless among the summer reveries of the trees. They rise patiently all around us, the greatest living
things in the vicinity. A "tree hymn" I composed a few years back tried
to enter the point of view of a tree (my backyard red maple, as I recall).
I wanted to imagine what it would be like to have no front or back, left
or right, eyes or ears:

> *An ear and eye spread out and floating*
> *half in the sky, half in the earth. Rootedness*
> *that branches down through minerals and fissures.*
> *Breathing and growing that leave no urge to move,*
> *a balancing in brightness, sap chugging in the dark,*
> *rough skin, a drowse that blurs the years and days,*
> *a streaming upward and a holding downward,*
> *ripple and tingle of buds and opening leaves*
> *white self ripped open by the lightning split,*
> *flexing and swaying by its monumental shadow.*

Trees in their summer splendor, standing alone or in small groups on a
meadow, make me think of Emily Dickinson and Charles Burchfield. I
love the ecstatic nature paintings of Burchfield. In their expressionis-
tic, confident response to this landscape, these seasons, this weather,

his paintings do for northern Ohio (and western Pennsylvania and the western end of New York) what Van Gogh did for the countryside near Arles and Cézanne for the region around Mont-Saint-Victoire.

Dickinson's poem about four trees has her characteristic combination of simplicity and mystery:

> Four Trees—upon a solitary Acre—
> Without Design
> Or Order, or Apparent Action—
> Maintain—
>
> The Sun—upon a Morning meets them—
> The Wind—
> No nearer neighbor—have they—
> But God—
>
> The Acre gives them—Place—
> They—Him—Attention of Passer by—
> Of Shadow, or of Squirrel, haply—
> Or boy—
>
> What Deed is Their's unto the General Nature—
> What Plan
> They severally—retard—or further—
> Unknown—

Susan Howe, in *My Emily Dickinson,* says: "This is the *process* of viewing Emptiness without design or plan, neighborless in winter blank, or blaze of summer. This is waste wilderness. Nature no soothing mother, Nature is annihilation brooding over" (21). It seems to me that words like *emptiness* and *blank* and *waste* and *annihilation* are out of place here. Far from "Emptiness," the trees have each other, have their meetings with sun and wind, have God as a neighbor, have their interactions with shadows, boys, and squirrels, all of whom tend to appreciate them.

Much more to the point is what Guy Davenport says about this poem in his book *Charles Burchfield's Seasons,* where he is comparing Burchfield's wonderful painting *The Three Trees* to the Dickinson poem. "It is the raw fact of the trees' existence that Dickinson focuses on," he argues, "making a piercing riddle of that fact." Burchfield's painting is almost certainly an allusion to Dickinson's poem, and Davenport suggests that it may contain an encoded image of his monograph signature. A little imagination can also make his three trees form the initials E. D.! I agree with Davenport that "Burchfield's trees are beings, presences, silent and majestic cohabitants of the earth with the lion and the robin. They are alive in a different way, secretly in public view." So, we might add, are Emily Dickinson's trees. And "secretly in public view" characterizes her poems as well.

The soil in my yard, where trees like the red maple and wild cherry do so well, is mainly clay. The glaciers that formed this landscape left us this clay soil, but they also left periodic ridges in which the soil is more sandy. I learn from my colleague, the biologist Tom Sherman, who has been writing a book called *A Place on the Glacial Till,* that these ridges, which run roughly east-west and occur every few miles as you go south from Lake Erie, are the beachy shores of ancient postglacial lakes.

These beach ridges, in this case from ancient lakes named Whittlesey and Warren, offer the best farming in our area. Lots of our roads run along these ridges, and driving them means passing truck gardens, greenhouses, vegetable stands, orchards, and other such evidence of their productive soil.

Among the first spring products of those glacial ridges are the strawberries. Around the second week of June this crop begins to arrive in sensational fashion, with stands selling berries and U-Pick signs at the biggest berry farms. The arrival of the strawberries in June, like the asparagus that comes in April and May, is one of the most welcome events of the year. It isn't just the taste of this fruit that entrances us. The color and the unusual fragrance are factors as well. I like to have them on the seat beside me as I go home, letting their smell fill the car.

And surely strawberry pies, tarts, and other such concoctions delight us partly because their redness is so enticing. If you couldn't eat a bowl of strawberries, for some reason, but could still sniff it and admire the shape and color of the berries, you'd have a significant percentage of the pleasure they afford.

Nancy Willard has a fanciful poem about how the strawberry seceded from God's creation and set up a rival creation of its own, with its own stars pocking its body, its own green north pole, and a mandala inside that you find by halving it horizontally. "Pick a strawberry," her poem advises, "as if you were paying court." Good advice, for that activity involves bending over and carefully releasing the berry from the stem.

Apparently, the strawberry isn't technically a berry, or even a fruit. It's "a swollen stem end dotted with black fruit (the 'seeds')," according to *The Cook's Book,* by Howard Hillman. Of course, the "seeds" don't look black on the berries we buy, but green. Inside is a world of deep red juice that stains your fingers and delights your tongue. I almost never eat strawberries during the rest of the year, and that doubles the pleasure of their short June season. I like them on cereal in the morning, and I have always loved making batches of fresh, homemade strawberry ice cream, trying to come as close to Italian gelato as I can. Recently I've discovered that strawberries are extremely good with balsamic vinegar, another Italian tradition, and I think a dessert composed of strawberries, yogurt, sugar, vinegar, orange peel, lemon zest, and Cointreau is a June phenomenon worth making two or three times a week during the brief June strawberry season.

Cherries follow the strawberries closely, around the middle of the month. I usually find myself picking and eating sweet cherries as June, three-fourths over, brings Midsummer Eve around. This is a holiday I got into the habit of celebrating because I researched it once, in the process of writing a book on Shakespeare's *A Midsummer Night's Dream.*

My affinity with this ancient solar festival might have come about any-
way, but delving into the Elizabethans' sense of it rapidly fostered its
presence in my own life. It helped me realize how vigorously the ancient "pagan" holidays, especially those connected to the solstices—
the time around Christmas and the time of late June—have survived
from religions now forgotten, with old customs and rituals and meanings all tangled up among the religions and the "secular" holidays that
have "replaced" them.

My research into Midsummer customs revealed not only the survival of very old customs in Shakespeare's time, like building bonfires
and rolling burning wheels stuffed with straw and rags down from hill-
tops, but also a sophisticated awareness of what these customs had once
symbolized—the apogee of the sun and various magical ways of in-
suring its continuity and beneficence. The Elizabethans knew that the
solar religion that gave rise to the customs was gone and that their
continuance of the rituals was thus a mixture of assimilation, contradiction, and nostalgia. They seemed sometimes highly aware of the
modified meanings—what had been mythically literal became, in effect, poetically metaphorical—and sometimes simply unconcerned
about them.

Edmund Spenser seems to have arranged to be married around Midsummer largely in order to be able to write it up in his splendid "Epitha-
lamion," a poem in which he is singing to himself ("So I unto myself
alone will sing"), but fully intending to be overheard: he published the
poem the next year, along with the love sonnets that supposedly docu-
ment the courtship leading to the marriage. In this very remarkable
midsummer and marriage poem, Spenser plays with his subject and
with the interaction of the personal and the communal. The fact that
it's the longest day of the year, for instance, delays the natural desires of
the bride and bridegroom for the consummation of their nuptial night.
The community celebrations of Midsummer—bell ringing, bonfire
building, divination, flower decking—become events that the poet can
pretend are all in honor of his wedding and his bride. The old tradition

that spirits are abroad in the woods on Midsummer Eve, and that divinations and transformations are possible, though dangerous, becomes a pretext for his invoking a night-blessing and exorcism.

The result is as sophisticated a handling of the meanings of folklore and the survival of old rituals into a "modern" world as one could wish for:

> Ring ye the bels, ye yong men of the towne,
> And leave your wonted labors for this day:
> This day is holy; doe ye write it downe,
> That ye for ever it remember may.
> This day the sunne is in his chiefest hight,
> With Barnaby the bright,
> From whence declining daily by degrees,
> He somewhat loseth of his heat and light,
> When once the Crab behind his back he sees.
> But for this time it ill ordained was,
> To choose the longest day in all the yeare,
> And shortest night, when longest fitter weare:
> Yet never day so long, but late would passe.
> Ring ye the bels, to make it weare away,
> And bonefiers make all day,
> And daunce about them, and about them sing:
> That all the woods may answer, and your eccho ring.

The reason Spenser locates Midsummer on "Barnaby the bright" (St. Barnabas's Day), June 11, is that that was concurrent with the solstice by the old calendar. A. Kent Hieatt, in his *Short Time's Endless Monument*, argues persuasively that Spenser's poem is numerologically symbolic, its twenty-four stanzas matching the hours of the day, its 365 long lines matching the days of the year, and many other such touches reinforcing its function not only as a marriage celebration but a cunning little model of time itself, intricately constructed and intended to be "for short time an endless monument," as its last line claims. In other words, while Spenser is playful he is also intensely serious, putting everything he knows and believes about time and its meaning into his own wedding poem.

And what about the night, the shortest of the year? Midsummer Eve was traditionally a time when people went out to the woods to make love, to practice divination, and to gather magical seeds like those of the fern and oak that were supposed to bloom once a year on the summer solstice. There they were apt to encounter spirits who might practice mischief on them. The strange lights they glimpsed in the woods could be marsh gas and other forms of natural phosphorescence, but they were often explained as mischievous characters like "Jack-with-a-lantern" and "Will-with-a-wisp," who led them astray ("laughing at their harm," as Shakespeare's Puck puts it) and into swamps. For Spenser, of course, a wedding night should be undisturbed by dreams, noises, spirits, and disruptions of any kind:

> *Let no lamenting cryes, nor dolefull tears,*
> *Be heard all night within nor yet without:*
> *Ne let false whispers, breeding hidden feares,*
> *Break gentle sleepe with misconceived dout.*
> *Let no deluding dreames, nor dreadful sights*
> *Make sudden sad affrights;*
> *Ne let housefyres, nor lightnings helpelesse harmes,*
> *Ne let the Pouke, nor other evill sprights,*
> *Ne let mischivous witches with theyr charmes,*
> *Ne let hob Goblins, names whose sence we see not,*
> *Fray us with things that be not.*
> *Let not the shriech Oule, nor the Storke be heard:*
> *Nor the night Raven that still deadly yels,*
> *Nor damned ghosts cald up with mighty spels,*
> *Nor griesly vultures make us once affeard:*
> *Ne let th'unpleasant Quyre of Frogs still croking*
> *Make us to wish theyr choking.*
> *Let none of these theyr drery accents sing;*
> *Ne let the wood them answer, nor theyr eccho ring.*

It is a tenderly ironic consideration of magical thinking and acting that both acknowledges the fictive nature of the magic and yet allows for its importance in expressing the human interaction with nature and the supernatural. I found it fun to contemplate from a scholarly perspective, but also, and more to the point, quite relevant to my own life and my own poetry.

That frogs and owls and storks, on the one hand, can be conjoined in a "spell" of exorcism with dreams, house fires, lightning, Pucks, witches, and hobgoblins, suggests a continuity of the natural and the supernatural with the human imagination and the activity of the poet. That's why it's such fun to consider Spenser's poem next to Shakespeare's handling of the same holiday in his play.

The poetry of Shakespeare's comedy is richer and more evocative than anything he had written previously. It is as if the subject allowed him to bring together the lyrical and theatrical sides of his talent. His own knowledge of the natural world, as one who grew up in the country, around woods and farms and in a peasant culture, serves him admirably. So does his familiarity with the folklore about fairies, pookas, and household spirits that he probably heard around the winter fire from his mother and grandmother. His delight in bringing together apparently unlike manifestations of the imagination, such as the mythical Theseus and the folkloric Robin Goodfellow, gleams unmistakably through the plot, characters, and language of the play. Its long speeches are like opera arias where the audience is intended to succumb to the evocation of a natural world shot through with supernatural and imaginative meanings that reinforce the human connection to nature:

> Be kind and courteous to this gentleman:
> Hop in his walks and gambol in his eyes;
> Feed him with apricocks and dewberries,
> With purple grapes, green figs, and mulberries;
> The honey-bags steal from the humble-bees,
> And for night-tapers crop their waxen thighs,

And light them at the fiery glow-worms' eyes
To have my love to bed, and to arise;
And pluck the wings from painted butterflies
To fan the moonbeams from his sleeping eyes.
Nod to him, elves, and do him courtesies.

Did Shakespeare and Spenser know of each other's handling of Midsummer as a metaphor for art's meaning and value? Almost certainly. The temporal coincidence of the poem and the play would be otherwise too hard to explain. Spenser was married in 1594 and published his poem the next year. The date given for the first performances of the *Dream* is 1595, though it is sometimes conjectured the play was written in 1594, while the theaters were closed. Most scholars also accept the idea that it was first performed on the occasion of an aristocratic wedding, as part of the matrimonial festivities.

Is one work a source for the other? We will never know. What we do know is that some of the best poetry in our language came out of this felicitous conjunction of marriage, holiday, theater, and poetry.

The summer solstice, as ancient holiday and as natural moment for celebration, continues among us. I've always thought that the American love of fireworks on Independence Day, so close to the solstice, may partly be a survival of the lights in darkness associated with the old solar festivals. In any case, our family fell into the habit of having a party on the longest day, complete with a few fireworks. This summer, as it happens, we celebrated the solstice in Italy, on top of a mountain in Umbria, with sparklers and a small bonfire, and one of my oldest friends fell in love with one of my newest ones. Several years ago, my heart still heavy with grief, I doggedly organized a party, mostly because my grown children still seemed to expect it, and found myself falling in love with the woman whom I would marry near a winter solstice a few years later:

At our Midsummer party
we tried to have all kinds of light:
a bonfire, candles, Tahiti torches,
fireflies adding their dots on the dark;
we set off pinwheels, Roman candles,
brandished sparklers—and later, above embers,
we were content with starlight.
I was a little miserable. I thought
myself on the other shore of love;
the pinwheels were for the sun's renewal,
not for mine. My mind went back
to the sun's other birthday,
that Christmas Eve we read "The Dead"
and watched the snow in the floodlight.

Love makes the world precious? Yes,
and loss of ego brings on love,
snow sifting off the roof
to blow where the night wind takes it . . .

Georgia came to that party, and something about it must have triggered the start of our relationship, which began a couple of weeks later, on the Fourth of July, which is surely Midsummer's North American echo and afterthought. From being on the other shore from love, I was suddenly in its very midst again. The ancient magic of Midsummer continues to assert itself, and it's like a secret handshake with Spenser and Shakespeare each time I celebrate it, a gift they have given me from four hundred years ago.

JUNE RECIPES

Four Summer Noodle Dishes

As the weather gets warm I resort more frequently to Asian cuisine, especially from hot countries where dishes are often served at room temperature and their flavors are selected and balanced to deal with the fact of heat. Even in June there are enough warm evenings to make a cool dish more welcome than a hot one. Combine that with my family's love of noodles, in almost any form, and you get this set of variations on noodles, drawn from a variety of hot-weather cultures. The first 2 can also be served hot and would be just as welcome in cold weather.

●

Shanghai-Style Vegetable Noodles

This comes from a *New York Times* article about Michael Tong, a New York chef and restaurant owner (Shun Lee and Shun Lee Palace). I've made a few changes.

8 ounces fresh noodles
2 tablespoons peanut oil

2 scallions, cut in 2-inch lengths
1 cup chives, cut in 2-inch lengths
1 sweet red pepper, cut in 2-inch lengths
2 cups napa cabbage, sliced crosswise
　　in ½-inch rounds
½ cup chicken stock (or vegetable stock
　　if you want to be fully vegetarian)
2 tablespoons dark soy sauce
1 tablespoon sugar
freshly ground pepper
1 tablespoon sesame oil
1 cup cubed yellow squash or zucchini
2 cups fresh spinach, rinsed and drained

For the noodles you can use fettuccine or the oriental noodles, Japanese or Chinese, you find fresh sometimes in the supermarket. You can also use dried pasta, such as linguine or spaghetti. Cook the noodles al dente, drain them, mix in a little sesame oil, and set them aside.

Over high heat, add the oil to the wok and bring it to the smoking point. Remember that hot, explosive frying is one principle of oriental cooking, so don't hesitate to get your wok as hot as your stove allows. Add the scallions, chives, and peppers. Stir-fry quickly. Add the cabbage, stir-fry for about 30 seconds. Push the vegetables up on one side and add the noodles to the wok. Keep the noodle pile and the vegetable pile apart. Add the chicken stock, the soy sauce, the sugar, the pepper, and the sesame oil. Put the squash on the vegetables and the spinach on top of the squash. Cover the wok and cook at high heat for 2 minutes.

Uncover the wok and remove the noodles, spreading them on a platter. Mix the vegetables and the sauce together and take them off the heat. Taste for seasoning. Pour the vegetables and sauce over the noodles. Serve immediately or allow the dish to come to room temperature and serve it as part of a "cool" meal. It will be good either way.

●

Singapore Nonya Noodles

This is also vegetarian. Coconut milk is fairly high in cholesterol, but having it once in a while in a dish such as this seems justified. Again, you can use almost any kind of fresh or dried noodle that is handy or that suits you.

—◦◦◦—

8 ounces noodles
4 ounces green beans
2 carrots
salt
4 cloves garlic
2 shallots
3 tablespoons ginger
2 fresh chilies (I use jalapeños
   and remove the seeds)
1 tablespoon peanut oil
$\frac{3}{4}$ cup coconut milk
$\frac{3}{4}$ cup chicken or vegetable stock
3 tablespoons fish sauce
freshly ground pepper
2 scallions, minced

Cook the noodles al dente, mix in a little oil (I like sesame for this), and set aside. Have a pot of boiling salted water and a strainer handy. Snap the ends off the beans and cut them in half if they are long. Plunge them in the boiling water for 2 minutes. Drain and chill immediately with cold water. Cut the carrots into similarly sized pieces and cook them the same way, 2 minutes in the boiling water and then cold water to stop the cooking. You can do the noodles in the same water, either first or after you've done the vegetables.

Make a purée in the food processor of the garlic, shallots, ginger, and chilies. Heat a wok and add the peanut oil, bringing it up to the smoking point. Add the garlic paste mixture and stir-fry a couple of minutes. Add the coconut milk, stock, and fish sauce. Grind in some pepper. Boil this mixture a couple of minutes; it will thicken and gain flavor. Now add the noodles and simmer them in the sauce for a minute or 2, letting them absorb it. Add the beans and carrots and stir until heated through. Check the seasoning and put in a serving bowl. Sprinkle chopped scallions over the dish and either serve immediately or later, at room temperature.

●

Noodles with Peanut Sauce

There are many recipes for this dish, a universal favorite, and if you make it regularly in the summer you will have fun exploring variations of seasoning and ingredients. I like to make it with fresh noodles, fettuccine from my pasta maker, or the Chinese egg noodles that are now available in many supermarkets. This version is pretty close to John Thorne's, in *Outlaw Cook,* and his whole chapter "Dandan Noodles" is recommended reading.

—◦◦◦—

4–5 cloves of garlic
small knob of ginger, peeled and sliced
$^{1}/_{2}$ cup peanut butter (chunky is best)

1 tablespoon brown sugar
3 tablespoons sesame oil
chili powder or fresh chili, to taste
3 tablespoons dark soy sauce
2 tablespoons vinegar (rice wine,
    wine, or Chinese black vinegar)
$\frac{1}{2}$ cup chicken or vegetable stock
noodles, cooked

Put everything but the stock into a food processor and blend, adding stock a little at a time to achieve a fairly liquid consistency (like light cream, says Thorne). If the sauce sits for a while, the flavors will marry better. Mix it with cold cooked noodles and top it with any combination of the following: chopped scallions, crushed roasted peanuts, chopped chives, fried shallots, coriander, cucumber strips, bean sprouts, or toasted sesame seeds. If you want meat in the dish, you can boil or microwave boneless, skinless chicken breasts and add them, cut in strips. Or you can have a roast pork tenderloin handy (see p. 151) and cut some slices into strips to add to the dish.

●

Thai-Style Noodles

Again, this dish is subject to many variations based on what's available and what you like. It is very good with rice noodles, which make a nice change from egg noodles and pasta, but what kind of noodle you choose is up to you. The easiest way to make this is to have a wok or pot full of simmering water and a wire-meshed Chinese ladle or colander insert. You cook your ingredients in the water and then dump them into the bowl you'll serve from, which already contains the sauce that will flavor them. The completed dish is tossed and topped with peanuts and coriander. At the table diners spice up their individual bowls of noodle "salad" with sugar, chili powder, fresh chilies in vinegar, and fresh chilies in fish sauce, the traditional "four flavors" of so much Thai cooking.

2 tablespoons peanut oil
2 garlic cloves, minced
1 shallot, minced
1 tablespoon pickled ginger shreds or
   preserved radish (*tang chi*)
1 tablespoon fish sauce
1 tablespoon light soy sauce
1 teaspoon sugar
1 large handful of bean sprouts
8–12 ounces noodles, rice or otherwise
assorted meats—e.g., sliced roast pork,
   pork balls, fish balls, fish cakes
2 tablespoons crushed peanuts
chopped fresh coriander, to taste

Fry the garlic and shallot in the oil until lightly browned, then set aside. Put the ginger shreds or preserved radish, the fish sauce, the soy sauce, and the sugar in a serving bowl and stir well. In a pot or wok of boiling water, immerse the bean sprouts for 5 to 10 seconds. Dump them in the serving bowl. Immerse the noodles. (If they are rice noodles you will have soaked them first and they will only need a few seconds; if they are fresh or dried noodles, use whatever cooking time you need to get them al dente.) Add them to the bowl, pour over the garlic and shallot oil, and mix. Immerse any other ingredients that need heating or cooking—pork balls, fish balls, fish slices, etc. Add them to the serving bowl. Cold roast pork doesn't need this treatment but can go straight to the bowl and is usually arranged on top. Sprinkle the whole thing with ground peanuts and coriander and let it sit at room tempera-

ture until you are ready to serve. Diners help themselves to bowls full
of noodles and add the following, to taste:

> 1 or more fresh chilies (I use jalapeños),
>   chopped, with 4 tablespoons fish sauce
> 1 or more fresh chilies, chopped,
>   with 4 tablespoons vinegar
> chili powder
> sugar

Other vegetable and meat combinations are easy to come up with. The
appeal of this dish is the way diners can spice it to taste—it is rather
bland without some generous helpings of the condiments listed
above—and the ways you can vary ingredients according to availabil-
ity. Pork balls and fish balls are sold frozen in Asian grocery stores, and
they generally need 3 or 4 minutes in the boiling water. Here follows a
simple roast pork recipe that will provide the kind of cold cooked meat
that is a great ingredient for any of the cold noodle dishes in this group.

●

Chinese Roast (Barbecued) Pork

> Any small pork roast will do for this, though lean pork
> is desirable and boneless is preferable. I tend to buy a
> pork tenderloin, which is pricey, but you can stretch it
> out over a week of cooking or more. It will keep in the
> refrigerator a week, and can be frozen wrapped in foil
> and thawed for use; it's good to thaw it right in the foil.

—◈—

> 1 small pork roast, preferably boneless and lean,
>   e.g., a tenderloin, approximately 2 pounds
> 2 garlic cloves, minced
> 2–3 tablespoons dark soy sauce

2 tablespoons rice wine or sherry
1 teaspoon sugar or brown sugar
salt
pepper, black or white
1 teaspoon ground star anise

Combine the garlic with the rest of the ingredients and rub this marinade into the roast. Let it stand at least an hour. Roast the meat on a
rack over a pan that contains the marinade and $\frac{1}{2}$ cup of water, starting
with the oven at $425°$ and reducing the heat to $350°$ after 15 minutes.
Allow about 30 minutes a pound. It's good to baste the meat as it cooks,
especially in the last hour, either with the marinade or with sesame oil.
If you like it really crisp, you can broil it, basting as you go, or you can
cook it slowly and then raise the temperature at the end, basting frequently with peanut oil.

The meat slices best after it has had a chance to cool. It is very good
by itself, dipped in plum sauce or hot Chinese mustard or soy sauce,
and it can be used in all sorts of stir-fry dishes as well as the noodle
dishes given above.

●

Fresh Green Beans

I think this is the perfect preparation for fresh beans,
picked in the garden or bought from a local produce
stand. Much depends on exact timing in cooking and on
the lightness of the seasoning. Once again, hats off to
Marcella Hazan for this recipe!

—◈◈◈—

1 pound fresh string beans
4 quarts boiling water
salt
olive oil
lemon juice

While the water is coming to a boil, you can snap the ends off the beans, pulling away any strings. If you do it a little ahead, soak them in cold water for a while.

When the water is boiling, add 2 tablespoons of salt, let it come back to a boil, and drop in the beans. Cook uncovered, at a moderate boil, for exactly 7 minutes—or 6 if the beans are very young and fresh. Drain the beans promptly and run a little cool water on them to stop the cooking. Put the drained beans in a bowl. Add a little salt, enough oil to coat them nicely, and just a whisper of lemon juice. Serve at room temperature as a salad or second course.

Strawberry Variations

Homemade Strawberry Ice Cream

I think the basic difference between American ice cream and Italian gelato is that Americans like the creaminess to come first and the flavor to follow along behind, whereas Italians like the flavor foremost. Since that's my own preference, I aim for results that feature the flavor, as pronounced as possible, of the main ingredient—in this case fresh-picked strawberries. This *gelato di fragola* is pretty much based on Marcella Hazan's recipe.

1 quart fresh strawberries
1 cup granulated sugar
½ cup heavy cream, milk, or yogurt

Wash the strawberries as little as possible, or not at all. Stem them and
cut the big ones in half, putting them in a blender container as you go.
One quart may be a little too much for a blender, in which case you can
save the leftover for topping or for your breakfast cereal. When the
blender is almost full, add the sugar and the cream. The mixture is now
ready for whatever home ice-cream freezer you use. It shouldn't be frozen too hard, and we usually start the freezing process just before we
sit down to dinner. With someone minding the freezer, doing the occasional crank with the paddle, we usually have a cold, soft, and incredibly tasty dessert by the time the meal is coming to its conclusion.

●

Strawberries with Yogurt and Balsamic Vinegar

This recipe is adapted from the now defunct magazine
Wine and Food Companion. It was contributed by a chef
from the New York restaurant Palio, one Andrea Hell-
rigl. It is what Italians would call *raffinato*.

———ఇ∾ᴑᴑ⌢———

½ quart (1 pint) strawberries, plus 20 extra for garnish
2—3 cups sugar
10 tablespoons balsamic vinegar
zest of 1 orange
zest of 1 lemon
1 tablespoon Grand Marnier or Cointreau
1 pint plain yogurt

As in the gelato recipe, I like to work with a quart of fresh-picked
strawberries; if I have some left over, that's fine with me. About half the

quart, cleaned and stemmed, should go into a blender with 1 cup of the sugar and 5 tablespoons of balsamic vinegar. Blend and pour into a bowl. Add the grated zest, the liqueur, and the yogurt. Stir well and set in the refrigerator to chill.

The rest of the strawberries, or as many as you want to use (5 or 6 per serving is a good guide), should be mixed with the remaining sugar (1 cup or more, depending on the number of strawberries and your own sweet tooth) and the remaining balsamic vinegar. Stir to make sure the strawberries are well coated with the sugar and vinegar and put them in to chill and marinate for at least an hour.

To serve, spoon the yogurt mixture into wide serving glasses or shallow soup dishes. Garnish with 4 or more strawberries. The mixture the strawberries have marinated in can be dribbled over the yogurt surface in an attractive fashion.

JULY

The Thunder Moon

.   .   .   .

I'm on my knees, weeding the garden. In this wet heat, everything seems to flourish, which means that giant weeds—crabgrass, purslane, wild sorrel, thistles—appear among my peppers and eggplants almost overnight. The threadbare saying, "It's not the heat, it's the humidity," is one of the world's grim understatements. The expressive words *muggy* and *sultry* get a bit closer. Once your body has responded to the heat by producing a film of perspiration, the humidity guarantees that it will stay. You begin to think you can never be dry again.

Conscious as I am of the sun's late afternoon glare, I can hardly miss the presence of a large shadow as it ripples silently across the garden and over my bent form. I look up, shading my eyes with my hand. It's a turkey vulture, sailing along, looking for a carcass to dine on.

Turkey vultures, often called buzzards, always return to our area on an exact date, March 17, and to an exact place, Hinckley, Ohio. A friend of mine debunks this as myth, and no doubt there's a little leeway about dates, but the basis for it is factual and historic. Hinckley was the site of a huge bear and wolf hunt in 1818. The wild animals, deer and smaller game included, were driven into a circle and slaughtered,

.   .

and the frozen carcasses that nobody wanted for meat were left. Imagine the melting, followed by the decomposing, and the vultures it must have drawn from far and wide. Ever since, like the swallows to Capistrano, they have come back to the same spot each spring. Amazing to think that birds can "know" dates and "know" places in that way, that they can behave in a fashion that lets us endow them with emotions like nostalgia.

In any case, people watch for their annual return now, and celebrate. The Cleveland area prides itself a little on the offbeat perversity of celebrating these carrion birds and their history at Hinckley.

Ugly as the turkey vultures may seem, with their little naked heads and curved beaks—both built for scooping out dead carcasses—and gruesome as their diet may be, they are nature's cleaners and garbage collectors. They are also gorgeous in flight, iconic outlines out of Native American art, riding the thermals and scanning the countryside. Where one appears, several others are not far away, and you will sometimes see smaller birds harassing them, especially crows, who have a vested interest in carrion, too. I'm told that vultures rely mostly on their sense of smell rather than on keen sight. If you deal in decaying carcasses, especially in summer heat like this, smell seems like a sensible choice.

This hot weather varies, running a narrow gamut between pleasant and nearly unbearable. Some Indians called July the Heat Moon, others called it the Thunder Moon. Both names are utterly appropriate. After a really hot day, a passing thunderstorm is especially welcome if it cools the world off a little. I used to enjoy standing outside and getting drenched, but I've learned to be wary of the lightning. Lightning is five times hotter than the fire of the sun. There is a visionary quality to the way huge snaking networks illuminate the whole night sky for a second or two, a sudden blinding map of energy accompanied by tremendous cracks and booms of thunder. The lightning strings, which are not much thicker than a pencil, sometimes run horizontally, covering five to ten miles of sky, sometimes vertically, sometimes both at once.

We need the "thunder moon" to balance the "heat moon." Summer is as harsh as winter, and lots of elderly people die during our heat waves. But out of the heat, the humidity, and the violent electrical storms come the bumper crops of corn, wheat, soybeans, rye, and hay.

The vulture sees all this as he glides over us. Take him as a spiritual presence, cruising the summer skies. He'd like the livestock and people that perish in the heat set out for him to dine on. Summer and heat are his own form of feasting, and even the thermals on which he rides effortlessly upward are provided by the ground heat, rising and forming invisible twisting columns.

I pause to admire the huge sky, blue as a lake and populated by mammoth clouds, high-piled thunderheads stretching north and south as far as the eye can see. Here I am in the heart of summer, feeling quite content to be at home. After a whole year abroad, living in Wimbledon, England, from 1967 to 1968, I was enchanted by my rediscovery of the American summer, and I wove the details of it into a love poem for my wife:

LOVE SONG
for Chloe

I guess your beauty doesn't
bother you, you wear it easy
and walk across the driveway
so casual and right it makes
my heart weigh twenty pounds
as I back out and wave
thinking She's my summer
peaches, corn, long moondawn dusks
watermelons chilling in a tub
of ice and water: mirrored there
the great midsummer sky
rolling with clouds and treetops
and down by the lake

the wild canaries
swinging on the horsemint
all morning long.

The birds feed exuberantly, while the abundance of crops and the huge leafy canopies of the trees push the wonder of growth and vegetation into the foreground of our sensuous life. Day's drawing out into longer and longer twilights puts us in a transitional world where our awareness is enlarged and ready for wonder. It's a spiritual picnic, and it feels quite effortless.

Some years later—it was 1982—I found myself returning again, from a briefer trip to England, and also recalling a summer three years before that in Italy. I came from an English June to an American July and was recalling an Italian July as well. I tried to triangulate the three experiences, incorporating the beauty and abundance I had found in each place, along with the eeriness, the strange ways in which the past interlocks with the present. My own environment, I decided, could be just as rich and phantasmagoric as those European ones:

THREE WALKS

1. Near "Appleby,"
Axminster, Devon, June 1982

A path, a garden, a country lane
with a very old lady and her daughter,
the whole evening holding tremulous
as though it might never end.
A codger watering his broccoli
talks up the art of gardening as
we gaze at his cabbages and gooseberries.
By his garden wall and along the lane
foxglove is speechlessly in bloom,
herb Robert, hogweed, eglantine,
everything, even the grass and cuckoo-spittle,
touched with the slow welling-up of life.
When we come back I hear again

some thrush in the deep shade
making a music as intricate
as what we were walking through.

2. Near Arcidosso,
Tuscany, July 1979

Maybe I like this city for being
nearly unknown, off in the mountains.
Over and over the cuckoo calls from the chestnuts
this sleepy midday. Red-and-lemon posters
for a circus, ORFEI, plaster every wall,
and I can imagine a humdrum Orpheus
ambling the narrow street to the bakery,
pausing to stare
at the round fountain where a stone mask
blows a thin rope of water
into a basin, a rope without ends.
He would climb to the old castle,
baking in sunshine, where
the air is alive with bees
that build in the crumbling masonry.
What would he make of it all? Would he stand,
his eyes blurring with tears,
looking back through the smoke of time
at the men and women, come and gone,
who have seen how the earth is lovely
and seen how its meanings desert them?

3. Near Lorain and Oberlin,
Ohio, July 1982

Backward and forward in time, as if
by way of England and Italy I've come
to stand in the K-mart parking lot
while Cassiopeia hangs askew
beyond the cornfields, come to hear doves

calling all morning in the rain
like very tired cuckoos.
Tomorrow, the Fourth of July, I'll go
mushroom-gathering in the cemetery
to the rumble of summer thunder
among the distant dead, Huron Weed, Amanda Peabody,
and the newer dead I knew, George Lanyi, Jean Tufts,
and if it's not so time-caressed
still I will pause there, startled
as though I stood on my own heart
in nature's haunted house,
as again, in the long-drawn evening,
with the fireflies signaling——
commas, hyphens, exclamation marks——
and the skyrockets in the distance——
foxgloves, fountains, bees,
constellations and mushrooms
hung for a second or two
on the dim sky above the trees.

If my "reality" is not so "time-caressed" as those I visited in England and Italy, and if it contains absurdities like the K-Mart (they've since built an even bigger one), it is nevertheless mine, not someone else's, the one place where I really do seem to stand on my own heart to confront what Emily Dickinson called "nature's haunted house."

In many ways, the unsettled and exhilarated mood of July is set by the Fourth. In a small town, that means municipal fireworks displays, so similar from year to year that they become confused with each other, while the exceptions—the year it rained them out, the year the town was broke and couldn't afford to have them, the year they were set off in the afternoon for some forgotten reason—intermingle in the jumbled communal memory.

When I look at poems I have written in July, I find that they often reflect the hallucinatory effects of these small-town Fourths, something of that vulture's perspective on the landscape. They contain that mingling of past and present, dead and alive, permanent and ephemeral, I explored in "Three Walks." They echo the strange dispersals the self experiences in summer, the sense that your own borders are breaking down and you are mingling with the landscape, with its history and its unspoken throngs of dead. Here's a July segment from "Water Diary":

> my eyes heavy   the plumtree burning
> muscles in my neck twist and I
> reach toward you   even in summer air
> your face is cool   a winter window
> steelwork   we drive off the city lies
> in haze behind but this
> hot mist is everywhere
> unsketching the little towns
> and the field with their cows and flies

I called those diary entries "dictations," as though I was a kind of secretary to the unconscious and the landscape, taking a letter. In the same way, I found myself playing secretary to dead presidents. There's a sort of Mount Rushmore character to a lot of July's iconography, a part of the national psyche that I was picking up on in the huge, hazy, disorienting American summer. Here is a "dead president" poem:

WOODROW WILSON

> I pull on the tight clothes and go walking
> rectitude misting around my figure
> carrying the book of shadows a low moon
> crosses the power stations the refineries
> and in the needle mountains there are lakes
> so cold and clear that the dead who sit
> at the bottom in buggies and machine-gun nests
> look up past the trout who nibble their shoulders

164

> to see the eclipse begin the dime-sized shadow
> sliding across the sun the insects settling
> across the bears in their yokes the antelopes
> acting out all their desires old lady
> who smothers her young in her iron robes
> you have wrung my thin neck a thousand times
> and taken my pinch-nose glasses but
> I come back again with the gliding Indians
> settlers who have forgiven all their tools
> the shabby buffaloes wild sheep wapiti
> the inland sea that looks at the sky all day
> with only a widgeon's wake to disturb it
> the V dividing away from itself
> all night under trembling constellations

The poem seems to posit the *idea* of America as a kind of destructive ideal, a pursuit of perfect freedom and exemplary democracy, a Miss Liberty who smothers her own young and recurrently strangles idealists like Wilson. The land itself, meanwhile, is a much larger reality, filled with its own past and harboring its own spiritual effervescence, a democracy of *being*. That greater reality allows Wilson to return, inhabiting it as a positive presence, mingling with the other victims of the idealism, all of them released from imprisoning beliefs and responsibilities. That happened to Teddy Roosevelt, too, in the companion piece I wrote. Perhaps both presidents spoke to me as they were roaming around, giant ghosts on the Fourth of July, figures in a parade or pageant my imagination was playfully constructing for itself.

It was also July when I wrote the opening section of "In My Own Back Yard":

> July, I'm dozing in sun on the deck,
> one thrush is singing among the high trees,
> and Li Po walks by, chanting a poem!
> He is drunk, he smells unwashed,
> I can see tiny lice in his hair,

and right through him
a brown leaf in the yard
flips over flips
again lies still
all this time
no wind.

Am I claiming that July is the best time for encountering ghosts, whether of politicians or T'ang dynasty poets? I think the point is more the way that summer's hallucinated effects—the heat, the haze, the sleeplessness and consequent somnolence, even the chance to dream and swing in a hammock or a deck chair—dilate the imagination and make us more alert to spiritual realities that sometimes arrive in forms as vivid and particularized as their material counterparts.

Encountering ghosts had a special meaning in this current July because it opened with a death in the family. My wife's only nephew, her sister's sixteen-year-old son, skidded on a wet road near his Pennsylvania home, crashed into a telephone pole, and died instantly. Cutting a young life off so abruptly, on the threshold of its promise and in the midst of its energetic unfolding, feels very different from deaths like that of my mother at eighty-eight. The transition that involves our letting go of the body, the corpse, and redefining the dead person as spirit, in whatever form, a transition basic to human life and death, varies greatly in its cultural manifestations, but there has to be some kind of poetry in it, some elements of spiritual transformation and release.

The viewing, the funeral, and the burial of our nephew Ian took up most of a hot, steamy, occasionally rainy July Saturday. By the end, after we had put the casket (handmade by the boy's father) into the red earth of the quiet country graveyard, we were exhausted and a little giddy. That night we all ended up eating and drinking too much at a long table in a dark, friendly restaurant. Life was beginning to reassert itself. People pick up and go on because they really have no other choice. We weep for our strangeness.

One incident from the funeral stands out vividly. At the service the local Unitarian minister had spoken movingly, without clichés and with an extraordinary command of metaphor and spiritual insight, about what had brought us all together there and how we might try to deal with it. All his experience and insight were brought to bear on that crucial transition from body to spirit. In the period when the congregation was asked to contribute thoughts, I spoke some lines from Rilke, fetched up from my memory the night before as I lay awake, trying to deal with this death:

> *Of course it is odd*
> > *to live no more*
> > > *on the earth*
> *to abandon customs*
> > *you've just begun*
> > > *to get used to*
> *not to give meaning*
> > *to roses*
> > > *and other such*
> *promising things*
> > *in terms of*
> > > *a human future*
> *to be held no more*
> > *by hands that can*
> > > *never relax*
> *for fear they will drop you*
> > *and even to put*
> > > *your name to one side*
> *like a broken toy.*
> > *Strange*
> > > *to wish wishes no longer.*
> *Strange*

to see things
        that seemed to
belong together
        floating in every
                direction.
It's very hard to be dead
        and you try
                to make up for lost time
till slowly you start
        to get whiffs
                of eternity.
But the living are wrong
        in the sharp
                distinctions they make.
Angels, it seems,
        don't always know
                if they're moving among
the living or the dead.
        The drift of eternity
                drags all the ages of man
through both of these spheres
        and its sound
                rises over them both.

After the service, the minister and I had a moment to shake hands. "Those lines you spoke meant a lot to me," he said.

"But they hardly even needed saying," I told him, "after what you said. They were like a paraphrase of your remarks."

"Well," he said, looking me right in the eye. "I have lung cancer. I'm dying. Maybe that explains it."

I will never forget this encounter, an instant of powerful exchange with a total stranger. It was, to put it in Rilkean terms, like meeting an angel, just for a moment—the central moment, for me, of a turbulent, grieving, mystifying weekend.

So spiritual realities, particularized in a summer landscape, make up a characteristic population in July and in July's poems, at least in mine. The vulture cruises everywhere, smelling the landscape for death. Sometimes, though, he comes as a butterfly. One July, after hearing that Vladimir Nabokov had passed away in Switzerland, I wrote an elegy for him. This time the grief was miniaturized, like fireworks seen from a distance. I could be celebratory about someone whose art would long outlast his life. Nabokov was much on my mind because I had taught a course devoted entirely to his fiction in the spring semester of that year, and the America I found myself wandering around in was consequently tinged and tinted with his sardonic, festive, and unpredictable imagination:

THE DAY NABOKOV DIED

1

I looked up from my weeding
and saw a butterfly, coal black,
floating across Plum Creek. Which facts
are laced with lies: it was another day,
it was a monarch—if it was black
it must have been incinerator fluff.

A black hinge, opening and shutting.

2

Elsewhere the sunset lights
bonfires in hotel windows, gilds the lake,
picks out false embers where it can:
watch crystal, drinking glass, earring.
"Nabokov," someone calls, "is dead. . . ."
What would you give to be in, say, Fialta,
hearing the rhythms of a torpid coast?
Or on the porch at the Enchanted Hunters,

conversing in the shadows with Sirin?
Sneezes, lachrymose sighs. Chuckles and coughs.
When at a loss for words, try waving
one helpless hand before your face.

Walking the dog, I saw a hawkmoth too,
big as two hands, resting under a streetlight.

   3

In the skyscraper across the lane
an aproned man sets up his easel
at the window opposite and cocks his head.
What does he see? A dwarf
mixing a violet powder, a fat
landlady playing patience, a little girl
brushing a velvet coat, in tears,
three people having sex. In short,
the world. Ourselves. Aren't all of us
some form of Maxwell's Demon,
particle sorters, systems
so self-enclosed they work too well to work?

Grandmaster, slip into your fiction like
Houdini diving through a pocket mirror.
Here's wonder, but no grief. And even so,
you'd not have liked this poem. Wan child
in a sailor suit, man running by
waving a gauzy net, tall fencer, pedant,
hotel mensch, empty suit of clothes . . .

One exile more. One language still to learn.

Good literature brings us, often quite playfully, up to the limits of what
we know and don't know, the thresholds where life and death tend to
mingle and interpenetrate. "Angels, it seems, / don't always know / if
they're moving among / the living or the dead." Nabokov was acutely

conscious of human suffering, in all forms and phases, yet he chose not so much to dwell on it as to look for ways to vault beyond it.

What July sometimes seems to offer us is an enlarged and tingling reality. The sky feels bigger because, filled as it often is with huge clouds—building thunderheads spread out across whole counties and states, some close, some very distant—we can be more conscious of its size. The sun rises on a vigorous, dew-streaked world, steaming with growth and death, and it sets very extendedly, often with huge pur-ples, prolonged golds and wild reds, not to mention the orange hues of the ubiquitous (in our parts, at least) daylily. It sets on a world already half-asleep, alertly dreamwalking. Thunderstorms rouse us suddenly with their loud cracks and blinding flashes, and then put us back to sleep as they patter away into the distance. Ghosts walk across our minds and hearts, lingering in our sunlit or moonlit yards. Vultures cruise, near and distant.

We reach out, hoping to touch the ultimate truths, trying to put our fingertips on the live cheek or sloping shoulder of being, but we reach forever, touching nothing. Around us is the strange company of ani-mals, historical figures, geological eras, and meteorological phenom-ena. The V of the duck's wake divides away all night, under trembling constellations. The same water will reflect the great midsummer sky of clouds and treetops.

I hate to see July disappear over the drugged, enchanted horizon. I want it to linger a few days more. On the other hand, August won't be very different.

JULY RECIPES

Daylily Buds, Two Ways

These are pretty much adapted from Billy Joe Tatum's *Wild Foods Field Guide and Cookbook.* Her basic recipe has you wash, stem, and simmer the buds for 20 minutes before using them in a recipe. I find that's too long and prefer no more than 5, if any. Sometimes I steam them.

●

Stir-Fried Daylily Buds

Obviously, this can be varied considerably according to available ingredients. If you see wild garlic budding when you pick the lily buds, you can readily substitute it for the garlic in this recipe.

3 cups fresh-picked daylily buds

2 tablespoons peanut oil

3–5 cloves garlic

2 tablespoons minced ginger

3 cups shredded kale or similar green (spinach, etc.)

2 tablespoons vinegar

2 tablespoons soy sauce

1 tablespoon chili paste or hot oil
1 cup water or chicken stock
½ cup chopped peanuts or whole sunflower seeds

You can blanch or briefly simmer the buds on the stove or in the micro-wave, but don't overdo it, especially if they are young and tender. Drain them and dry them on paper towels. Heat the oil to very hot in a wok or frying pan and throw in the garlic and ginger to fry explosively for 30 seconds or so. Add the lily buds and the kale or other green. Stir-fry vigorously to coat with the oil and seasonings. Add the vinegar, water, chili paste, and soy sauce. Cover and cook for 3 to 4 minutes. Uncover, add the peanuts or sunflowers, and serve hot or at room temperature. Good over rice or noodles, obviously.

●

Lily-Bud Fritters

This is like the preparation Italians give to zucchini blossoms.

———

2 cups cooked drained daylily buds
1 cup flour
2 teaspoons baking powder
salt
½ cup milk
2 eggs

You can steam or boil the daylily buds until you think they're tender enough. Be sure to squeeze as much moisture out of them as you can. Combine flour and baking powder, adding a pinch of salt. Beat the eggs with the milk and then whisk in the flour mixture. In a deep fryer or pan, heat the peanut oil (or other cooking oil) to 350°. Dip the buds in batter and fry in oil until golden brown. Drain on paper towels and salt lightly, keeping finished ones warm while you deep-fry the others. Serve immediately. A dip of something like soy and vinegar will go well with these.

●

Zucchini and Basil Pasta Sauce

This is another one of Marcella Hazan's standbys, slightly adapted.

—⟨⟨⟨⟨⟨⟨⟩⟩⟩⟩⟩—

3 or 4 small zucchini, 1 pound
   or more
vegetable oil for frying
1 pound pasta (fusilli, ziti,
   rigatoni, etc.)
5–6 tablespoons olive oil
1 tablespoon flour
½ cup milk
salt
½ cup shredded basil
1 egg yolk
¾ cup grated Parmesan or
   Romano cheese

Cut the zucchini into finger-sized sticks. Fry them in hot oil, in batches that don't crowd the pan too much. Drain on paper towels. Meanwhile, you can be heating the water for the pasta. Boil the pasta as you prepare the final stage of the sauce.

Mix the flour into the milk. Heat the olive oil (Hazan uses half butter, and you can do that or substitute margarine), then whisk in the flour and milk mixture, a little at a time. After it thickens, add the fried zucchini, then add salt to taste and the basil. Heat and stir the mixture, then, off heat, add the egg yolk and the grated cheese. Taste for seasoning and add to the cooked, drained pasta. I pass the pepper grinder at the table and, sometimes, more grated cheese. But you might not want either; the flavor of the basil, the zucchini, and the pasta together is very delicate, and too much seasoning could spoil it.

●

Basil Pesto

This is a standard recipe, but I include it here for reference in subsequent recipes that will call for it.

———

2 cups fresh basil leaves, tightly packed
2 garlic cloves
½ cup olive oil
3 tablespoons pine nuts
1 tablespoon salt
½ cup grated cheese, Parmesan,
    Romano, or both
2 tablespoons butter

Put the basil, oil, garlic (peeled and chopped into smaller pieces), and pine nuts in a food processor and blend, scraping down the sides if necessary. Put in a bowl and add the cheese and butter. It is customary to mix a couple of tablespoons from the pasta cooking water in to insure a soupier texture. Serve on pasta, on bruschetta, or as a seasoning for minestrone (see below).

●

Summer Minestrone

I used to think vegetable soup was a great winter dish, but Italians have made it a national summer favorite, when, after all, the vegetables tend to be particularly fresh and succulent. They make it in the morning and

let the servings sit out in bowls until the soup reaches
room temperature. I make it in the middle of the afternoon for serving at dinner time. Leftover soup can be reheated and cooled for serving in the same way. In both
cases, the flavors marry and the results are marvelous,
often served with some rice or pasta added, or a slice of
bread, and a lacing of pesto.

—◦◦◦—

beans—either 8 ounces dried navy, great northern,
    or cannellini that have been soaked overnight and
    cooked for 1 hour with a piece of ham or bacon,
    or 1 pound fresh beans (cranberry, borlotti, or
    fava), shelled, which will yield about 8 ounces
$\frac{1}{2}$ cup olive oil
1 medium onion, chopped
   1 stalk celery
1 large carrot, peeled
2 garlic cloves
1 bunch of Italian parsley, about 4 tablespoons
    chopped
1 large potato, peeled and diced
$\frac{1}{2}$ pound cabbage (red or savoy, preferably),
    shredded
$\frac{1}{2}$ pound green beans, peas, kale, or zucchini,
    or combination of any two
1 pound tomatoes (14 ounces if canned)
salt and pepper
1 cup cooked Arborio rice and/or 6–8 bread slices
pesto (see preceding recipe)

If the beans were dry, they should be cooked and ready when you start
the rest of the soup. If they are fresh, cook them separately in salted
water for about 20 minutes. In either case, then, you will have a pot of
cooked beans standing by in their cooking broth.

First you cook an *odori,* meaning that you have chopped the onion, celery, garlic, carrot, and parsley and are sautéing them in the olive oil. When they are starting to brown and soften, you can add the cabbage, potato, green vegetables, and the tomatoes, which you'll have peeled, seeded, and puréed (you can use canned tomatoes, but that seems a shame in the summertime). You can use a blender or pass them through a food mill, and you can use the same food mill or blender to do the same thing to about half of the cooked beans.

Add the beans, both whole and puréed, after the vegetables have cooked about 15 minutes. Add the bean cooking broth as you go to achieve the consistency you want. Taste for salt and pepper, cook a few minutes more, then turn off the heat.

Add the cooked rice if you are using it. If you are using bread slices, toast them, rub them with garlic, and put them in either a large tureen or (my preference) individual serving bowls. After the soup has cooled for a while, put it in the serving bowls and let it come to room temperature. It should sit for an hour or 2 before serving. Serve with a streak of pesto on the surface and, depending on how cheesy your pesto is, a sprinkling of grated cheese.

●

Pasta with Ricotta Pesto

In this version you add 3 tablespoons of ricotta to your pesto, making it a little milder. The pasta Hazan recommends is a version of the lasagna noodle, in other words, quite broad. I use the disk on my pasta maker that produces 2 long strips, about 2 inches wide, and cut them into squares. After cooking the pasta, I spread some on a platter, smear on ricotta pesto, add more pasta, then more pesto, etc., so that the sauce and pasta are layered. I add 3 to 4 tablespoons of the pasta cooking water to give the pesto a fairly liquid consistency.

Eggplant Riff—Six Recipes

I know some people don't like eggplant—it has, among
other things, one of the most unfortunate names in the
language. But this is just idiocy, since this vegetable
adapts itself to so many flavors and treatments. Call it
aubergine and try again. The texture may take a little
getting used to, but if you try these 6 recipes and still
don't like it, you need to have your head and taste buds
examined!

●

Italian Baked Eggplant

This is very simple and very good. Slice 2 or 3 eggplants
in ½-inch slices, stack in a colander, salting each layer,
and let them drain for an hour. Rinse them off, dry
them, and put them in a large baking or roasting pan.
Add olive oil liberally and make sure it coats the slices
on both sides. Roast in a 425° oven for 10 minutes, then
turn the slices and roast another 10 minutes. Transfer
them to a serving platter and dress with lemon juice

(2 to 3 tablespoons), salt, pepper, and oregano. I use both dried and fresh oregano on this dish, which may sound like herbal overkill to some. I do not peel the eggplants if they are young and relatively fresh and tender. Serve at room temperature as an appetizer or as an accompaniment to meat dishes.

●

Caponata

There may be as many versions of this as there are families in Italy. This one is adapted from a delightful book by Jo Bettoja and Anna Maria Cornetto, *Italian Cooking in the Grand Tradition*. Their version makes a lot, since it keeps well in the refrigerator and has many uses, as an appetizer, side dish, or snack. It freezes well, too.

───ɷɷ───

> 4 medium or 3 large eggplants
> 4–5 plum tomatoes
> 4 sweet peppers, 2 red and 2 yellow if available
> 4 small zucchini
> 2 large red onions
> ½ pound fresh mushrooms, portobello or
>   wild meadow mushrooms
> 2 tablespoons capers
> 1 cup green olives (pitted, with pimentos
>   okay)
> 2 bay leaves, fresh if possible
> salt and pepper
> ½ cup vinegar (cider, red wine, or white)
> 1 teaspoon sugar (some people use more,
>   liking a sweeter caponata)
> ½ cup olive oil

Peel and cube the eggplants, sprinkle with salt, and let them drain for an hour. Rinse the cubes and dry them. Put the tomatoes, split lengthwise, in a pan and simmer for 10 minutes. Put them through a food mill and add a pinch of salt. Cut the peppers into squares, the onions into slices, and the mushrooms into halves (quarters if they are large). Peel and dice the zucchini.

Preheat the oven to 350°. In a large roasting pan mix the eggplant cubes, onion slices, pepper squares, diced zucchini, and mushroom pieces with the tomato sauce. Add the capers, olives, and bay leaves. Mix again. Add the vinegar, olive oil, and sugar, mixed. Sprinkle with salt and pepper. Bake for 1½ hours, stirring the mixture 2 or 3 times during the cooking. Let cool and serve at room temperature with bruschetta slices, or as an accompaniment to grilled meat dishes (chicken, pork, fish), or as a lunch snack along with hard-boiled eggs.

●

Hunanese Hot and Sour Eggplant Salad

It's important to let the eggplant flavor come through, so don't overdo the seasoning of the dressing on this.

—⟦∾⟧—

3–4 long oriental eggplants
or 2–3 standard ones

Dressing
3 tablespoons soy sauce
4 tablespoons vinegar
2 tablespoons sesame oil
2 tablespoons chili paste
1 tablespoon sugar
2 tablespoons peanut oil
1 tablespoon minced ginger
1 tablespoon minced garlic

1 tablespoon minced spring onion
1 tablespoon rice wine or sherry
1 cup chicken broth

Steam the eggplants until tender. Cool. Peel the eggplants and cut them into thin strips. Arrange on a serving platter and pour the dressing over. Garnish with chopped coriander and chopped peanuts.

●

Asian Eggplants

This recipe is for the long, narrow eggplants, a lighter or more lavender hue. You find them in Asian groceries, and I have learned they aren't hard to grow. They don't need to be salted to remove the bitterness, and they are seedless. This and the other Asian recipes can be adapted, however, to our larger eggplants; you just need to remember to slice, salt, and drain them for an hour.

——◦◦◦◦——

3–4 long eggplants
olive oil
½ cup chopped fresh basil
3 garlic cloves, finely chopped
½ cup vinegar

Quarter the eggplants, coat them with olive oil, and either grill them over charcoal or roast them in a 400° oven until well browned.

Layer the eggplant slices in a dish, adding garlic, basil, and vinegar on each layer. Refrigerate, covered, for several hours or overnight. Serve as a salad at room temperature.

Vietnamese Charred Eggplants
with Sweet and Sour Sauce

My source is Nicole Routhier's *Foods of Vietnam*.
I've made a few small changes.

—◦◦◦—

3–4 firm eggplants

2 teaspoons sugar

2 tablespoons white vinegar

1 tablespoon fish sauce

2 small hot peppers, jalapeño or red chili,
  seeded and shredded

3 tablespoons peanut oil

5 garlic cloves, crushed

1/2 cup shredded basil

freshly ground black pepper

Prick the eggplants with a fork and grill them. If you don't have a charcoal fire going, just put them right on the stove, electric or gas, and keep turning them until the skins are black all over and the flesh is soft. It will take 4 to 5 minutes. The blackening is important because it imparts a roasted taste to the eggplant flesh, but I suppose you could do it in a very hot oven or under a broiler. Cool on a rack. Peel the charred skin and cut the eggplants into finger-sized strips.

While the eggplants are grilling, combine the sugar, vinegar, fish sauce, and chilies in a small bowl.

Heat the oil in a skillet or wok. When it is smoking, throw in the garlic and stir-fry a few seconds. Add the eggplant strips and cook, stirring, for about 2 minutes. Throw in the sauce and cook for another minute or 2. Add the basil and remove from the heat. Place the mixture on a serving platter and sprinkle with black pepper. I usually serve the dish at room temperature. You can make the dish hotter by leaving the chili seeds in. Very good with rice.

Middle Eastern Eggplant Purée

The similarities between seasonings used in this Middle Eastern recipe and those used in the Asian recipes—garlic, lemon juice or vinegar, a fresh herb—are interesting to consider. This is a recipe to which you can add tahini (sesame paste) to achieve the famous and "vulgarly seductive" (according to Claudia Roden, whose *A Book of Middle Eastern Food* is my main source here) dish called baba ganoush (a seductive name, if you ask me), or you can add yogurt. The latter dish is sometimes decorated with fried meat balls, cumin, and cinnamon.

3 medium-sized eggplants
3 tablespoons olive oil
3 tablespoons chopped parsley
2 garlic cloves, crushed
juice of 1 lemon
salt and pepper

Grill the eggplants according to one of the methods described in the recipe above. Again, you want soft flesh and blackened skins. You can peel them under cold running water, and you should try to squeeze out the bitter juices as you are doing so.

Put the peeled, squeezed eggplants in a food processor, along with the oil, garlic, parsley, lemon juice, salt, and freshly ground pepper. Purée, tasting and adjusting the seasonings as you go. This is an appetizer or a salad. It's really good on toast or as a dip, and so are its variations with tahini and yogurt.

Three Bread Salads

Here we go with the peasant food again. In summer, if you are lucky enough to have stale bread around and you don't want to make a hot soup (but see the cold minestrone recipe above, p. 174), you can use it for any of these salads.

●

Fatoosh

I've seen "fatoosh" spelled several ways. It seems to be Syrian in origin.

———

4–5 slices stale bread, toasted and
    broken into small chunks
juice of 1 lemon
1 large cucumber or 2 small ones,
    preferably the "burpless" English kind
3–4 tomatoes, chopped
3–4 spring onions, minced
1 sweet pepper, red, green, or yellow,
    diced

1 cup mixed chopped parsley, mint,
    and coriander
2 garlic cloves, crushed
½ cup olive oil
salt and pepper

Peel, dice, salt, and drain the cucumber for ½ hour or so. Put the toasted bread chunks in a salad bowl and sprinkle them with the lemon juice. Add water if the bread needs more liquid for softening (it should be soft but not mushy). Add the cucumber, tomatoes, onion, pepper, parsley-mint-coriander mix, and garlic. Add olive oil, salt, and pepper. Mix. Chill or serve at room temperature.

●

Israeli Bread Salad
(*Toureto*)

No tomatoes in this one, and it is usually puréed.

⟝◦◦◦⟞

½ small loaf of stale bread
1 large English cucumber
2 garlic cloves, crushed
4 tablespoons olive oil
juice of 1 lemon
salt and white pepper
paprika

Soak the bread quickly and squeeze out the excess water. Put the bread, cucumber (peeled, chopped, salted, and drained), garlic, olive oil, and lemon juice in a food processor and blend. Chill. Serve garnished with more olive oil mixed with paprika, salt, and pepper, and dribbled over the surface.

Panzanella

Marcella Hazan's version of this Italian classic has you
fry the bread cubes in olive oil before adding them to
the salad. This makes the texture crunchier and the
salad more appealing, but it also is naughtier in terms of
fat content. I let it depend on what else we're eating,
and I sometimes compromise by frying half the bread
and soaking the other half in water.

⌒∘/∘/∘⌒

½ loaf stale bread, cut into large (1-inch) cubes
1 clove garlic
4 anchovy fillets
1 tablespoon capers
pinch of salt
5 tablespoons olive oil
1 tablespoon wine vinegar
½ sweet pepper, diced
½ cucumber, peeled and cubed
1 large or 2 medium-sized tomatoes, cut
   into chunks
½ sweet onion, sliced thin and soaked in 2–3
   changes of cold water

If you are frying some or all of the bread chunks, use vegetable oil, and
keep a close eye on them, as they will brown fast. The ones you aren't
frying should be soaked quickly in water and then squeezed dry.

Put the garlic, anchovies, and capers in a blender or a mortar. Blend
or mash to a pulp. Put in a salad bowl. Add the salt, olive oil, vinegar,
and diced pepper, mixing with a whisk or fork. Now add the bread
chunks, cucumbers, tomatoes, onion, and toss thoroughly. Chill and
taste for seasoning just before serving.

AUGUST

Love and Survival

· · · · ·

August is vast. The last month of summer kicks up to a new level of extravagance and abundance, as though to make sure the season has a chance for full impact. Whatever was big gets bigger. Whatever was tiring gets exhausting. Whatever was true gets truer.

Take the mosquitoes. They were already bad. Today, following a rain that must have totaled three or four inches overnight and well into the morning, a rain that flooded local basements and sent rivers surging toward the lake, I am considering how their population will now grow exponentially. I have to make myself remember the haiku by Issa in which he expresses gratitude to be bitten by "this year's mosquitoes"—because it means, of course, that he has lived for another year.

Or take the produce. We were already starting to experience large quantities of corn, tomatoes, zucchini, peaches, and other such delectables. Now they double their numbers, so that you have bargains at the roadside stands and neighbors bringing bags of their own surpluses. There's a large basket of cucumbers sitting out by the entrance to our subdivision with the single word *FREE* attached to it.

You begin to think about how to use things up. This is the time when

· ·

people start canning, baking zucchini bread, freezing pesto, sun-drying (or oven-drying) tomatoes, making jam and pickles—all ways of preserving the expanding cornucopia. They are looking ahead to winter, but they are also responding to the fact of sheer plenitude.

I like to go out in the country in August, driving those roads that traverse our glacial ridges, to see just how the peaches are coming. A tree-ripened Red Haven peach is an incomparable sensation of taste, smell, and color, with no way of telling where one leaves off and another begins. It's the time of year to pick blueberries, to sample corn, and to see how good the tomatoes, melons, cucumbers, and green beans have become.

My own gardens, meanwhile, are yielding round purple and long lavender eggplants, golden peppers, green-going-red ancho chilies, and tiny, bright red cayennes. I stand in their midst, feeling possessive, lucky, infatuated.

My country forays also take me into fields and ravines—wild blackberries are ripe now—where I stop to marvel at the sheer size some wildflowers attain. It is no longer a matter of delicacy or fragility. If finding seasonal wildflowers meant scanning the forest floor in spring, it now entails looking up, pushing through, even feeling dwarfed by. Queen Anne's lace, for example, is everywhere, and its waist-high or chin-high blooms are flat and wide and white, with a tiny purple flower at the very center. Postblooming, they form delicate green nests, cages, balls, and cups that are complex and fascinating, no two alike. Those explain such folk names as "bee's-nest plant" and "crow's-nest." Queen Anne, incidentally, is not the English queen but Saint Anne, the Virgin's mother and patron saint of lace makers. The little purple flower was thought to be a drop of blood, pricked by the lace maker's needle.

Ironweed, an old favorite of mine, blooms a very distinguished deep red-purple, on stalks that can tower six or seven feet. Joe-pye weed, with its magenta-pink flowers, rises just as high and higher, several varieties of it, and there is something equally huge called horseweed. I suppose ironweed was named for its strength and durability. The taller version has been given the appropriate Latin names—my guides vary on the terminology—of *Vernonia altissima* and *Vernonia gigantea*. Oh tall Vernonia, giant Vernonia, durable purple iron maiden, goddess of my Ohio Augusts.

A wonderful plant called boneset, which blooms white around our swamps and river bottoms in August, sounds as though it must have been used to help mend broken bones. In fact, it was another fever antidote, particularly for dengue fever, which was popularly known as "break-bone" ague—you shook so hard it looked like your bones might snap. Just about everybody used to dry boneset stalks and flowers in their attics, ready to make a horrible-tasting concoction for any family fevers.

Ironically, one of these plants, white snakeroot, while it was used by the Shawnee as an antidote for snakebite, was itself the cause of a terrible illness that ravaged whole populations of southern and Midwestern settlers, the so-called milk sickness, the "trembles" that killed so many children and took away Abraham Lincoln's mother, Nancy Hanks Lincoln, when the family lived in Indiana. Snakeroot contains a toxin that was transmitted through the milk of cows that browsed on the plant.

Wildflower names and their "found poetry" are intermingled, for me, with issues of love and survival. In Vermont, one summer, Margaret and Chloe and I kept a list of all the wildflowers we found and identified. We took short walks and rested often, looking up names in our field guides. Some of the flowers we found were natives of Vermont's Green Mountains, but many, even most, were the same ones that grow around here. Two things struck me—the variety of their names, and the affinity, for me, that they seemed to have with the stars (consider what "aster" means, after all), all the vivid, distant summer constellations:

IMAGINARY POLAROID

In this picture I am standing in a meadow
holding a list of fifty-one wildflowers.
It is Vermont, midsummer, clear morning
all the way to the Adirondacks.
I am, as usual, lost. Misplaced. But happy,
shaggy with dew. Waving my list.
The wind that blows the clouds across these mountains
has blown my ghosts away, and the sun
has flooded my world to the blinding-point.
There's nothing to do till galaxy-rise
but name and gather the wildflowers.
This is called "pearly everlasting."
And this one is arrow-leaved tearthumb!
Hawkweed, stitchwort, dogbane, meadow rue . . .
The dark comes on, the fireflies weave around me,
pearl and phosphor in the windy dark,
and still I am clutching my list,
saying "hop clover, fireweed, cinquefoil,"
as the Milky Way spreads like an anchor overhead.

Knowing the names of things, being really knowledgeable about your environment, has a centering or anchoring effect. And if stars and wildflowers got twisted together in my imagination, it was partly through visual analogy. A field of blooming Queen Anne's lace is constellated like a night sky. So, for that matter, is a simple patch of lawn with white clover blossoms studding it, a common enough July/August sight if you glance down toward your feet.

The starry skies can easily become an August preoccupation. The mosquito population I mentioned earlier actually seems to get a little discouraged on lengthening and cooling August nights, so that you can wander around outside. You will naturally find yourself stargazing, looking up. If you wildflower-gaze by day and stargaze by night, you are naturally going to enjoy mixing them up a little.

That is partly why I set my long backyard poem, "Night Thoughts," on an August night, the eleventh, in 1991. The nights of the tenth through the twelfth of August see the earth at the peak of its annual passage through the asteroid belt that gives us the Perseid meteor shower. Every year that brings people out to lie on blankets or tilt back in their lawn chairs to watch and count the meteors that streak the sky several times a minute. It is like a ghostly, meditative echo of the Fourth of July fireworks.

I found out about the Perseids when I spent a summer working at a resort in Maine, between my sophomore and junior years in college. We were on an inland lake, near Waterville. On a clear August evening, the eleventh or twelfth, round about midnight, I took a rowboat out on the quiet lake and lay back to watch the night sky.

I was not disappointed. Every few seconds a streak of light, short or long, momentarily altered the tranquil features of the heavens, striping the blackness and introducing sudden motion among the quietly blazing stars and planets. It was impossible to see every meteorite, since as you turned your head to watch one occur, say, toward the east, another might be starting in the north. The asteroids must be very dispersed, because while the Perseids take their name from the fact that the meteorites seem to be coming out of the constellation Perseus, in my own experience they are widely scattered across the night sky.

After a while I gave up trying to count or categorize them. I just let the boat drift free, rocking slightly on the dark water where the stars and light streaks were of course all mirrored. History and circumstance seemed to fall away, subsumed by the hugeness and ancientness of what I was experiencing. If the imagination is "imprinted" by certain unforgettable events, that was certainly such a moment for me. On the one hand I had a pretty good scientific understanding of what was actually occurring in the night sky as the planet passed through the asteroid belt. That did nothing, on the other hand, to diminish the sense of magic and spiritual community that heightens the senses, raises the hairs on the back of the neck, and seems to create an intuitive understanding of myth, the imagination's ancient and time-honored means of containing the uncontainable. The midnight stillness, dis-rupted occasionally by the wavering calls of loons, the smell and feel of the cool dark lake beneath me, the dim forest all around on the shore, and the lit vault of stars with its sudden meteor streaks—I felt at home in it, felt that sense of unity and harmony we spend our lives seeking and only occasionally experience.

I've written twice about other aspects of that summer. The first was about the weekly ice-cream making, in a group of prose poems called "Four about the Letter P":

Hauling a cake of ice from the ice-house, hosing off the sawdust, shaving it to slush that is packed around the can and dasher and sprinkled with rock salt, taking turns with the crank, doing this every Sunday morning through a whole summer so that some hundred people may have ice-cream with chokecherry sauce, and never once thinking "This is a piece of the river."

The block of ice, fetched on a Saturday and kept under a tarpaulin in a shed, always left me a little astonished at how it was able to maintain its size and cold temperature in hot weather. We put it in a washtub and used a long-handled scraper to shave chips from it as we needed them. The finer the shavings, the better the results in terms of the interaction of ice and rock salt. I remember that my friend Fred and I used to read to each other as we took turns cranking those Sunday middays, waiting for the large batch of ice cream to slowly stiffen.

My other poem about that time in Maine is much more recent, just a few years old. It brings together a number of random associations:

POEM FOR ADLAI STEVENSON
AND YELLOW JACKETS

It's summer, 1956, in Maine, a camp resort
on Belgrade Lakes, and I am cleaning fish,
part of my job, along with luggage, firewood,
Sunday ice cream, waking everyone
by jogging around the island every morning

swinging a rattle held in front of me
to break the nightly spider threads.
Adlai Stevenson is being nominated,
but won't, again, beat Eisenhower,
sad fact I'm half aware of, steeped as I am
in Russian novels, bathing in the tea-
brown lake, startling a deer and chasing it by canoe
as it swims from the island to the mainland.
I'm good at cleaning fish: lake trout,
those beautiful deep swimmers, brown trout,
I can fillet them and take them to the cook,
and the grateful fisherman may send a piece
back from his table to mine, a salute.
I clean in a swarm of yellow jackets,
sure they won't sting me, so they don't,
though they can't resist the fish, the slime,
the guts that drop into the bucket, they're mad
for meat, fresh death, they swarm around
whenever I work at this outdoor sink
with somebody's loving catch.
Later this summer we'll find their nest
and burn it one night with a blowtorch
applied to the entrance, the paper hotel
glowing with fire and smoke like a lantern,
full of the death-bees, hornets, whatever they are,
that drop like little coals
and an oily smoke that rolls through the trees
into the night of the last American summer
next to this one, 36 years away, to show me
time is a pomegranate, many-chambered,
nothing like what I thought.

I know I was struck, when I wrote this, at the vividness of my recollection. The fact that I could remember a summer thirty-six years away more precisely than one that was, say, two or three back, helped affirm a sense of time as more than simply linear, like Borges's notion, in one of his stories, of a garden of forking paths, where distant events and other possible outcomes coexist, pathways in a maze. The sense of self and the continuity of identity, as I have been contending, are based on the action of memory. Memory is not infallible, or even very reliable, but it may be a microcosm, showing us time's elasticities and multiplicities.

Looking back at this poem, understanding it more clearly as an elegy of sorts—for Stevenson, for the fish, for the yellow jackets, for the world of the 1950s, for the always receding past—I comprehend my choice of final image more clearly. The pomegranate is the traditional fruit of the dead, associated with the underworld. Its many-chambered aspect, which links it here with the hornets' nest, also implies the presence of death everywhere in time and experience. It is a Rilkean image, finally: death as fruit, as a part of life, growth, and nourishment. *In my father's house are many mansions.* Lots of them are graves and catacombs. *Angels don't always know if they are moving among the living or the dead.* People don't either. *In the midst of life we are in the midst of death.* And vice versa? These are ideas I understood better when I wrote the poem than I did when I lived it. Time is a pomegranate. Many-chambered. The older you get, the more fruit there is to nibble on, the more there is to nourish you. Eating your own life, you are also eating your own death.

August has also meant, on and off over my years in this area, time spent at Lake Erie, in a cottage. Oberlin Beach, where professors have had summer places over the years, was close enough that we could stay in touch with our jobs, amuse the children, and get some writing done. We never owned a cottage, but we often rented. Friends from town would drop in, and boat owners sometimes visited by water.

Lake Erie in the sixties was supposed to be a dire place. People spoke of its "death" from chemical pollutants, and it seemed to have a dim future. On the south shore, the effects of wind and weather were eroding the shoreline and threatening lakeshore cottages and properties. But the lake still offered a haven in late summer, where we could get away cheaply.

Life at the lake was pleasant precisely because it was largely uneventful. Hot days could be regularly punctuated by cooling swims. A late-night dip, just before bed, was especially refreshing. Breezes came off the lake, and thunderstorms from Michigan and Canada made for a grand show, night or day. So did the gradual progress of the long ore and grain boats, shaped like the lake itself, many of them going in or out of the nearby port of Huron. At night we could stroll out and look at the stars, grill a simple meal and eat the local corn and peaches, play cards or mah-jongg, and then sleep soundly. By day we could work—I always seemed to get good writing done—bask, lie around reading, or go off on minor expeditions.

A favorite expedition was to the area upstream of the mouth of Old Woman's Creek, which emptied into the lake right next to Oberlin Beach. We spent happy hours paddling around a wetland area that was teeming with plant and animal life.

In the summer of 1963, in August, Chloe and I, newlyweds then, came back from an expedition up Old Woman's Creek to some terrible news. My best friend, Newell Ellison, had been shot and killed while walking his dog in Washington, D.C. We set off almost immediately for his funeral. This was the first death of someone close I had had to face. Its suddenness was devastating. Newell and I had been graduate students at Yale together, and then he had come to Oberlin to teach in 1962, one year after I started. He had been best man at my wedding, and we were both looking forward to the next year of teaching together and encouraging each other with our work on doctoral dissertations.

The following summer, as the anniversary of Newell's death approached, we were once again staying at Oberlin Beach. I was reading Eugenio Montale, the great modern Italian poet, for the first time and with a great sense of excitement. Very little of Montale's work was available in translation then, so with an Italian-American dictionary and a few literal translations in *The Penguin Book of Italian Poetry,* I was going back and forth between the Italian text and what turned out to be my first serious efforts at translation.

What excited me about Montale was the way he was able to make landscape and place stand for human emotions without romanticizing or anthropomorphizing his subject. The complexity of the world around us—its storms, pollutings, and mysteries, its desolations and its beauties—matches up with the complexities of our lives and emotions in his work in a fashion that feels both revelatory and (as with all the best poets) effortless. In the opening section of "News from Mount Amiata," for example, Montale invokes the mountainous region of Tuscany very vividly, and, since it's a kind of letter and a kind of prayer, we understand that the speaker is trying to explore his own feelings by noting precise details:

> *Bad weather's fireworks become*
> *the beehives' murmur at the other end*
> *of evening. The room has wormy beams*
> *and the smell of melons*
> *floats up through the planks. Delicate*
> *smoke signals, rising from a valley*
> *of gnomes and mushrooms toward the summit's*
> *diaphanous cone, cloud up the pane,*
> *and I write you from here, from this distant*
> *table, from the honeycomb cell*
> *of a sphere hurtling through space—*
> *and the hooded cages, the fireplace*
> *where chestnuts explode, the veins*
> *of mold and saltpeter, are the frame*
> *into which you'll soon burst. The life*
> *that stories you is still too short*
> *if it contains you! The gleaming background*
> *highlights your icon. Outside it rains.*

How simple, and yet how effective, to report on your surroundings, to sketch them in expertly as a way of capturing a mood. I don't know if the poem was written in August, but it felt like that, like vacation time, languid and abundant, like the month in which summer is poised for its last pleasures before the year turns toward the fall. The "icon" could be a picture of a loved one, a special snapshot of someone the speaker is anticipating being reunited with; it also carries a metaphysical charge, making the poem a little bit like a prayer to someone who can bring more order and organization to this beautiful, bewildering world. The poem closes:

> *This Christian brawl with its*
> *shadowy words, its mere lament,*
> *what does it bring you from me? Less*
> *than the millstream, that burrows softly*
> *in its concrete sluice, tears away.*
> *A millwheel, an old log: the world's*
> *last boundaries. A heap of straw*
> *breaks up: and coming late*
> *to wed my vigil to your deep*
> *sleep that greets them, the porcupines*
> *drink from a thread of pity.*

Is this a world in which two lovers long to be together, or is it a world in which the presence of divinity seems precarious, a "deep sleep" that produces only a thread of pity for the immense human suffering that fills it? Water can grow scarce in summer; pity is hard to come by in wartime. The final image is ineffable and unforgettable, and it resonates as no direct statement about history, politics, love, or metaphysical longing possibly could, long after we have put the poem down.

With this reading of Montale as background, with the anniversary of deep grief to unwrap and ponder, with the ambiguous landscape and lakescape in which I was "estivating," I found myself suddenly able to write a kind of poem that felt more natural and more inclusive than poems I had written previously. It seemed to touch on my grief, on the beauty of the world around me that I found spiritually nourishing, on my wonder at my own impending fatherhood, just about three months away. Because it brought together many strands of interest and preoccupation, I sensed its importance to me, as a writer and as a person. Montale gave me the precedent for weaving together my grief, the mystery of death, and the natural world I felt so deeply involved with:

LATE SUMMER: LAKE ERIE

Nearly a year since word of death
Broke off the summer: as if a goddess
You followed respectfully
Should turn and stun you with her look.

We can go back to Old Woman's Creek,
Easy canoeing except where lotus
And waterlily choke the way:
Rose mallows massed on the banks, around
Bends, the sudden rise of ducks,
Invisible bitterns, the silent, ponderous
Heron, our kingfisher escort,
And, under the still, flowering
Surface, death: the orange carp
Crowd toward the killer lake.

I swore I'd write no letters to the dead.
It's only myself I want to tell
Things are about the same. The wind
Still pounds and stumbles around the cottage,
The lake is streaked and rumpled, dead
Fish wash up to the beach, our summer
Is the same, sweet, easily murdered pleasure.
I wade in the supple breakers, I'll
Paddle again on the creek. Now,
This morning, I walk to the road;
All to the south the dazed, hot landscape lies,
Under its piled thunderheads,
Dreaming of love and survival.

I seem to spend my Augusts musing, not so much searching out questions of love and survival as living comfortably among them. The month's excess makes me feel princely, privileged. I experiment with lazy forms of food preparation, like recipes in which you let the sun cook your food for you—tomatoes, zucchini, eggplants. Before I can bring myself to eat a peach, I may spend several minutes smelling it, rolling it around in my hand. I even take a magnifying glass to its suede-smooth skin, discovering that it is yellow-orange, with millions of tiny red dots on one side, and red, with comparable sprinklings of yellow dots, on the other. But words like *red* and *yellow* do not do justice to the hues of brick, old Tuscan wine, contusion, copper, lamplight, candle flame, lemon, and sunrise that somehow all inhabit this one piece of fruit, the whole of it downy with a bloom of fuzz that catches and holds the light.

This sultry weather is more conducive to reverie than activity, though the line between the two is never firmly drawn. Musing on a steamy August evening, out for a walk, or simply sitting on the screened porch, I can revisit Vermont and Maine or walk the beach at Lake Erie, gazing at meteors, part of a lakescape with ore boats and thunderheads. Half in the past and half in the present, I find myself pondering endings. They can be abrupt and terrible, like the end of Newell Ellison's life. They can try to climb to insights, like my night among the Perseids and my recognition about time at the end of "Poem for Adlai Stevenson and Yellow Jackets." They can resonate the way those porcupines do for readers of Montale or the way that image of the Milky Way does for me in the Vermont poem.

The ending of "Late Summer: Lake Erie" feels a bit ungainly. It's a young man's work, a self-conscious gesture toward the whole United States from its "northern shore," claiming that all of us and everything around us, including the clouds and the landscape they pass over and rain on, long for just two things: love and survival. A porcupine would have been better as a closing image, or a skunk, like the one Robert

Lowell took from Montale's model to close his own landmark poem, "Skunk Hour."

Love and survival. Now I have put down the peach and am pondering a plum, nearly the same size and a deep purple-blue, glossy, fresh, and cool. About to take a bite, I decide to look at it instead under the magnifying glass. A small surprise awaits me there: I find a replica of the night sky, as if it, too, could become a globe, black-purple starred with gold and silver specks and an occasional blue cloud, sprawling like a galaxy. It's as if, if I wait, I may glimpse a meteor.

Three Sun-Cooked Vegetable Dishes

There is something satisfying about using the heat and glare of the summer sun to help you with your food preparation. These dishes sit outside, uncovered, so you have to put them in a sunny place where they won't be disturbed. The first is a tomato sauce for pasta. The other 2 produce vegetables—zucchini and eggplant, respectively—that can be served like a salad or as appetizers and antipastos.

●

Sun-Cooked Tomato Sauce for Pasta

This is a variation on the uncooked summer tomato sauces for pasta that sometimes go under the name of *pasta estivi*. Those are often refrigerated and combined at the last minute with the hot cooked pasta, the 2 temperatures meeting in the middle. You can do that with this dish, if you like. The point is that the sun-cooking brings out the flavors of the ingredients more fully.

2 pounds fresh ripe plum tomatoes
(or other kinds, if you prefer)

½ cup capers
1 cup pitted black olives, calamata or similar
2 handfuls of basil leaves, cut in ribbons
½ cup olive oil
2 cloves garlic, chopped
salt and freshly ground pepper
1 pound pasta

Boil some water in a pan, dip the tomatoes in for a minute, in batches, then peel, seed, and dice them. Put them in a big bowl and add the capers, olives, basil, half the olive oil, the garlic, and some salt and pepper. Put the bowl outside in the hot sun, uncovered, for 3 hours or so.

When you are ready to eat, bring the bowl in and cook the pasta. Mix it with the rest of the oil and then with the sauce. You can chill the sauce after you've "cooked" it, if you want, and add it to the pasta while the pasta is still quite hot. You can also leave it lukewarm or at room temperature, putting it on the pasta when the latter has cooled. If you're dying to make this dish and it's raining outside, put it in a warm oven for the required time, or in a warm place like your hot-water-heater closet. It will be almost as good.

●

Sun-Cooked, Marinated Zucchini

The "cooking" here is to sweat the moisture out of the zucchini slices. You then grill or fry them and put them in their marinade. How long you marinate is up to you—overnight is fine, but an hour or so works pretty well, too.

———

3 medium-sized zucchini
coarse salt
peanut oil, for frying

1 handful of mint leaves
freshly ground pepper
$\frac{1}{4}$ cup white vinegar
2 tablespoons balsamic vinegar
1 teaspoon sugar
2 garlic cloves
2 tablespoons olive oil

Wash the zucchini, cut off the ends, and then slice them about a $\frac{1}{4}$-inch thick. I like to slice them lengthwise, using a mandolin. Salt the slices, put them on a tray or trays, 1 layer, and put the trays in the sun for at least an hour. Blot off the moisture with paper towels, and either grill the slices, brushed with a little oil, or fry them gently in peanut oil until they are lightly browned. Put them in a serving bowl. You can layer them now, but you should put mint leaves, cut up, along with pepper and just a little more salt, all over each layer. Boil the vinegar, sugar, and garlic for a minute, then add a little olive oil. Pour this mixture over the zucchini. At this point you can put them back in the sun for an hour or 2, until you're ready to serve, or you can cover and refrigerate them for a longer marinating (e.g., overnight).

●

Sun-Cooked, Marinated Eggplant

For this dish you follow all the same procedures as in the recipe above, except that you use fresh oregano instead of mint. Peel the eggplants? Only if the skin seems exceptionally tough. I would rather leave it on even if, when it comes time to eat, I decide to eat everything inside it and leave the rim of skin uneaten. It helps the slices hold their shape through the 2 steps of cooking and the third step of marinating.

Cold Rice Salads

In hot weather, cold salads with rice or pasta as their
base can be one-dish meals. Italians tend to serve rice
salad as an appetizer or a buffet entry, and that's fine,
but on a hot evening when nobody is terribly hungry,
it can readily become a main dish, accompanied by
stuffed tomatoes or marinated zucchini and a white
wine chilled almost to the freezing point. The same is
true of the rather mild Thai "fried rice" I've included
here (see recipe below). It can be served hot, but it
doubles nicely as a cold salad in hot weather.

●

Italian Cold Rice Salad

This is based on Marcella Hazan's, which I like for its
delicacy and visual appeal. Substitutions of all kinds
are possible, though—for example, tuna instead of
chicken; celery instead of, or in addition to, the pepper; and, of course, nuts: toasted pine nuts or toasted
chopped walnuts. A vegetarian version might use tofu

and hard-boiled eggs as another possibility, chopped fine. Keeping the ingredients small is important because they seem to go better with the rice that way.

—◦⁄◦⁄◦—

1 cup raw rice
1 whole chicken breast, or 2 halves,
    boneless and skinless
1 sweet pepper, red, yellow, or green, diced
1 dozen black olives, pitted and diced
1 dozen green olives, pitted and diced
1 cup Swiss or similar cheese, diced
1 small dill pickle, diced
1 tablespoon mustard, Dijon or similar
2 tablespoons balsamic vinegar
6 tablespoons olive oil
salt

You can be dicing the ingredients while you are bringing a couple of quarts of salted water to a boil and cooking the rice therein for about 12 minutes. Drain the rice and rinse it with cold water. Mix the dressing—the mustard, vinegar, olive oil, and a little salt—and combine it in a bowl with the rice, mixing well. Add the other ingredients —chicken, olives, cheese, pepper, pickle, and anything else you've decided on, for example, pine nuts—and mix thoroughly. You don't need to chill this salad. If you do, bring it to room temperature before you serve it.

●

Thai Rice Salad

This is fast, easy, and fairly bland. You can dress it up and spice it up in various ways, but it is awfully nice by itself or balancing a spicy cold salad of chilies, eggplants, and tomatoes.

3 cups cold cooked rice
3 tablespoons peanut oil
3 garlic cloves, chopped
1 onion, chopped
1 cup cooked shrimp
3 tablespoons fish sauce
3 tablespoons tomato ketchup
2 tablespoons white vinegar
1 tablespoons Tabasco sauce

Garnishes
chopped coriander and/or basil
cucumber
fried shallots
chopped peanuts
chopped hard-boiled egg

Heat the oil in a wok or large frying pan. Fry the garlic briefly, then add the onion. When the onion is golden, add the shrimp and the fish sauce. Stir in the rice, mix it all together, add the ketchup, vinegar, and Tabasco sauce, and when it is heated through, put it in a bowl or on a platter. Let it come to room temperature before serving, and garnish or decorate it with the cucumber, peeled and cut into strips, the chopped herbs, and the peanuts, shallots, or chopped egg.

●

"Vitello" Tonnato

I put *vitello* in quotes because I almost never make this Italian hot-weather classic with veal anymore. I make it with pork roast (*maiale tonnato*), turkey breast (*tachino tonnato*), or with chicken breasts (*pollo tonnato*). This way I don't have to depend on the market having one specific kind of cut of meat. This is a great dish for company, and while it requires some advance work, it isn't really that hard.

———✦———

1 3-pound boneless pork roast,
   1 3-pound turkey breast, or 3 pounds
   boneless, skinless chicken breasts
1 carrot
1 celery stalk
1 medium-sized onion
6 tablespoons olive oil
salt and pepper
1 cup white wine
2 cups stock

If you're using a pork roast, chop the onion, celery, and carrot finely in a food processor and sauté in a casserole or deep pot in the olive oil. After a few minutes add the pork roast (or a veal roast if you want to be absolutely authentic), salted and peppered, and brown it on all sides for 10 to 15 minutes. Add the wine, stock, and enough water to just about submerge the roast. Bring it to a boil, reduce to a simmer, cover the casserole or pot, and cook for about 2 hours. Let it cool in its broth and then refrigerate. You can do this the day before you plan to serve the dish or on that morning. When you are ready for the final preparations, slice the roast in thin, even slices, dip the pieces in the sauce, and put them on a platter. Put the rest of the sauce on top and garnish. Refrigerate, covered with waxed paper or plastic wrap, until ready to serve.

If you are using turkey breast or chicken breast, place it in the stock, wine, and water along with the carrot and celery, cut in large pieces, and the onion, halved and peeled. Add some salt and a few whole peppercorns. Poach the turkey breasts until done. Let cool in the stock and proceed as above. If you are using chicken breasts, you may not be able to slice them; you could leave them whole or cut them into large strips.

The Sauce

1 egg
1 teaspoon dry mustard
¾ cup light vegetable oil
    (safflower, corn, canola, etc.)
2 anchovy fillets
1 can (7-ounce) tuna
2 tablespoons capers, rinsed
    and drained
½ cup stock from the meat

Put the egg, mustard, and a little salt and pepper in a blender or food processor. Blend for 30 seconds, then add the oil slowly, in a thin stream, with the motor running. You'll get a light mayonnaise. Now add the anchovies, the tuna, the capers, and the stock. Blend again until the sauce is smooth. Some cooks smear the bottom of the serving plate thickly with a third of the sauce, add the meat in slightly overlapping layers, and pour the rest of the sauce on the top. I prefer to dip each piece of meat in the sauce and then put it, sauce side down, on the platter. Then I pour the remainder of the sauce over the whole. You can garnish with parsley, capers, green peppercorns, or anything else that seems appropriate. I sometimes sprinkle a little paprika over, too. Cover the platter (I prefer waxed paper to plastic wrap, which tends to pick up too much of the surface) and refrigerate until you are ready to serve it.

●

Fresh-Picked Sweet Corn

Maybe a recipe is hardly necessary, but I'll include it
because I think it's great to serve with a dish like the
one given above, and I find there's a certain amount of
confusion about how best to cook it.

—⊷⊶⊷—

8–12 ears of young sweet corn

Buy the corn in mid- to late afternoon if you can, from the grower, and
preferably a high-volume seller, which will mean the corn is picked
several times a day and hasn't been sitting around. Fanatics will tell you
you should pick it and rush it straight to the pot. The sugars begin to
turn to starches right away when it's picked. But I find it's sweet enough
anyway, so I content myself with trying to buy it pretty fresh and cooking it as quickly and simply as possible.

Bring a large pot of lightly salted water to boil. When it is boiling,
add the ears of corn, put a lid on the pot, and take it off the fire. The
corn will be cooked in about 10 minutes, but it can sit in the water
longer if you aren't quite ready to serve it. Serve with butter, salt, and
pepper available for individual preferences.

●

Blueberry Frozen Yogurt

As summer goes on, I continue experimenting with
approximations of true gelato. Sometimes the results
don't feel all that Italian, but they are successful in their
own right. I feel that way about my blueberry frozen
yogurt.

—⊷⊶⊷—

1 pint fresh-picked blueberries
¾ cup sugar

juice of $\frac{1}{2}$ lemon

3 tablespoons triple sec or similar liqueur

2 cups plain yogurt

Wash the blueberries and pick them over. Put them in a blender with the other ingredients and purée. Chill in the refrigerator until you are ready to put the mixture in an ice-cream maker. One very nice presentation of this is to scoop out several oranges (1 for each diner), saving the top as a lid. Fill the oranges with blueberry yogurt when it is mostly frozen, replace the tops, and put them in the freezer until you are ready to serve them. The pulp and juice you scooped out of the oranges can be blended with milk or yogurt and ice to make a refreshing summer drink.

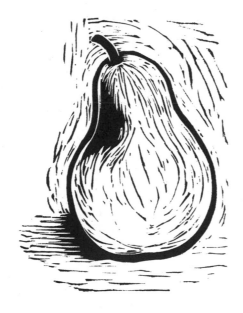

Peaches and Red Wine, Two Ways

As I mentioned, the peaches of August are one of our greatest treats around here. Tree-ripened, not needing to be shipped anywhere, they are fragrant, sweet, and exceptionally delicate in flavor. Eating them raw or cut up on cereal is probably the simplest and best way to enjoy them, but I include here 2 desserts that combine them, very simply, with another of my favorite foods.

●

Peaches in Red Wine, Cooked

You need a pan for this that will hold the peaches in a single layer. Use 1 peach for each diner, up to 8.

1 cup red wine
½ cup brown sugar
pinch of ground cinnamon
2–3 cloves
grinding of black pepper
1 teaspoon vanilla extract or 2 tablespoons liqueur
6–8 peaches

Bring the wine and brown sugar to a boil and stir to dissolve the sugar. Add cinnamon, cloves, pepper, and peaches and cover the pan. Simmer the peaches, poaching them, for about 8 minutes. Remove them from the sauce and let them cool. Reduce the sauce until it is syrupy, and add the vanilla or liqueur. Let it cool, too. When the peaches are cool they will peel easily. You can serve them whole, halved, or sliced, with the sauce poured over them.

●

Peaches in Red Wine, Uncooked

In this recipe you simply skin the peaches (dunking
them for a minute in boiling water makes the skins easy
to remove), slice them in a bowl, and add the wine,
sugar, and spices. The amounts from the recipe above
will work well here, though you may need to increase
the wine if you use a lot of peaches.

Both these dishes can be served over vanilla ice cream.

SEPTEMBER

Clouds out of Old Dutch Paintings

. . . .

A COUNTRY POSTCARD

September here, a haze on things,
diamond mornings, dying corn.
We have green fields here, white-flecked,
we have blue fields here, chicory,
yellow fields, four kinds of goldenrod,
and a man in a white shirt
and a red face
a man made out of words
stands by the B & O tracks
listening for the express
that disappeared west
before the tracks
began to rust.

There's a stillness
this morning, that the man
made out of words must walk through
listening

. .

as he wades
in chicory, alfalfa,
wild carrot, goldenrod,
the nodding, growing,
dew-decked, soon-to-die
words.

It is certainly true that the September light is a combination of haze and brilliance. The dew gets heavier now and shows up on bright mornings in diamond-glints everywhere on the ground and foliage. Droplets of mercury stand trembling on my rose leaves when I go out in the morning. Days can start misty and then be burned clean and clear by a less hot but more dazzling sun. It must be the lessening humidity and the cooling nights that make these swings from early dew and haze to a gleaming midmorning clarity so pronounced. The air loses all its excess moisture, drying out speedily, and the results are crystalline distances, a blue sky of great depth and concentration, and clouds that possess intricate detail for miles. Pouring over everything, the sunlight maintains an almost blinding, effortless brilliance.

These gleaming days seem for a while just a pleasant modulation of the summer heat, a pendulum swing back toward the weather of June, as if the summer were going to recapitulate itself, a film run backward. Certain signs, however, show the close observer what is really coming —not early summer, but the prelude to the cold. The roadside weeds are browning. Patches of grass have started to turn yellow and dun, though that is partly a result of late August drought. A few fields are already empty, full of stubble or even replowed for next year, and the corn that hasn't yet been harvested is tipped with a sea of tan tassels and mixes its vigorous green with more and more dry, bleaching leaves every day. Some trees are starting to show yellow edges on their high green leaves, an effect that will grow more pronounced as the nights drop toward the fifties and then the forties, heading toward the frost point. The two huge black walnuts in my father's backyard are already starting to shower small yellow leaves down whenever there's a breeze.

They are always the first to lose their foliage and the last to put out new leaves in spring. High on their spreading, dramatically angled limbs I can see the green walnuts, fat and round, clustered like testicles. They will drop, on the yard and occasionally on the roof, with loud thumps, all through the fall.

Everywhere I turn, small signs of the new season appear. I will turn around and find one whole branch of a sweet gum suddenly gone yellow or orange. Or I'll be strolling around my yard, and a huge brown sycamore leaf, like a crumpled page from an old folio, will drift down past me. As I pick it up to inspect it, another will float past.

Insects are especially active now, with an accompanying sense of preparing for the cold. Yellow jackets are everywhere, hovering over trash containers and around picnic sites. I keep seeing crickets underfoot, and I know from experience that a few of them will soon show up in the house, chirping away.

Outside, the grasshoppers whirl up as you walk, looking in flight like drab, army-surplus butterflies. They seem just right for the dry, crackly, springing texture of September, whirring up suddenly when I inspect my garden for ripe tomatoes, peppers, and eggplants. They usually fly a parabola of six or seven feet and land, watchful and ready to spring again if you approach them. I find them perched on every plant and can see the ragged edges of leaves that are the results of their eating.

POEM ABOUT HOPPING

Rabbits in Alabama hop
Into clumps of Syrian grass
To nibble the stalks, thinking of
Sorghum, hardly noticing autumn.

Along the Great Divide the bighorn
Sheep hop casually from rock to
Rock in the wind and glare, seriously
Considering leaping silver rivers, as

Salmon in crazy waters jump
Upstream for love—oh it's

A nervous country. When you
Walk through stubble, the hub

Of a wheel with grasshopper
Spokes, or sit over bowls of excited
Cereal, what can you say to your heart
But, Down sir, down sir, down?

Certainly this poem's exuberance is partly sexual. I was newly and happily married when I wrote it. But I was also celebrating American energy. We're a bustling nation, and we even like noisy breakfast cereal. America's nervous dash and restlessness had their dark side in that year, with a presidential assassination impending.

Years later, writing the middle section of "Poem in Three Parts," called "Dancing in the Dark," the section that deals with the universality of motion and change, I found myself waxing retrospective:

> 4
> *"Rabbits in Alabama hop," I wrote in 1963,*
> *happy enough between two deaths: a summer friend*
> *and a November president. New-married, love-sheathed,*
> *I could feel the planet's wobble and bounce*
> *as I walked my dog through weeds and stubble*
> *grasshoppers spraying in every direction*
> *so that I called myself "hub of a wheel,"*
> *teasing my sturdy little ego*
> *tingling along like a streetcar,*
> *not yet in the undertow of fatherhood,*
> *soft-shoe in the cornfield, dust-mote dance,*
> *loving the action I saw spread out—*
> *a map of this generous, jumping bean country.*

Not everything is hopping. Fruit is simply hanging there, ripening slowly. Up on the glacial ridges between this town and Lake Erie, the orchards are yielding their harvest. Peaches continue a little way into September, but they are gradually replaced, first by the pears and then by the apples. Whenever you can get these fruits at the orchards where they are grown, ripened on the trees before picking, you get bursts of unforgettable flavor. The pears are juicy and sweet, yielding but not too soft. Biting into one is an amazing sensation of luxury and seduction, and you can see why wasps sometimes burrow into fallen pears and stay there, losing themselves in pleasure and intoxication. A couple of ripe pears, some Stilton or Brie or Gouda, and perhaps a glass of port: one fine way to welcome autumn!

The apples come in waves, from Early Blaze on through Empire, Jonagold, Ida, Melrose, and Winesap. To bite down on a fresh, hard, slightly chilled, and recently picked apple is to experience an explosion of flavor in your mouth that resembles the impact of a particularly fine white wine, a Meursault or Montrachet, or an especially big chardonnay. It's eating, but it's also drinking, the imbibing of an ambrosia or essence that makes you think this fruit might well have been forbidden in paradise because it harbored so much sheer sensuous pleasure.

After a good rain, the orchards will offer another reward. Some kinds of mushroom become abundant, and orchards are one excellent place to find them. My family has emerged from local orchards with boxes and paper sacks full of meadow mushrooms (popularly known as "pink bottoms," because their gills when young are a dusky rose color), horse mushrooms—the large version of the meadow mushroom—and puffballs, some of them almost the size of basketballs. You can dry the meadow and horse mushrooms, but the puffballs can't be saved: you eat them when you find them, and the very best way is to cut them in slices or slabs, which you dip first in beaten egg and then in cracker crumbs before you fry them.

Other mushrooms are turning up now, too: the exotic and amazingly meatlike sulfur shelf, ranging in color from sulfur yellow to a gorgeous orange and growing on tree trunks; the parasol mushrooms that so often show up under pine trees, delicate in their flavor and also good for drying; and the shaggy manes, or lawyers' wigs, which belong to the inky cap family, meaning they will deliquesce into wet black piles if you don't get around to eating them. The inky caps are best, I think, with eggs, scrambled or in omelets. They don't mix well with alcohol—they can produce indigestion and nausea—so you do better to have them for a breakfast or brunch.

It's a clear, vivid September morning, with a slight breeze out of the southwest. Margaret, who is visiting for a day, is going with me to see if we can still pick some blackberries at a farm near the lake. We enjoy the September landscape as we drive along, the trees still mostly green, the cornfields growing browner, and a huge indigo sky with clouds the size of ocean liners.

The berry farm proves to be a sizable patch of land where raspberries, blueberries, and blackberries are grown and people are encouraged to pick their own. This is the very tail end of the season, and the young proprietor is a little surprised to have customers on this cool weekday morning. The blackberries are plentiful, he tells us, though near the end of their season. The blueberries, which we inquire about, are in his opinion too ripe: we're welcome to pick as much as we like, for free.

Working along the blackberry rows first, we find ourselves delighted

218

by their size—some are almost as big as ping-pong balls—and a little disappointed by their flavor. Huge clusters weigh down the berry canes, and you almost feel that the plant is grateful when you relieve it of four or five big blackberries. The air is pungent with the smell of crushed, fermenting berries on the ground, and a few wasps and yellow jackets cruise around, investigating.

The blueberries turn out to be marvelous, so we fill two baskets with them, unable to resist the offer of free fruit. Fortunately, Margaret is a veteran pie baker, and she decides to combine the blackberries, blueberries, and some Concord grapes she has brought with her into enough filling to make four pies.

The Concord grapes and the blueberries both have a kind of cloudy bloom on their deep-blue skins, similar enough that they look like different-sized cousins. I hold a blueberry between thumb and forefinger, admiring its mottling. A planet of deep-blue seas and snowy continents. A new world of New World fruit. Certainly the blueberries and Concord grapes combine well, along with the blackberries, for a spectacular result in Margaret's pies, which leak a staining purple juice and draw raves at a local potluck supper, when I take the largest, messiest pie to sit among the assortment of desserts.

~

As the cold closes in, the garden's yield narrows. Tomatoes are no longer ripening, so just a few green ones sit, a little forlornly, on their vines. I pick the last few eggplants shortly before the first frost, which comes just a day or two after the official first day of fall, the equinox. It's a light frost, not that different from other early mornings when the dew on the ground is wet but white, the color of snow or ice. The whitened grass always makes me think of Tu Fu's autumn poems. In one he says, simply and memorably, "from now on / the dew will be white." From now until spring, he means, when the world starts itself up into life and growth again. In another, he is watching an almost new moon rising, probably right around the time of the autumnal equinox:

NEW MOON

Such a thin moon!
In its first quarter

219

a slanting shadow
a partly finished ring

barely risen
over the ancient fort

hanging at the edge
of the evening clouds

the Milky Way
hasn't changed color

the mountain passes
are cold and empty

there's white dew
in the front courtyard

secretly filling
the drenched carnations.

The apparently casual skill here always intrigues me. Tu Fu makes the moon new but then immediately old as well by virtue of its associations with the ruined fort and the evening clouds. The little roundnesses or parabolas of moon crescent and ancient fort shape are echoed in the circular carnations. Meanwhile, the poet expands the scope of his panorama on up to the galaxy overhead and on out to the distant mountains, with their deserted passes, before circling back to his own house and the emotions suggested by the cold attacking the carnations.

Still, as the cold nights come and the frosts begin, certain parts of the garden do well. The kale has never looked better. The same is true of the arugula, which will continue to produce for the next month or two. It sends me back to a favorite recipe. Nothing could be simpler than the "poor person's soup" that contains only potatoes, bread, a handful of arugula, and some salt, pepper, and olive oil. The presence of the arugula transforms the mixture into something that smells a little like chicken soup. Adding the bread last makes it rather thick, and you end up eating something that has the consistency of porridge. I serve it on a Sunday evening, followed by a salad of greens that has some poached salmon on top and a vinaigrette of cracked peppercorns, along with a simple Italian *vernaccia.*

I found some broccoli rape when I went to buy the salmon. Greens flourish in this bracing weather, and the bunches of rapini, with their bright green leaves and yellow buds at the top, looked especially appealing. Combined with spinach, the broccoli rape becomes the stuffing for little *consums,* a kind of dumpling made of *piadina,* an ancient stone-griddle flat bread. The flat bread used to be cooked on a hot stone or tiles, but we moderns can use an iron skillet if we regulate the heat carefully. The chewy breads should come out a little scorched, but not burned. I can make the breads round and flat and serve them with the garlicky, slightly bitter mixture of greens on the top, or as a side dish. Sausages are good with this meal, too, fried up or grilled. It's especially fun, though, to stuff a round piece of dough, folding it over to make a half-moon shape, the *consum,* and cook it on the hot, dry surface, turning it now and then.

I reflect, as I work, on what a very ancient process this must be, predating both the kitchen and the stove. Unleavened bread, a variety of field greens, and a hot surface to cook on. The recipe has surely survived from the Etruscans! And cooking it links me with them, poor disappeared race, in the long reaches of the cultural imagination.

Mary Young, my mother, would have been ninety this year, on September 29. I spend a fragile and gorgeous blue day missing her as I move through my various tasks, longing to see her as I did not realize I could, startled by my childish need, and contented to realize how deep and lasting is my love. How I wish I could tell her now what she meant to me! Sitting outside with some students, talking to old friends who are visiting, seeing a production of *Romeo and Juliet,* shopping for a dinner party, walking the dog, or simply turning my face up to the benign midday sun, I am always a little to one side of myself and my life this month. It is the mechanism of seasonal change. It is the knowledge of growing older. It is the skein of losses that gradually come to characterize our life.

I associate this sense of things with the French poet Jean Follain, who wrote so simply and perceptively about ordinary moments of life and routine in terms of the recognitions and epiphanies they can produce. Like William Carlos Williams, he is a poet of the ordinary and everyday who can transform our sense of reality by pointing out the simplest objects and the most unlikely people as profound and touching. Here is one of his poems, as translated by W. S. Merwin:

DAWN

A house roof and the star
growing pale above it
held the glance of a man
who felt himself caught again
in the delicate play of causes
the signs farther down
disclosed their golden words
the wood, the iron, the stone
enforced their presence
a wide open window
showed the ochre wall and the cupboard
and the hand laying an iron spoon
on the china of a plate
where it was chipped long ago.

How simple that spoon is! It becomes a spoon from my mother's kitchen, where she cooks while I play contentedly, four or five years old, with pots and pans and graters and beaters she has let me drag out of the cupboards and drawers. The "delicate play of causes" (*fin jeu des*

causes) is what we always seem to be sensing in Follain's poems, moments when people pause and find their awareness growing, taking in
past and present. A melancholy joy comes off these little poems, like

the steam and aroma from a stew or a stockpot.

How could I not try to import Jean Follain to Ohio? Couldn't his obsessed characters, alone with their suddenly enlarged awareness, be
my own neighbors?

SUITE FOR JEAN FOLLAIN

1

In September there come to Ohio
clouds out of old Dutch paintings
above weeds in gold confusion
in overlooked orchards apples
drop in the wild grass
a baby strapped in a station wagon
stares at the checked jackets
of hunters stooping to gather
groceries spilled on the sidewalk.

2

Never came back to visit
says the old woman out loud
lugging a bucket of feed
across the empty farmyard
beyond her a shed is collapsing
terrifically slowly a cow
is chewing without expression
white stars pass
from a burst milkweed.

3

The evening has turned the blue
of a milk of magnesia bottle
and the big American flag

is snapping against itself
in front of the courthouse
looking up at the window
where she undressed he thinks
of wrens and tent revivals
and statues from ancient Egypt.

4

A wet stone beehive
stands in the middle of the garden
beyond the wall delivery trucks
occasionally pass
a smell of burning leaves
reminds the mailman of childhood
a fish jumps in the reservoir
in the graveyard clumps of honey mushrooms
blacken slowly in rain.

September is full of noticings and longings. Beauty and abundance are everywhere, but we are distracted from them by memories and losses. The person or persons who did not come back to visit that old farm woman—her children? her brother or sister?—aligns with the sexual yearning of the boy looking up at the window and the postman's reverie of his childhood. Meanwhile, clouds, weeds, fish, and mushrooms have lives and meanings of their own. The apples drop in the grass, the blue of evening is unforgettably deep, and the milkweeds, if we will only mark them, know how to live and die.

Fresh Puffballs

You know puffballs for sure when you slice them crosswise, into $\frac{1}{4}$- or $\frac{1}{2}$-inch slices, because they have no incipient stem. (If there is one, you have a very young stemmed mushroom, and it might be edible— a meadow mushroom, for instance—but it might be an amanita and you should check.) If the puffball's inside is discolored, it is past its best and you should reject it; you want a consistent chalky white.

———

1 pound fresh puffballs, any size
1 egg, beaten lightly
$\frac{3}{4}$ cup crushed cracker crumbs or
    bread crumbs
3–4 tablespoons butter or margarine

Slice the puffballs as described above. Dip the slices in the beaten egg, then in the cracker crumbs, and fry in the butter until brown on both sides. Serve as an appetizer or a side dish.

Shaggy Mane Omelet

If you find 2 or 3 shaggy manes, with their long, flaky, gray-white domes, you can bring them home, clean them off, sauté them briefly in a little butter, and add them, along with salt and pepper, either to scrambled eggs or to an omelet. The results will be delicious. If you get lucky and find a few more, you might want to make this slightly more ambitious version:

2 cups sliced raw mushrooms
   (shaggy manes may be mixed
   with meadow mushrooms)
2 tablespoons diced onion
3 tablespoons butter
4 eggs
3 tablespoons cream
salt and pepper
3 tablespoons grated cheese,
   Swiss or similar (optional)

Sauté the mushrooms and onions gently in the butter for about 5 minutes. Meanwhile, beat the eggs (not to foaminess; a whisk or fork is enough) and add the cream, a pinch of salt, and a grinding of pepper. You can also add some grated cheese at this point. Turn up the heat and add the egg mixture to the onion-mushroom mixture. Swirl the egg mixture to cover the bottom of the pan, and let it rest while the bottom cooks. When it has set a little but the top is still soft, fold the omelet over on itself. Cook another minute or 2, depending on how soft you like it, then transfer it to a dish. Serves 2, 3, or 4 people, depending on how hungry they are.

●

"Leif Ericson Pie"

I'm no expert on piecrusts. It's one of the gaps in my repertoire, and I will remedy it one of these days. A friendly colleague has even given me a careful, step-by-step, supposedly foolproof recipe. Meanwhile, though, I either don't make pie—I learned some time ago that I would have to be careful about indulging in desserts—or I have a helper—Margaret, Georgia, Darby—who can do a crust. Or I buy a frozen crust at the supermarket, feeling guilty about it.

The point of this recipe is the filling we invented from our adventure in picking late berries and combining them with Concord grapes. I think the ingredients for 2 pies would be something like the following:

—⟨ᴓᴓ⟩—

2 cups Concord grapes
3 cups blueberries
4 cups blackberries
3 cups sugar
$^{1}/_{2}$ cup tapioca

The grapes must be skinned and seeded, using the following method: separate pulp from skins, reserving skins. Cook the pulp until the seeds loosen. Strain through a colander. Combine the pulp and skins with the fruit, the sugar, and the tapioca. Mix thoroughly. Fill prepared pie shells.

Poverty Soup

This *zuppa dei poveri* is from Marcella Hazan's second
volume. Three simple ingredients—potato, arugula,
bread—make a marvelous combination. Try to use
really good olive oil with this.

——◎◎◎——

4 medium-sized potatoes
3 cups water or 2 cups water and
  1 cup chicken broth
1 large bunch of arugula
½ loaf stale Italian bread
salt and pepper
olive oil

Peel and dice the potatoes and put them in the water. Bring to a boil and
cook for about 10 minutes. Add the arugula, washed and chopped,
along with some salt. Cover the pot and cook another 10 minutes. Add
the bread, remove pot from heat, and let stand, covered, for 5 to 10
minutes. Serve in bowls, adding a grinding of pepper and a couple of
tablespoons of olive oil on the top of each bowl.

Poached Salmon Salad

The salmon for this dish can be steaks or a fillet. It is
poached in the oven or microwave, then dressed with a
peppercorn vinaigrette, and served over salad greens.

——◎◎◎——

4 salmon steaks or 2 1-pound fillets
½ cup white wine

1 tablespoon black peppercorns
¼ cup raspberry or similar vinegar
coarse salt
½ cup olive oil

Salt the salmon fillets or steaks and put them in a dish with the wine. Cover with waxed paper or, if you are microwaving, plastic wrap. Poach in a preheated 450° oven for 7 to 10 minutes, or microwave for 4 to 5 minutes. Remove and let cool in the pan. The peppercorns should be crushed in a pestle and marinated in the vinegar, the longer the better. When you are ready to serve, separate the cooked salmon into bite-sized pieces and arrange attractively over the greens. Combine the vinegar and pepper with the oil, add a little salt, whisk, and pour over the fish.

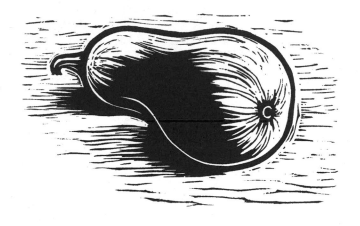

●

Consums
(Griddle Dumplings Stuffed with Greens)

These are not hard. You make the greens, then let them cool while you prepare the dough. For this one, too, I am indebted to Hazan's second volume. The balance

of greens—bitter rapini, earthy spinach, sweetish cabbage—is important to work out, but every cook will
have his or her preference about proportions, and you
can taste as you go. The amount of garlic is variable,
too. Other possible seasonings include lemon juice and
hot pepper. Experiment!

———⟨ᴑᴑᴑ⟩———

The Stuffing
1 pound fresh spinach
1 pound broccoli rape
½ pound shredded cabbage or chopped kale
salt and pepper
2 cloves garlic
½ cup olive oil

Wash the greens thoroughly. Leaving some of the water on them,
sprinkle them with some salt and put them in a large container in the
microwave. You'll need to do this in batches. Cook them on full power
for 3 minutes—first the spinach, then the rapini, then the cabbage
or kale (you can use Swiss chard as a substitute for any one of them).
Alternatively, you can boil the greens successively in salted water,
in batches, draining them, but the microwave method is a lot easier.
Squeeze the water out and chop the greens roughly.

Chop the garlic and sauté it lightly in the olive oil, using a large frying pan. Add the greens, stir-fry them, add salt and pepper, and let
cook for 5 to 10 minutes, turning frequently. Set aside to cool while
you prepare the griddle cakes.

The Dough
2 cups flour
3 tablespoons lard or olive oil
pinch of baking soda
1 teaspoon salt
½ cup warm water

I mix and knead the dough in my dough machine. If I didn't have that, I would use the food processor and the plastic blade that comes with it. Failing both, I would mix things together on a work surface (mounding the flour and putting the lard or oil, the water, the salt, and the baking soda into a crater in the center, then mixing and kneading for about 8 minutes).

Take a chunk of dough—about the size of an egg, Hazan suggests—and roll it out into a thin disk, 6 inches in diameter. Put about 3 tablespoons of greens on one half of the disk and fold the other half over, pinching the edges shut. If the seal doesn't stay tight during cooking, I find that's not a big problem. As you start cooking filled *consums,* you can be making more.

Cook them fast on a very hot griddle, 1 or 2 at a time. If you like black and brown spots on the dumplings, they will cook in just a few minutes with some turning needed to make sure all surfaces get cooked. If you don't want these burned spots, use a cooler griddle and take 6 or 8 minutes instead of 2 or 3 or 4. You can experiment as you go.

I like to serve these with grilled or broiled sausages as an accompaniment. I would imagine that the *consums* are also delicious filled with cheese, maybe a mixture of mozzarella and ricotta. Hazan says they can also be fried and are extraordinarily delicious when fried in hot lard.

●

Poached Pears

This is easy and can be prepared ahead of time. I serve it room temperature, but I think it would also be good warm or chilled.

—⟨ತ⟩—

6 ripe pears (fresh orchard Bartletts
    if you can get them)
1 lemon
4–6 tablespoons sugar

2 cups red wine
1 stick cinnamon
6 cloves
1 vanilla bean

Squeeze the lemon and add the juice to a bowl of about 1 quart of cold water. Peel each pear and halve it, removing the seeds and stalk. Put the halves in the bowl of lemon and water as you work. Heat the wine and add the sugar, cinnamon, cloves, and vanilla. If the pears are quite sweet, go easy on the sugar. Drain the pears and add them to the wine, making sure they are all more or less immersed. Simmer covered for about 10 minutes. Cool the pears in the wine. To serve, arrange the pear halves attractively on a plate or platter and strain some of the thickened wine over them.

●

Pears with Cheese and Walnuts

Best when the pears are coming from the orchards, but good any time of year.

4 pears
¼ cup goat cheese
¼ cup Gorgonzola
2 tablespoons cream or milk
lemon juice
¼ cup chopped walnuts

Do not peel the pears. Halve and core them and rub them with lemon juice. Mix the 2 cheeses, adding the milk or cream to achieve a spreadable consistency. Spread each pear half with the cheese mixture and sprinkle with walnuts.

OCTOBER

Subtle Bustle

· · · ·

This might well be our finest month. It's partly the silent explosion of color in the foliage of the deciduous trees. It's partly the way that foliage drifts intermittently to earth, with the season seeming now to accelerate toward winter and then to brake and park, arriving at prolonged, occult pauses, temporal backwaters and time warps, indolent warm days when leaves lie around on the ground, casting light upward, and the afternoon stretches out endlessly toward lucid evenings and brilliant nights. In such intervals, the season feels as though it will last and last, even while you are acutely aware that it cannot.

October's contradictions are tart, astringent. We may experience a similar paradox with spring's turning into summer, but that is less fraught with rueful consciousness, less charged with agreeable melancholy. Autumn's hesitations and changes in October are skittish. They leave us happy and pensive. Keats captured this simultaneous sense of slow ripening and approaching cold with lyric exactitude:

TO AUTUMN

Season of mists and mellow fruitfulness,
  Close bosom-friend of the maturing sun;

· ·

234

Conspiring with him how to load and bless
   With fruit the vines that round the thatch-eves run;
To bend with apples the moss'd cottage-trees,
   And fill all fruit with ripeness to the core;
      To swell the gourd and plump the hazel shells
With a sweet kernel; to set budding more,
   And still more, later flowers for the bees,
   Until they think warm days will never cease,
      For Summer has o'er-brimmed their clammy cells.

Who hath not seen thee oft amid thy store?
   Sometimes whoever seeks abroad may find
Thee sitting careless on a granary floor,
   Thy hair soft-lifted by the winnowing wind;
Or on a half-reap'd furrow sound asleep,
   Drows'd with the fume of poppies, while thy hook
      Spares the next swath and all its twined flowers:
And sometimes like a gleaner thou dost keep
   Steady thy laden head across a brook;
   Or by a cyder-press, with patient look,
      Thou watchest the last oozings hours by hours.

Where are the songs of spring? Ay, where are they?
   Think not of them, thou hast thy music too,—
While barred clouds bloom the soft-dying day,
   And touch the stubble-plains with rosy hue;
Then in a wailful choir the small gnats mourn
   Among the river sallows, borne aloft
      Or sinking as the light wind lives or dies;
And full-grown lambs loud bleat from hilly bourn;
   Hedge-crickets sing; and now with treble soft
   The red-breast whistles from the garden-croft;
      And gathering swallows twitter in the skies.

The poem epitomizes, and is epitomized by, the month of October. For me, it is the finest of Keats's great odes because it has the firmest and most realized sense of place. It also has a remarkably quiet ending, a world stilled so that distant and almost imperceptible sounds can be heard. It gathers and hushes the spirit, dispersing our awareness into the environment as a kind of figure for death: death as a soothing emissary of change and integration. Keats knew in his heart how ill he was.

I have this great poem memorized. I wanted to take the sounds of autumn, all the music Keats captured, inside me, possessively. Then I could reproduce them whenever I felt like it. I recite the poem, or parts of it, when I'm walking, raking, driving the car, or drifting off toward sleep.

If rapid change and leisurely prolongation coexist in October, so do happiness and sadness, in an inextricable mixture one develops a taste for, growing older. "Where are the songs of spring? . . . thou hast thy music too," wrote Keats, aware of his own illness and impending death. "Lord: it's time. The summer was very large. / Lay your shadow on the sundials now / and let the winds loose in the meadows," wrote Rilke, teaching himself to welcome change, decline, and death. "I sing the fall, it is the human season now," wrote Archibald MacLeish, meaning by "human" the awareness in the aging human being that life is brief and death is on its way. The chorus of poets, remembered and overheard, grows and swells into a murmuring choir during these fall days. Tennyson offers his perspective, derived from Homer: "The woods decay, the woods decay and fall. / The vapors weep their burthens to the ground. / Man comes and tills the field and lies beneath, / And after many a summer dies the swan." Melancholy as his thought may be, it is shot through with music, with all his rich enjoyment of autumn.

What the poets tell us, again and again, is that the synthesizing of extremes—of emotional highs and lows and of the elastic experience of time—feels holistic, feels exhilarating, gives you a sense of expanded awareness and consciousness. And all around you the color proceeds with its seasonal deepening, its remarkable variations. Staring into my own backyard and the ones that adjoin it shows me bursts of orange, bronze, lemon yellow, and scarlet. If I try to make out shapes in these newly transformed trees I see rearing lions, great purple fountains, gaudy candelabras, and huge ochre harps. And then come rain and wind, and the motley-colored leaves shower down, littering the ground with light and color that fade slowly, fade rapidly.

I want to be a scarecrow, fall equivalent to my January snowman, as much a part of all this as I can be, tipped in a field, performing my own demented dance of love as the wind blows me this way and that. My children and I used to stuff my old clothes with fallen leaves, put a carved pumpkin head on top, and set this puffy effigy against a tree in our backyard. In an early poem called "Evasions," exploring the connections between the weather and seasons on the one hand and the deepest parts of the self on the other, I closed the poem with three odd couplets:

> *Didn't I say the weather*
> *Would gather me back together?*

> *Was it at Halloween*
> *I carved my face, scooped my brain?*

> *A seedy, saffron pumpkin,*
> *Lined with the wind, I grin.*

So the pumpkin becomes the guardian spirit, the head of the ephemeral figure who stands for us and playfully connects our sense of the sacred with our immediate environment. Saint Pumpkin, as Nancy Willard calls him. Sometimes the sacred *is* the local, and perhaps the more often the better. The jack-o'-lantern's face is the enigmatic mask for our ambivalence toward change, beauty, and death. It grins at nothingness. It contains nothingness—or perhaps a guttering candle. No wonder I have come back to this subject more than once.

Children dive into leaf piles. They want to nest, want to be buried, want to hibernate. Squirrels and chipmunks hustle around gathering nuts, torn between eating and storage. Woodchucks fatten themselves until they can hardly waddle. The wind is gentle, then harsh, then gentle again. Leaves star the air. Birds squabble over last berries on the bushes. Everywhere in this area, especially because of the sugar maples and red maples, the world is lit by silent yellow and scarlet explosions, great lungs of lemon and flame, standing casually in the woods or at the edges of yards. The wind rustles through these trees-turned-lamps as though amazed at their metamorphosis, their heatless conflagration.

Out on the produce stands, along with the increasing varieties of apples and the piles of different-sized pumpkins, the winter squashes make their annual appearance. This is a vegetable I have only recently come to love. Like eggplant it is unfortunately named, at least to appeal to a child or a poet. If it were called, say, calabash or cucurbit, wouldn't I have come to love it sooner? Jimmy Durante, nose like a squash, used to intrigue us when I was a child, closing his radio program by saying tenderly, "Good night, Mrs. Calabash, wherever you are." We would melt at the mystery, tenderness, and humor of this. He could never have said, "Good night, Mrs. Squash."

We should call it by its real, and longer, name, *asquatasquash* or *isquotersquash,* a Narragansett word. Meanwhile, the individual names for the different varieties of winter squash are colorful and, usually, metaphoric: *acorn, butternut, Hubbard, spaghetti, buttercup,* and *turban.* The turbans are often treated like gourds—that is, used as decoration—but they can serve both purposes and are quite delicious. Inside, like the butternuts and the acorns, like the buttercup (a subdivision of turban), they harbor a golden-yellow light, echo of the maple leaves and pumpkins, a gold that flares out when you cut them open. The color is deeper, running toward orange, in the pulp around the seeds, helping you discern what you should scoop out before you cook it. Nothing is much simpler than cutting a squash in half, or, if it is big, in several pieces, wrapping the pieces in plastic wrap, and microwaving them for about seven minutes. You can bake them in the oven, too, of course. Or steam them. The result can be eaten straight from the shell, with a minimum of seasoning (salt, pepper, maybe a little sour cream or yogurt, and, for some folks, brown sugar or maple syrup). The flavor is nutty, sweet, and direct, a taste of autumn. The cooked squash

can also be riced or puréed for various combinations. And these calabashes, these winter cucurbits, whatever we call them, also make
great soups.

My latest discovery is a butternut squash risotto I picked up from one
of my food magazines. The flesh is treated two different ways, which
gives a variety to the texture, and the adaptation to microwave lets me
put the whole thing together inside an hour on a golden afternoon, as
the light retreats and the crows carry on their harsh conversations in
the swaying, glowing trees. The next day I try a new recipe for a spaghetti squash that I picked up on the same foray to a favorite orchard.
The treatment is actually Vietnamese, a kind of unpredictable salad
marrying several flavors—mint, coriander, peanuts, vinegar, shrimp,
and, of course, fish sauce—and I reflect, as we eat it, on the cultural
marriages that have made these New World hard-rinded squashes
grace dishes from Italy and Vietnam. For all I know, spaghetti squash
may *be* Asian, like the winter melon, but since it turns up among the
acorns and butternuts and pumpkins, I take it as one more triumph
of pre-Columbian agricultural experimentation. All these calabashes,
gourds, isquotersquashes were probably developed first on those remarkable terraces in Cuzco.

Did the Incas, I wonder, sense the innate comedy of these vegetables? Besides being local color, inside and out, in our dying autumn
gardens, they are half curios, decorations, objects of contemplation
among which the pumpkin has more or less accidentally, because it's an
icon for a human head, been elevated to star status. "Are you sure that's
edible?" I hear customers say at produce stands, examining a turban
squash or a wildly striped and speckled version of the acorn. "Are you
sure?"

A late October afternoon, a Sunday, somewhere between cold and
warm. The light comes from a great distance as the sun recedes west.
It's nearly horizontal, but it still feels powerful. More and more leaves

are underfoot. You smell them, you scuffle through piles of them, you watch the wind stir and rotate them, and yet, when you look up, the trees still seem full, oaks glowing bronze, sweet gums a rusty red, maples flaring gold and shining bloody. A few gnats, darning the air a little desperately in this last warmth. Neighbors raking and stopping to lean on their rakes and chat with passersby.

A call for my wife about a cancer patient. Someone else is dying, fading with the fatal golden season. Most of us have death at some level of our consciousness as we walk through these beautiful scenes, shot through with so many reminders of last things and imminent endings. As we amble toward the melodrama of All Souls and Halloween, we can even joke about it, teasing ourselves a little, as I did here:

OCTOBER COUPLETS

1

Again the cold: shot bolt, blue shackle,
oxalic acid bleaching a rubber cuff,

a cow-eyed giantess burning roots and brush,
the streak and smash of clouds, loud settling jays,

crows roosting closer—my older-by-one-year bones
have their own dull hum, a blues; it's all plod,

but they want to go on, above timberline,
to boulders, florets, ozone, then go free

in the old mill that the wind and the frost run
all day all night under the gauze and gaze of stars.

2

Somewhere between sperm cell and clam shell
this space cruiser takes me places I'd rather

stay clear of: a planet all graveyard, mowed,
graveled and paved, bride-light and parson-shade,

or a milkweed, bitter, about to burst, or a dropped
acorn even a squirrel didn't want, browning to black,

and I have to learn to relax with it all, to sing
"Where the bee sucks, there suck I," though the lily

is sticky and choking, bees don't suck, and the sting
is a greeting you never recover from.

3

"Steam of consciousness," a student's fluke,
makes me see a lake, linen-white at evening,

some amnesia-happy poet all curled up
sucking a rock at its black bottom;

oblivion tempts everyone but I
would miss too much——whales and ticks,

the weather's subtle bustle, blue crab clouds,
my kite rising, paper and sticks, a silver ember,

while the poem's ghost waits by the empty band shell,
does a little tango, taps out its own last line.

4

But this fall rain, somehow both thread and button,
sewing itself to the malachite grass,

beading the clubs and brushes of the spruce——
all day I have sat as if gazing over water,

wind feathering the reservoir, stupid as a church,
and thought of summer: all those burst horizons,

mineral cities, rosy meat, clean seas and shaggy islands,
the wine cork popping in the grape arbor,

these things seem better and clearer than gods just now,
raspberries hung like lamps among their brambles.

5

These leaves, these paper cutouts drifting the yard,
stars, fish, mittens, saddles: the badges and epaulets

of emptiness—last night in my dream
I was the killer, the guard who failed to stop him,

and the child who froze and was spared: Nothing lasts,
sang the crowd, and I answered, It sure does;

Is nothing sacred, roared the statesman—I do
believe it is, said I . . . I wake and shave,

still full of my dreamflood—oh, skim milk sky,
oh, brown star curling in my hand . . .

We wander through October, picking up hues of beauty and hints of oblivion. Rain leads to reveries of summer and of the Mediterranean world where autumn is gentler, a little less freighted with death. We stand in our own yards, examining leaf shapes to see stars and mittens, saddles and fish, when we might be busy raking.

An old friend comes to visit for a few days in the third week of October. He is a painter from Tucson, curious about Ohio's contours and colors. We were in high school together and shared an Omaha landscape, and he remembers summers and falls with particular nostalgia, the buzz of cicadas as August wound down, the freshening cold and autumn bonfires that came in as each school year took up its rhythm. I take him around this area and find a rare pleasure in seeing my own world through an outsider's eyes. We drive through Amish farmland in Holmes County, fertile valleys dotted with old well-kept farms where teams of workhorses are being used to harvest the corn. The corn is still stooked here, so that some fields are lined with regular rows of what look like miniature tepees. On the hills and along the valleys, the foliage obliges us with striking colors, and the soft contours of the hills lead us on over the course of a long, sunny afternoon.

Alan notices things that I have never thought much about. One is how much the characteristics of New England are reflected in the architecture—Greek Revival houses, meetinghouse churches, shuttered barns—and general atmosphere of these little Ohio towns. Since New Englanders settled the area, especially Connecticut residents who had been burned out by the British troops in the war of 1 8 1 2, the similarity makes sense. He also notes that great extremes of wealth and poverty don't seem to be present. He is right: most of this area is tidy and just modestly well-off. The homes are kept up and the farms look cared for, but one doesn't see expensive cars or large mansions on the one hand or squalid poverty, rural or urban, on the other.

We drive along the shore of Lake Erie. The summer vacation season is over. Many places are shuttered or boarded up. Some boats have already been brought ashore for the winter. The lake is calm and huge. At Oberlin Beach we get out and walk around the old cottages, the deserted beach, and stand at the mouth of Old Woman's Creek. There's something calming about the whole scene on this mild October day, a promise of fair weather and future summers, a continuity of life and nature. Inland from the lake, at Milan, we visit the birthplace of Thomas Edison—a tiny brick house that reminds us again how small were the spaces in which people lived and raised families back then—and browse around in a couple of antique shops. Things we knew as boys, growing up together in Omaha, Coca-Cola trays and moon-topped gas pumps—are now considered antiques. World War II relics—do people think those are *old?* Our boyhood feels very distant. Alan, who is interested in folk art, buys a little figure, a doll carved out of walnut with arms that swing round on little pins. It was made as a toy, no doubt, but there is nothing childish about its look or meaning. Stiff and erect, its dark face has a steady, contemplative look, as if it were seeing a great distance. It reminds us of kachina dolls.

Seeing Ohio through his eyes has made me cheerful. I buy an acorn squash as I come back from taking him to the plane, and handle it reverently, pretending that it is a magical talisman. It is a deep green, the green of hemlocks and dark forests, and it has patches and flecks of orange, like an autumn sun through dark pines. Its shape emulates another wonderful autumn object, the fruit of the oak: I think of a student from the West Coast who just told me she was seeing real acorns for the first time, crunching them underfoot and then, realizing suddenly that they meant oak trees, looking up into a glory of changing leaves. What local charms do we take for granted, wherever we live, because we know them too well? Poets and painters, local talent or observant visitors, can sometimes make them new for us.

Another visitor is my sister, who comes in from California late in the month to help celebrate my father's ninety-second birthday. I think about how nice it is to have a birthday marked by things like the closing of the month, the end of the baseball season, the fall of leaves, and the onset of cold weather. Ninety-two such birthdays feels like a staggering number.

That thought takes me back ten years, to another prolonged, golden-yellow October afternoon. I was alone in the house for most of that month, still deep in my grief for Chloe but able to glimpse and foretell the happiness of a new life. I was also on the verge of completing the long poem "Poem in Three Parts." It had been almost two years in the writing and was the poem that eventually, along with the painful story of Chloe's illness and death, "Nine Deaths," constituted the bulk of the collection *Earthshine*.

Each part of this poem had sections organized around a particular theme: our ties to the earth, our autochthony, in the first, called "Broken Field Running"; the omnipresence of motion and, by extension, change, in the second, "Dancing in the Dark"; and the miraculous presence and meaning of light in the third, "The Light Show." Because the writing of this poem had coincided with Chloe's illness and eventual death, with my grief and then my eventual falling in love with the woman who had been her doctor, personal elements are inevitably threaded through what is mainly an impersonal series of meditations on philosophical and spiritual themes. I could contemplate the evidence in the world that corroborated my trinity of primary facts—autochthony, motion, and light—but I could not keep fear, grief, wonder, sorrow, and love from bursting into my meditations. Nor did I want to.

As October wound to a close, I had written what turned out to be the next-to-last section of "The Light Show." In it I imagined myself standing at a new vantage point, on the moon, to contemplate the sun and the earth, witnessing their relationship and meaning:

> 9
>
> *Earthrise: from its rubbled moon*
> *I'm watching the sun's third planet.*
>
> *It's blue and white, with flecks of brown and green.*
> *Vast weather systems swirl and mottle it.*
> *Moist, breathing through its fantastic*
> *membrane of atmosphere*
> *it crowds my heart with love.*
>
> *The world's suspended, Chekhov says,*
> *on the tooth of a dragon. Even that tooth gleams.*
>
> *I've come here to figure out how light*
> *streams to the wheeling planet,*
> *a solar blast, photons and protons,*
> *and helps it live. Morowitz*
> *and Lewis Thomas tell us*
> *that energy from the sun*
> *doesn't just flow to earth*
> *and radiate away: "It is*
> *thermodynamically inevitable*
> *that it must rearrange*
> *matter into symmetry,*
> *away from probability,*

against entropy,
lifting it, so to speak,
into a continually changing
condition of rearrangement
and molecular ornamentation."

Which is how I got here, I suppose,
some rearranged matter
imagining and praising
"a chancy kind of order,"
always about to be chaos again,
"held taut
against probability
by the unremitting
surge of energy"
streaming out of the sun.

Behind, above, below me, stars:
countless suns with the same meaning!

Before me, leisurely as a peacock,
the turning earth.

The final section came on a warm afternoon that seemed prolonged, almost endless, as October wound to a close. As I sat watching the yard out my window, various associations came streaming together in an experience that might well be described as mystical or visionary. I suddenly felt I was in the presence of Emily Dickinson, who was visiting me as a sort of tutelary spirit, reprimanding me a little for my flagging spirits. She wanted to help me accept the permanent loss of Chloe and the temporary absence of Georgia, to let me complete my poem. Perhaps she was even trying to tell me that all my losses were temporary and that loss itself is illusory. The sense of place, the spirit of acceptance, and the momentary perception of order also reconciled me to all the other spiritual seekers in my vicinity.

My afternoon experience was an extension of another visionary sensation I had had the night before, when I woke to a movement of pale light in my dark bedroom and realized it was a sheet of blank paper from my desk that the breeze—it was warm enough to have all the windows open—was lifting and dropping periodically, as if calling me to write one more page. That blank sheet of paper now came back suddenly, to join the bus and the visiting spirit of a fellow poet, as part of the set of light images with which I wanted to end my long poem:

> 10
>
> *It's a late October afternoon:*
> *warm winds and distant thunder.*
> *Leaves catch the sunlight as they shower down.*
>
> *Just over my outstretched fingertips*
> *floats Emily Dickinson, horizontal spirit:*
> *"See all the light, but see it slant"*
> *is what she seems to murmur.*
>
> *I don't know. All through these months*
> *I've been a well with two buckets:*
> *one for grief and one for love.*
> *Sometimes the daylight has bewildered me.*
>
> *A day as bright and intricate as a crystal,*
> *an afternoon that will not go away—*
> *one of Time's strange suspensions.*
>
> *The Gospel Lighthouse Church's lemon-yellow bus*
> *says "Heaven Bound" up front. They feel they know.*
> *Last night, what made me think*
> *we are continuous with a noumenal world*
> *was a sheet of blank paper in my midnight bedroom*
> *rising and falling in a midnight breeze.*
>
> *This afternoon my house*
> *is flooded with late sunlight*
> *and the next sheet of paper after this one*
> *is white, and is for you.*

The copresence of a thunderstorm somewhere in the vicinity and the brilliant late sunlight, strangely alive among the leaves, somehow matched the moods of grief and love that had been present in my life ever since I fell in love with Georgia. Someone asked me once if I hadn't intended to say "numinous," relating to the apprehension of the divine and divinity. That word is very close to what I had in mind, but I was drawing on my long-ago study of Kant and the idea that beyond the phenomenal world, beyond the reach of anything but intuition and pure thought, is another world, noumenal, past perceiving or understanding.

A well may have two buckets, and water from one may even taste different from water from the other, but they have, finally, the same source. That loss and love, death and life, this world and any other kind of world beyond, any afterlife, might ultimately be part of the same whole left me utterly happy and literally speechless. The next sheet of paper would have to be the reader's to inscribe or inspect. My task was done, and my poem finished. That was more than ten Octobers ago. The Gospel Lighthouse Church, I notice, is boarded up these days. The congregation has either gone to heaven or merged with another one down the road somewhere. October, orange and golden and mellow, is much the same.

Isquotersquash Riff—
Seven Winter Squash Recipes

Butternut Squash Soup with Goat Cheese

This is easy, fun, and subject to many variations:

1 large butternut squash
2—3 cups stock—chicken broth or similar
salt and pepper
chopped parsley, chives, or scallion tops
crumbled goat cheese, 2 tablespoons per serving

Preheat the oven to 400°. Cut the squash in half lengthwise, scoop out the seeds and stringy pulp, and bake the 2 halves, face down, on a baking sheet for about an hour. If the squash browns and starts to caramelize a little, don't worry; that will enhance the flavor.

When the squash is cool, scoop out the flesh and put it in a blender. Add about a cup of the stock to help it liquefy. If the squash is large or your blender small, you may need to liquefy in 2 stages. Add the salt and pepper as you go. (Tabasco sauce is an interesting alternative to the pepper.) At this stage you have the option of a purée, to accompany a main course, or a soup, depending on how much stock you add. If you intend to serve a soup, taste for seasoning and then set aside. Just before serving, heat to boiling point, pour into bowls, and garnish with crumbled goat cheese and parsley or chives. Other garnishes that are good include shaved Parmesan cheese, chopped black olives, crumbled bacon, hard-boiled egg, and sour cream. Use your imagination and whatever you have on hand.

●

Microwaved Acorn Squash

Again, the attractiveness of the recipe lies partly in the ease of preparation and partly in the variations you can introduce. Squash adapts readily to all sorts of sweet and savory accompaniments.

———

2 acorn squash (about the size
   of a grapefruit)
salt
paprika or cayenne pepper
grated cheese or brown sugar
cream or sour cream

Halve the squashes. Remove seeds and fibers. Wrap each half tightly in plastic wrap and microwave for about 15 minutes. Remove from oven, unwrap, and season each half with salt and paprika or cayenne.

At this point you can add brown sugar to the cavity if you like that, then run the halves under the broiler long enough to melt the sugar. You can do the same with grated cheese. Or you can simply add some cream or sour cream to the cavity and keep the halves warm until you are ready to serve them.

●

Acorn Squash Purée

Follow the above procedure for cooking the squash.
After you have unwrapped the halves, scoop out the
flesh and put it through a potato ricer. Stir in some
butter, some cream or sour cream, and a tiny pinch
of nutmeg. Balsamic vinegar is another possibility,
but go easy! Serve hot.

●

Vietnamese Spaghetti Squash Salad

I clipped this from a *New York Times* article of June 13,
1990. The recipe is attributed to Marcia Kiesel.

———⚬⁄⚬———

1 spaghetti squash, about 2 pounds
5-ounce pork loin, in 1 piece
$\frac{1}{4}$ pound medium-sized shrimp, shells on
1 tablespoon sugar
1 tablespoon white vinegar
$\frac{1}{4}$ teaspoon salt
2 tablespoons water
$\frac{1}{4}$ cup fresh mint, minced
$\frac{1}{4}$ cup fresh coriander, minced
$\frac{1}{4}$ teaspoon freshly ground black pepper
$\frac{1}{2}$ cup Vietnamese fish sauce
2 tablespoons chopped peanuts

Trim off both ends of the squash, peel, and cut in half lengthwise. In a
large pot of boiling water, cook the squash halves about 6 minutes. Remove the squash and cool with running water. Let the water continue

to boil, as you will cook the pork and then the shrimp in it. Separate the squash into strands (I use a fork). You should get about 4 cups.

Boil the pork for about 8 minutes. Remove the pork from the water and put in the shrimp for 2 minutes. Drain the shrimp, cool under running water, shell, and cut in half lengthwise. Cut the pork into julienne strips. Combine the sugar, vinegar, salt, and 2 tablespoons of water in a small bowl.

Put the squash, pork, and shrimp in a large bowl, adding the mint, coriander, and pepper. Add the vinegar mixture and the fish sauce, and mix well. Serve on plates or bowls, sprinkling each serving with peanuts.

●

Butternut Squash Risotto

This is adapted from the October 1995 issue of *Gourmet* magazine.

⸺◦∿∿◦⸺

1 small butternut squash
1 medium-sized onion, chopped
2 garlic cloves, sliced thin
1 tablespoon minced fresh ginger
3 tablespoons butter
½ cup Arborio rice
2 cups chicken broth
½ cup white wine
2 tablespoons chopped chives or scallion tops

salt and pepper
shaved Parmesan cheese for garnish
toasted squash seeds

Cut the squash in half. Remove seeds and fibers. Peel one half and cut the flesh into ¼-inch dice. Oil a baking pan and put the uncut half face down, then the diced squash next to it. Season lightly with salt and pepper. Bake in a 450° oven for 25 minutes. Let cool. Scoop the flesh from the uncut half and set aside.

In a microwave baking dish, melt the butter (about 1½ minutes), add the onion, ginger, and garlic, and cook for about 2 minutes. Add the rice and cook 2 minutes more. Add the broth and wine. Microwave 9 minutes. Stir in the diced and the scooped-out squash. Cook 9 more minutes. Remove from oven and stir in chives or scallion tops. Add salt and pepper to taste. Top with pieces of shaved Parmesan and toasted squash seeds (see recipe on next page), and serve.

●

Roasted Squash Wedges

This is extremely simple and should work with just about any squash you happen across, not to mention pumpkin.

———⟨∿∿⟩———

1 2-pound squash (acorn, Hubbard, golden
   nugget, butternut, turban, etc.)
a good olive oil
salt and pepper

Halve and seed the squash, discarding stringy pulp. Cut into wedges. Rub the wedges generously with olive oil and put into a baking dish, being careful not to crowd them. Salt and pepper. Roast in a 400° oven for 40 minutes, turning occasionally.

Toasted Squash Seeds

In all of the above recipes, the seeds removed from the squash or pumpkin should be thoroughly washed, set out to dry, and then toasted in a toaster oven or dry frying pan until brown and fragrant. Add some salt while they are still hot. The results can be used as garnish for some of the squash dishes, or served separately as a snack. This works for pumpkin seeds, too.

Grilled Steak and Potatoes, for Cecil Young's Ninety-Second Birthday

This recipe calls for a fireplace grill. It can be done outside if the weather is warm enough, and I suppose it can be done on a stove-top grill or in a broiler. I think it's worth investing in something like my fireplace Tuscan grill, though. During the winter months it cooks things like jerk chicken, swordfish, steak, and lamb chops

253

incomparably, and it also grills vegetables—peppers, potatoes, onions, tomatoes, yams—in a most appetizing way, giving them a smoky, slightly charred flavor that shouldn't be available only in summer!

—⦿⦿—

steaks for 4—strip, Delmonico, or rib-eye
4 baking or russet potatoes
olive oil
2 lemons—1 for juice, 1 to be cut in wedges
salt and pepper

The fire in the fireplace should be built early enough so that it will be in the ember stage when you are ready to cook, under control but quite hot. The potatoes should be baked for about ½ hour in a 400° oven, then quartered. Both the potatoes and the steak can be rubbed with olive oil, lemon juice, salt, and pepper and left to sit out for a while. It's easier to cook them separately, especially if you have a hot fire. Cook the potatoes first, turning them often, until they are nicely charred and mostly cooked. Then put them in a pan to one side of the fire or back in the hot oven. Now cook the steaks, about 4 to 5 minutes a side, depending on thickness and your diners' preferences. When you are ready to serve, drizzle a little more olive oil over the steak and the potatoes and serve with lemon wedges on the side.

Three October Apple Desserts

You can make these any time of the year, of course, with fresh apples from the store, like Granny Smiths. It's when they are plentiful in the orchards, though, in so many varieties, that it becomes fun to adapt them to some classic dessert recipes.

●

Microwave-Baked Apples with Maple Syrup

This is from Barbara Kafka's *Microwave Gourmet*. It combines 2 Ohio products with a marvel of modern technology for a quick and delicious result.

4 large apples, cored and peeled around the top
1 tablespoon currants
3 tablespoons walnuts
zest of 1 orange, grated
2 tablespoons orange juice
3 tablespoons lemon juice
¾ cup maple syrup

Put the apples together in a fairly deep dish. Mix the currants, walnuts, and orange zest together and spoon equal amounts into each apple cavity. Stir juices together with maple syrup and pour over apples. Cover with microwave plastic wrap and cook for 4 or 5 minutes, depending on the size of the apples. Serve warm with the liquid poured over the individual apples.

●

Apple Upside-Down Tart

This is a real classic of French cooking, and for good
reasons. My version is based on the one in de Groot's
The Auberge of the Flowering Hearth.

———⚬⚬⚬———

3 pounds apples, peeled and cored
1 cup sugar
4 tablespoons butter
1 recipe pie pastry (see below)

Make the pastry first and let it chill. Slice the apples ¼-inch thick.
Cook half the sugar with 3 tablespoons of water to make a caramel, and
pour it into the bottom of your baking pan (which should be straight-
sided like a cake pan rather than sloped like a pie pan), 9 inches in diameter and 3 inches deep. Distribute the caramel evenly, then lay the
slices of apple on, evenly and in some pattern that looks decorative
(e.g., out from the middle). Sprinkle the rest of the sugar over the
apples and dot them with the butter. Roll the pastry out ¼-inch thick
and cut out a circle 11 inches across. Drape this over the apples and fold
it over at all the edges, sealing the apples with the crust as much as
you can.

Bake the tart in a preheated 350° oven for 45 to 50 minutes. Check
to see if crust and liquid are done. The sprinkled sugar should caramelize, too. Let the tart cool for 30 minutes, and then turn it over onto a
platter. My first efforts at this have not been as beautiful to behold as
they would be in the hands of an experienced pastry chef, but they have
been wonderful to eat.

Pastry Crust
1¾ cups sifted flour
1 teaspoon salt

256

5 tablespoons butter

¼ cup sugar

1 egg

Mixing pastry is tricky, and I'm anything but an expert. I currently use my dough mixer, on its pastry setting, to combine the ingredients. The butter needs to be cut up into very small chunks, and the dough needs to be encouraged to form into a ball, finally, with about ½ cup of ice water, added a little at a time, after 7 or 8 minutes of mixing. The dough may get a few more kneadings with the heel of the hand, and some sprinkling of flour if it is too sticky. It's important not to knead it too much or it will get tough. Wrap the ball of dough in waxed paper and let it rest in the refrigerator until you are ready to roll it out.

●

Apple Brown Betty

I make this partly for love of its name, partly for its down-home delicious flavor.

—⟳⟳⟳—

1½ cups bread crumbs

¼ cup melted butter

2½ cups peeled apples, roughly
    chopped

¾ cup brown sugar

1 teaspoon cinnamon

pinch of nutmeg

pinch of cloves

1 teaspoon salt

1 teaspoon grated lemon zest

2 tablespoons lemon juice, mixed with
    4 tablespoons water

½ cup currants

Spread about a third of the bread crumbs on the bottom of a baking dish. Put in half the apples. Mix together the sugar and the cinnamon, nutmeg, cloves, lemon zest, and salt. Sprinkle half this mixture on the apples. Add half the lemon and water mixture. Sprinkle another third of the crumbs on, along with half the currants. Now add the rest of the apples and cover them similarly: the spice mixture, the lemon and water, the currants, and the bread crumbs last. Add the melted butter, cover the dish, and bake for 30 minutes in a 400° oven. Then remove the cover and give it another 10 to 15 minutes so that "Betty" will "brown." People serve this with cream, hard sauce, and custard sauce, but try it with this lemon sauce:

> ½ cup sugar
> 1 tablespoon cornstarch
> 1 cup water
> 2 tablespoons butter
> pinch of grated lemon zest
> 2 tablespoons lemon juice
> tiny pinch of salt

Combine the sugar, cornstarch, and water, and cook over a low flame until thickened. Remove from the heat and stir in the butter, the lemon zest, juice, and salt. Serve.

NOVEMBER

Bleach and Brownout

Haze, char, and the weather of All Souls':
A giant absence mopes upon the trees:
Leaves cast in casual potpourris
Whisper their scents from pits and cellar-holes.
RICHARD WILBUR, "IN THE ELEGY SEASON"

．　．　．　．

November is stately and cold, a little like a mansion that has been closed up for the winter so that the wealthy owners could go to Florida. One thinks of sheeted furniture and echoing rooms, of having a big place almost to oneself. When I move around outdoors, there is less evidence of life. The mourning doves sitting on the power lines look and sound lonely. Insects are nowhere to be found. The occasional owl heard at night or the rare cottontail disappearing from the glare of the car's headlights only stress the deserted feel of things. Plants grow more and more drab or naked, and some disappear altogether. There's a general sense of locking down and closing in.

I recall a short poem by Stanley Kunitz, "The End of Summer," that closes with these lines:

> *Already the iron door of the north*
> *Clangs open; birds, leaves, snows*
> *Order their populations forth*
> *And a cold wind blows.*

I have that cold wind all around me, and it seems to pursue me as I drive south to Wellington, running an errand, on an early day in November. The air is both fresh and bitter, and whenever I face into the chisel-sharp wind, my sinuses begin to throb and ache, an old winter malady that meant a childhood filled with hot packs and headaches.

Driving now along the empty back roads, taking in the bleak look of fields and windbreaks, I can't help considering how different the sky is on a cold and windy day. The clouds are low and crowded, complicated both as to shape and color. They churn and roll not far overhead, showing dove-gray and pearl, adding hues of purple, peach, oyster, rose, gunmetal, jade, and the dull violet-blue of bruises. Long and short, sometimes smooth and sometimes ragged, they fold over and displace each other in unpredictable combinations, hurrying by, opening sudden rifts into puffy ivory valleys and then closing them up again with intruding whale shapes. The pageant is beautiful above the stripped trees and bare fields, but it is chilling, too, unwelcoming. That iron door that has clanged open has no regard for us and our need to be warm and sheltered.

Now the *North* of North America really begins to make itself felt. This is the month of puritans and pilgrims, a time that is all too easily associated with self-denial, hard work, character building, and wood splitting, testing the spirit for survival through the winter. Part of me wants to go find a cave and hibernate till spring. Or migrate south.

Here on the far side of Halloween, autumn shows us a grimmer face. Now come those other holidays—All Souls, the Day of the Dead, Guy Fawkes Day—that parade the bones and skulls, that immolate the effigies, unmasking the vigor of death and the steeper pitch of decline. All Souls is only the next day, the thing that Halloween was the "eve" of, but already the world feels different. The sun rises on bleak, deco- rated graveyards. The wind grows brutal. Hard frosts blacken the last greens of the garden. I had this uncompromising side of autumn and its weird, crackling music in mind when I wrote this ghazal about it:

AUTUMN GHAZAL

Dressed all in cornshucks, I thread the marsh & meadow.
The rain comes widdershins. The brain's a sopping pumpkin.

Now meet Jack Bones, the tramp, and Hazel, the dusty witch;
His vinegar sizzle, her dripping crock of honey.

There's counterstress for walnut-crack. Light like a knife
Stuck in an apple. There's banging of cutlery and plates.

Blueface stares at bloodyface. Oily hands tear bread.
Miles of high-tension wires. Smoke haze, asphalt scuffle.

What are those frosty weeds? What's this smashed cottage?
Who dumped the soup of life? Who cracked this cheval glass?

Coming up from the lead-mine, seeing the bean-curd clouds,
Hearing the bruise-owl call, shopping for winter candles . . .

Sleep condescends. Light rills across wet spiderwebs.
It takes eight days to wheel this bulkhead into place.

Are those eight days the first eight days of November? Is the bulkhead a relative of Kunitz's iron door? The light that is like a knife and that rills across spiderwebs is more precious as the days shorten, and the wild colors of October are subdued, reduced to the gray of lead and the white of bean curd, the dun of smoke and sere leaves, the grainy black of asphalt. If red shows up, it's apt to be on a bloody face, someone who's been beaten up in a fight outside a bar on a cold night. We may play with all this grimness, as I did in my poem, but we are also letting it move into the foreground.

Customs and instincts run toward the occasions that can contain them. In Mexico, the Day of the Dead is celebrated with gruesome candies and cookies (skulls, bones, skeletons) and picnics in the cemetery that acknowledge the presence of the dead among us, their fantastic hold on us. In England, the custom of making an effigy of the early seventeenth-century traitor Guy Fawkes—long since transformed into a communal scapegoat for all the ills and bad luck that can be heaped on the declining year—leads to community bonfires, fireworks, and the ceremonious burning of the "old Guy."

It makes me wish we had a comparable holiday in early November, one that would move us to bonfire building. Even our old custom of burning the leaves, which used to give such a characteristic fragrance to the November air, is now generally banned by ordinance, mostly stemming from concern about acid rain. Our leaves get vacuumed up by a truck that prowls slowly through our neighborhoods on and off through the month, humming loudly. The sharp tang of their smell, smoldering and crackling in slow fires as homeowners stood nearby, leaning thoughtfully on their rakes, is mostly a thing of the past.

Things of the past. It's natural for memory to be doing its own slow dances in this month. I set my poem "Three Time-Trips" in November, beginning it with the sensation of walking on fallen acorns, a Proustian moment of memory-release, and closing it with a dog walk in a field where I have ambled, musing, on and off for many years. In between I recalled the streetcars of Omaha, wonderful lost transportation contraptions that I associate with my own puberty. This is not *ubi sunt,* wanting to go back or to have things back. Nostalgia is not the issue. The point is more the luxuriance that memory sometimes affords us, time shaped for once like a lucky horseshoe, giving us free vacations in the past:

THREE TIME-TRIPS

1

My shoes crush acorns.
I'm thirty-nine I'm seven.
Far down the yard
my father and a neighbor
sail horseshoes through the air.

The clank and settle.

And the past I thought would dwindle
arcs back to me, a hoop.

The men wipe their necks,
the boy walks round the oak:
sometimes our lives rust gently,
a long-handled shovel, leaned
against a sun-warmed wall.

2

Fourteen, I perch on the wicker seat
in a nimbus of misery, love's shrimp,
hearing the streetcar's crackle and hiss
as the drugstore turns on its corner.

And what was real? The whipped sparks,
the glove puppets, bobbing, the pocket dreams,
this poem-to-be, my father's wharf
of set belief, the wicker and shellac?

Learning to be imperfect——
that's erudition!
Like coolies in flooded fields
we wade on our own reflections.

3

November bleach and brownout. Acid sky,
falsetto sunlight, wire and fluff of weeds, pods,

bone and paper grass clumps. The dog bounds off,
stitching the field with her nose. Hound city.

It's thirteen years. Different dog, same field,
and double grief: dull for the slumped president
stake-sharp for my friend's ripped heart—faint
night cries in the mansions where we lived.

But the bullet grooves are gone, the first dog's dead,
and here is the field, seedy and full of sameness.
Speech fails, years wrinkle. Dream covers dream

that covered dream. My head starts up a jazz
I never could concoct. I have to grin. On the cold pond
the tinsmith wind is whistling at his work.

Incidental things will interest and even delight a poet in the midst of composing. I like the way one can veer toward and away from tradition these days. There's a movement toward rhyming in the poem's second section, the poem becoming more conventional as it attempts to be more epigrammatic and comprehensive. The third section is a ghostly sonnet, with the faintest of rhyme schemes and the traditional eight and six complication and resolution. These are incidental matters to most readers, and should be, but like the tinsmith wind the writer is a craftsman who naturally takes interest in the details of his medium and the particulars of his craft. And why a tinsmith? In freezing the pond he is making it into something like metal, both in look and feel. A blacksmith would be too ponderous, a goldsmith or silversmith too ornamental. The November wind, soldering and cutting, hardening and polishing, is almost a tinsmith by default.

A day and then a night of cold, drenching rain. November turns my thoughts to stews, simmering on the stove, filling the house with their smell, ladled over noodles or rice in the earlier and earlier darkness of the evenings. I suppose chili is among our most familiar American stews, originating in the southwest and Mexico and undergoing regional variations wherever it travels.

I have a good chili recipe from Craig Claiborne and Pierre Franey's *The New New York Times Cookbook,* which they credit to a cook named Margaret Field in San Antonio. It is somewhat austere, as chilies go—no beans, no tomatoes—and it is truly delicious. Mrs. Field says the meat must be in cubes and that rubbing the cumin and oregano between your palms as you add them helps bring out the flavor. You can have your beans and tomatoes on the side, or as last-minute additions, along with lettuce, sour cream, grated cheese, chopped coriander, and more hot sauce or red pepper flakes. This dish cooks three or four hours and is really best twenty-four hours later, reheated. I find myself making it on a slightly bleak November Sunday afternoon, to the accompaniment of a late Mozart opera, *La Clemenza di Tito,* in the background. When I pause from my cooking to glance outside, snowflakes are swirling and eddying outside the window, lending both depth and light to the winter air. Amazing how the music, the food, the snowflakes, and the season suddenly bind together, a chord of rightness as authentic and memorable as the chili. Could I have added a little chocolate? Maybe next time.

Another Sunday night I make a chicken dish that has a complicated and distinctive vinegar sauce. I got it from the French mountain cooking described in Roy Andries de Groot's *The Auberge of the Flowering Hearth.* He says it's a very old recipe from the Loire valley, invented by thrifty housewives to make use of red wine that had turned to vinegar in the hot weather. The good wine vinegar could be bottled and kept for some time, obviously, but this dish seems to me particularly good in the fall, as cold weather closes in. It's warming and fragrant, but there's also an austerity about the zing and pucker of the vinegar that feels right for the season. I recall my imaginary tramp, Jack Bones, and his "vinegar sizzle" as I putter around the kitchen, keeping watch over my aromatic sauce as it reduces and loses some of its sourness.

What's in season is partly a matter of what's available—fewer and fewer greens and green vegetables now, for instance, less variety of fruit—and partly a matter of habit, association, and taste. Chestnuts are starting to catch my eye at the store and out at the orchard. Surely that's because roasting them on a winter fire is such a distinct and seasonal pleasure, a companionable feasting while the wind howls and dances outside.

Ever since late summer, the birds have been migrating. In the old days, people thought that they hibernated, buried in mud or huddled in caves. Perhaps it was almost impossible to imagine the fabulous journeys birds undertook until we could fly long distances ourselves, though the Chinese poets of the distant past were keenly aware of wild goose migrations as a sign both of spring and of fall. In this part of the world, people began banding birds to find out where they went, and the answers sometimes proved astonishing. We are still piecing together details of the migration patterns and pondering their mystery.

The local purple martins, for instance, left in late August, headed all the way to South America. As September and October passed, other species and populations left on a schedule that rarely varies. And we have migrants arriving as well as leaving. Those who have come from farther north to winter here include juncos, some types of sparrow, and increasing numbers of Canada geese, who stay around at least as long as there's open water. Food is a factor in determining where birds go, and Canada geese that used to go farther south are now finding forage enough in this area, as well as ponds that are never frozen solid for very long.

For me, it's November that especially invokes this pageant. I will glance at the sky while driving or walking and see a line of ducks, wings cutting the air like efficient scissors, heading east and south. Or there will be a ragged V, more like a check mark, of geese, a little higher up, honking and flapping. The geese are always thrilling to watch, flying over, taking off from a pond in a group, or coming in to land. Galway Kinnell wrote about this in his poem "Ruins under the Stars":

> Sometimes I see them,
> The south-going Canada geese,

At evening, coming down
In pink light, over the pond, in great,
Loose, always dissolving V's——
I go out into the field,
Amazed and moved, and listen
To the cold, lonely yelping
Of those tranced bodies in the sky,
Until I feel on the point
Of breaking to a sacred, bloodier speech.

The highest flyers and the biggest birds in this fall migration pattern are the tundra swans, also called whistling swans. They come all the way from the high Arctic, from Alaska and the Aleutians and Hudson Bay, where they nest and raise their young in the summer months. The ones that pass over us cross the Great Lakes region on their way to Chesapeake Bay. Because they fly high and tend to avoid settled areas, traveling a lot by night, we seldom see these magnificent birds, long-necked and white, wild cousins of the birds that decorate parks and botanical gardens with their majestic swimming and fierce hegemony. But we do hear them. They are audible for long distances, approaching, passing over, and then disappearing south and east, and their clamor is puzzling if you don't know what you're hearing.

The night before my son, Newell, was born, November 16, 1964, I took a nervous walk from home to hospital, where Chloe was already in labor. It was a mild night, and as I walked I suddenly heard what sounded like a pack of beagles overhead, an uncanny chorus of yipping, high in the sky. These were the tundra swans, as I later found out, and this was their precise time of migration. There are probably many flocks, but there is one, at least, that flies over Oberlin every year at the same time. We began to listen for them around the time of Newell's birthday. On November 16 or 17, every year, we can catch their yipping and barking passage as they pass over us, flying high, and at night. We call them the barking swans, and Newell was delighted, even when very small, to have an annual event that helped chronicle his nativity. The fact that we couldn't see them, and that they tended to pass over by night, added to the mystery and fascination. Another mystery, to me at least, is why anyone would describe the noise these great birds make as "whistling." Ducks quack, geese honk, and these swans bark like a pack of foxhounds streaming through a valley, or a deep woods full of blue tick hounds on the trail of a raccoon.

In 1984, as November drew to a close, I was trying to complete a busy semester and care for an increasingly ailing wife. I was also writing sections for that long three-part poem about gravity, motion, and light that I have mentioned before. November saw me working on several sections of the middle portion, "Dancing in the Dark." I was willing to let myself be more than a little melancholy about change and mutability, implications of time and movement, because I was in the presence of mortal illness, concerned with it every day. And as I stared out at our increasingly wintry landscape, I thought of Edmund Spenser, whose eloquence when he wrote the "Mutability Cantos" for the sixth book of *The Faerie Queene* was probably commensurate with his own melancholy. Spurned in his efforts to get significant patronage at court, despite his having made Elizabeth, his capricious monarch, the very center of his projected epic, realizing perhaps that time and illness would prevent him from achieving the original twelve-book conception, Spenser must have felt discouraged from time to time. I imagined him watching Elizabeth dance at court—she loved social dancing—and feeling bitter about her association, through old age and whimsicality, with mutability rather than with the ideals he had shaped for her. After measuring my own mood and my sense that nothing would or could hold still, I shaped some words to console Spenser, deflecting my own mild sadness onto his larger enterprise and ambition:

> *Industrial sky this afternoon, gray rags*
> *swabbing a dim chrome button.*
> *I seem to hear a drum and tambourine.*

The branches are wiggling in thundery wind
and the last few leaves, washed from the trees,
sail through my line of sight.

Everything's moving. We never know that.
Molecules vibrate in the solid rock
out of our ken, an act of faith.

Even if helium freezes, Margaret tells me,
it's two degrees above absolute zero
and there's movement, however sluggish.

In the Milky Way's heart a magnet pulses.
Holy Ghost, spraying neutrinos and gamma rays,
come closer to our stethoscope!

.   .

Edmund Spenser has a headache
from trying to write The Faerie Queene:
Has come to court a little tipsy.

Watching the regal bitch
whirl through a wild lavolta
her face a grinning, red-wigged skull,

"I hear the music of the spheres,"
he mutters to himself,
"and it's the dance of death."

But life and death are tango partners, Ned,
mincing through figures, cheek to cheek,
we cannot hope to read.

                    More leaves spin by,
minnows off the willows, oak-brown batwings.
And the trees rock in the giant pulse. And hold.

The next section of "Dancing in the Dark" recalled a late November walk in London, with Charles Wright, one year earlier. He had just shown me a finished version of his poem "London Journal," one of the finest things he has done. We had lunch in a pub and then walked over to the Victoria and Albert Museum, where there was a Buddha he wanted to show me because it was in the poem.

It happened to be a day when the IRA set off a car bomb next to Harrod's department store, very close to where Charles was living that fall. Innocent shoppers were killed and maimed, and the devastation was terrible. Charles himself had crossed the street on his way to meet me, we later realized, dodging past a dumpster and putting his hand, to steady himself, on that very car that would explode a couple of hours later. These unforeseen risks somehow combined themselves, for me, with Chloe's very different kind of danger. She was home battling the nausea her chemotherapy regularly created. The whole event was sobering, reminding us again of the terrible contingencies that characterized the world we had been admiring that day:

> *A London Saturday. One year ago.*
> *C. and I walk through the V and A,*
> *happy to study replicas. Half a mile off*
> *the Irish Republican Army*
> *has car-bombed a street next to Harrod's.*
> *Blood*
> *and broken glass*
> *and a strange hush. Elsewhere,*
> *a waiter drizzles oil on a salad.*
> *In our flat near Baker Street*
> *my wife reads, turning pages.*
> *Bright fibers rim a shawl. Pink candles*
> *infuse a churchy gloom.*
> *Smell of ammonia from somewhere.*
> *A guard yawns. A madman squints.*
> *Hung by its feet,*

a pheasant sways in a butcher's window.
Leaves blow in the park.
Time bleeds.
Holly bushes glitter.

Once again I do not know
how this can be turned into words
and held steady
even for a moment:
it slides across your eye
and flickers in your mind.

You look up from the page.

Both consciousness and communication fascinate me because their very precariousness and ephemerality make them especially precious. How does one set of experiences and memories connect, if at all, to another? Imagination seems to save us, making us capable of sharing each other's moments and memories. Language is a swaying bridge of rope and fragile planks, hope and improvisation across a deep gorge of wild misunderstanding.

You look up from the page. Perhaps you look up into your own version of November's austerity, into temporal vistas that include cold skies, walks through brown weeds, festive Thanksgiving tables, the strange shapes into which memory bends time. Perhaps you stare into the fire, like Edmund Spenser, watching it dwindle and choke on its ashes. Perhaps your memories are quite different, yet you, too, can ponder the onset of raw winter, its geese and clouds and scarcity, its tinsmith wind, the shuttered mansion, the dim museum, the lonely reader, the broken glass, the brownout and the bleach.

Three Great Stews

San Antonio Chili

As I mentioned in the November chapter, this came to Craig Claiborne and Pierre Franey from a cook named Margaret Field, who lived in San Antonio. It's a classic and worth making in this large recipe because it is so good reheated.

———

5 pounds lean beef, in 1-inch chunks
   (chuck is best)
½ cup olive oil
½ cup flour
½ cup chili powder
2 teaspoons cumin seeds
2 teaspoons dried oregano
8–10 cloves garlic, minced, or small
   jar of already minced garlic
4 cups meat stock—
   e.g., canned beef broth
salt and pepper

The Beans

1 pound dried pinto beans
1 large onion, chopped
chunk of salt pork, approximately ¼ pound

Heat the oil in a deep casserole. Add the meat and cook, stirring, until it is lightly browned all over. Mix the flour and chili powder together and sprinkle the mixture over the meat, stirring constantly to coat it evenly. Add the cumin and oregano (Mrs. Field strongly recommends rubbing it between your palms as you sprinkle it on). Add the garlic. Cook, stirring, for another minute or so, then add the broth, plus salt and pepper to taste. When you've brought it to a boil, partly cover the dish and set it on a simmer for 3 to 4 hours.

While it's cooking, prepare some pinto beans to go with it. Soak the dried beans for an hour, then put them in water with the onion and salt pork. Cook for 2 hours, then taste for salt.

Serve your chili and beans separately. Diners can mix them if they want to. The following condiments should accompany both: chopped fresh tomatoes, shredded lettuce, sour cream, grated Cheddar cheese, chopped fresh coriander if you can get it, and hot sauce or hot pepper flakes.

●

Lamb Navarin

Lamb stews are not common in this country, as they are really intended for mutton, which needs longer cook-ing. However, I have a sentimental fondness for this dish, which was one of my first successful forays into French cooking when I was just starting out. It opened my eyes to the possibilities of long-cooking dishes that combine meat and vegetables. My adventure began

with Julia Child's *Mastering the Art of French Cooking,* and
that is the ultimate source for this recipe. Do I need to
point out how well this is accompanied by a really good
red wine?

———⌘———

3 pounds lamb for stew (shoulder, breast, leg:
    a mixture is actually best)
3 tablespoons olive oil
1 tablespoon sugar
3 tablespoons flour
salt and pepper
3 cups meat broth—e.g.,
    canned beef stock
3 tablespoons tomato paste
3 cloves garlic, crushed and
    peeled
1 bay leaf
1 tablespoon rosemary
6 carrots
6 small potatoes
6 turnips
12–15 pearl onions, peeled, or
    3 large onions, quartered
1 cup peas, fresh or frozen

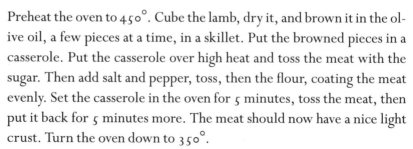

Preheat the oven to 450°. Cube the lamb, dry it, and brown it in the olive oil, a few pieces at a time, in a skillet. Put the browned pieces in a
casserole. Put the casserole over high heat and toss the meat with the
sugar. Then add salt and pepper, toss, then the flour, coating the meat
evenly. Set the casserole in the oven for 5 minutes, toss the meat, then
put it back for 5 minutes more. The meat should now have a nice light
crust. Turn the oven down to 350°.

    Pour out any excess olive oil from the skillet in which you browned
the meat. Add the broth and bring to a boil, stirring and scraping up

the cooking juices. Pour the liquid into the casserole and, over heat, mix in the tomato paste, garlic, rosemary, and bay leaf.

Cook the lamb for an hour in the oven, with the casserole lid askew. Then you can add the vegetables. At this stage Julia Child recommends straining the sauce and skimming the fat, but I sometimes skip that if the meat has not been very fatty in the first place. The potatoes go in, peeled and cut into 1-inch chunks (or ovals, according to Julia Child), along with the carrots and turnips, similarly treated, and the onions. Mix the lamb and vegetables thoroughly and return to the oven for another 1 to 1½ hours. Add the peas for the last 10 minutes.

Serve from the casserole or a hot platter, accompanied by rice, noodles, or bread.

●

Beef with Beer

The Belgians have a knack for cooking beef stews with beer, but this is in fact an Irish recipe, or my adaptation of it.

—⟨⟨⟩⟩—

2 pounds round steak or chuck,
    cut into 1-inch squares
3 tablespoons cooking oil
3 tablespoons flour
4 large onions, coarsely chopped
1 pint lager or ale
2 tablespoons fresh parsley, chopped
1 tablespoon thyme
1 tablespoon brown sugar
1 tablespoon vinegar
1 beef stock cube
salt and freshly ground black pepper, to taste
2 thick slices of bread
3 tablespoons Dijon mustard

Roll the meat cubes in the flour and fry in batches in the cooking oil until brown on all sides. Transfer the brown pieces of meat to a casserole. Fry the chopped onions in the same skillet you used for the beef and add them to the casserole. Pour the lager into the skillet and bring to a boil, scraping and deglazing. Add the parsley, thyme, brown sugar, vinegar, the beef stock cube, and some black pepper. Taste for seasoning and add salt as necessary. Pour over the meat (if the beef cube hasn't dissolved, don't worry—it will). Spread the slices of bread with mustard and place them on top. Cover the casserole and bake it in a slow oven, around 300°, for about 3 to 3 ½ hours.

●

French Chicken with Vinegar Sauce

This is an old recipe, as Roy Andries de Groot suggests. You want to use a good-quality wine vinegar here, and you can mix in some red wine of your own to achieve a slightly mellower result, although the lengthy reduction of the sauce has that effect, as well.

—ᵒᵛᵒᵛᵒ—

1 chicken cut into serving pieces (I usually
    buy a small roaster and do this myself)
salt and pepper
4 tablespoons butter
4 cloves garlic, unpeeled
4 tablespoons chopped parsley and chives
1 tablespoon tarragon
1 teaspoon thyme
1 ½ cups red wine vinegar (or 1 cup red
    wine vinegar plus ½ cup red wine)
2 ½ cups chicken broth

2 tablespoons tomato paste
¾ cup milk with 1 tablespoon flour
    mixed into it

Make this in a large skillet that has a lid. Dry the chicken pieces, sprinkle them with salt and pepper, and brown them in the butter. As they brown, add the unpeeled garlic cloves. Stir well and, after a few minutes, add the parsley, chives, tarragon, and thyme. Mix well, then put the cover on the skillet and simmer for about ½ hour.

Take out the chicken pieces and keep them warm in a bowl in a low oven. Turn up the heat under the skillet and, when it is quite hot, add half the vinegar, scraping and deglazing. Add the chicken broth and tomato paste. Mix well and bring to a boil so you can begin reducing it. Stir frequently. When you have reduced it by about half, taste to see if the vinegar has mellowed. If not, cook longer. Strain and return to the pan. Squeeze the pulp out of the garlic skins and put it into the sauce. Add the milk mixed with flour (this is my substitute for heavy cream, by the way). Cook, tasting and adjusting the flavors, adding the rest of the vinegar to taste, and more tomato paste if you like. Return the chicken to the pan and baste with the sauce. Cook another 10 minutes or so, with the cover on if you feel your sauce is the right consistency or off if you feel it's a little thin. Serve on a hot platter sprinkled with more chopped parsley and chives.

Four Potato Recipes

November is a good time to remember how plentiful, cheap, and various potatoes can be. At my house, we don't hesitate to make them a main course, along with a salad and fruit dessert, when we are trying to eat lightly and watch our weight.

●

Baked Stuffed Potatoes

A well-known presentation, but easy to overlook.
It combines the things you like about baked potatoes
with the things you like about mashed potatoes.

4 baking potatoes
4 cloves garlic, unpeeled
1 tablespoon parsley
1 tablespoon butter or margarine
1 tablespoon salt
freshly ground pepper to taste
1 cup grated Cheddar cheese

Bake the potatoes and the garlic cloves for an hour in a 350° oven. When they have cooled enough to handle, cut the potatoes in half lengthwise and scoop the insides into a bowl, keeping the shells intact. Mash the insides with the parsley, butter, roasted garlic pulp, salt, and pepper. Spoon the mixture into the shells, sprinkle with grated cheese, and return to the oven for 10 minutes or until golden brown.

Latkes

Potato pancakes are irresistible, and these are my own favorite. The recipe makes between 40 and 50, depending on the size you like, and I guarantee you they will disappear rapidly into the mouths of your diners.

—◁◁◁—

6 baking potatoes
2 onions
5 eggs
2 teaspoons lemon juice
1 cup flour
1 tablespoon salt
freshly ground pepper
1 cup cooking oil
sour cream
applesauce

Peel the potatoes and cut them into large chunks. Do the same with the onions. Put both through the shredding disk of a food processor and then into a large strainer. Press to squeeze out the excess moisture. Beat the eggs in a mixing bowl. Stir in the lemon juice and the onion-potato mixture. Add the flour gradually until you have a thin batter; you may not need the whole cup. Season with salt and pepper.

Heat the oil until quite hot. Fry the latkes by dropping a large spoonful of batter into the oil and flattening it a little with the spoon. Don't crowd the latkes; you can fry 5 or 6 at a time in a normal-sized skillet. They will take 2 to 3 minutes to brown on one side and another 2 minutes after you turn them. Drain them on absorbent paper. You can keep them warm in the oven while you are frying the rest of the batch. Serve accompanied by sour cream and applesauce on the side.

Potato Gratin

This is what Americans call scalloped potatoes. The main difference is that the American recipe would tend to call for milk and Cheddar cheese, whereas this one, French, uses stock and Gruyère.

2 pounds potatoes (just about any kind
   seems to work for this recipe)
2 tablespoons flour
1 cup grated Gruyère cheese
salt and pepper
2 tablespoons butter
2 ½ cups stock (chicken, beef, or
   vegetable, preferably homemade)
1 clove garlic

Rub a 9 × 13-inch baking dish with a cut clove of garlic, then butter it. Peel the potatoes and slice them thinly and evenly (a mandolin is much better than a food processor for this step). Do not soak them in cold water as you would frying potatoes; you want to keep their starch. Toss them in a large bowl with the flour and then arrange them in the baking dish. After each layer (you should have 3), add salt and pepper, the cheese, and some of the butter. Be sure you have plenty of cheese (and some butter) for the top. Pour the stock over the top and bake in a 350° oven for about 75 minutes. The top should be golden brown and the potatoes quite tender.

Potatoes Anna

This could also be called "skillet galette," since it uses a
regular American cast-iron skillet. The tricky part of
this recipe is achieving a crust on the potatoes that stays
unstuck and makes them easy to unmold, an attractive
cake, browned and patterned with the swirled effect of
the layered potatoes. I've tried a number of recipes, but
this is mainly based on Julia Child's, which is usefully detailed, as usual.

—◦◦◦—

3 pounds potatoes
½ pound butter
salt and pepper

Clarify the butter (heating it to separate the clear liquid from the milky
stuff). Heat the oven to 450°. Peel and slice the potatoes (about ¼-inch
thick). Spread them to dry on paper towels; the drier you can get
them, the better. Set the skillet over fairly high heat and put in about a
third of the clarified butter. Starting from the middle of the pan, arrange the potato slices in overlapping circles, first clockwise and then
counterclockwise, working out to the rim. When you've got 1 layer,
brush it generously with more of the butter and add salt and pepper.
Now start a new layer, working from the outside in, using the same
technique of alternating the direction of your circles. Add more butter, salt, and pepper. Continue until you run out of slices. You should
have a slightly higher center, which will reduce during cooking. As
you've built up your layered cake, you've also been gently shaking the
skillet from time to time to make sure the potato surface is not sticking
to the bottom (and sides, as you build it up).

Butter the bottom of a heavy saucepan and use it to press the cake
down and force the layers together. Put the skillet on a baking sheet

and put a (buttered) lid on it, then set it in the oven for 20 minutes. Take the lid off, check the sides and bottom of the cake to free them up if they are still stuck, and cook uncovered for another 20 to 30 minutes. If you're lucky, your potato cake will unmold onto the baking sheet and then slide onto a buttered serving dish. If it's stuck, you may need to dig around gently to get it free. If it's really stuck, you have 2 options: serve the thing in its pan and cut it into wedges, or unmold it and serve it looking messy. It will still taste delicious.

If I am fortunate enough to come by a truffle, white or black, I slice it very thin and put the slices around on the potato layers as I build them up. Some cooks also do this with slices of cheese, like Gruyère.

Three Side Dishes for the Thanksgiving Table

All 3 of these come from an article I clipped out of the *Cleveland Plain Dealer* some time ago. We don't make all of them every year, and we introduce variations, but all have proved reliable and popular at our table.

●

Holiday Brussels Sprouts

This vegetable can vary wildly in quality, which may explain some people's dislike. When they are bad they can

taste bitter and harsh, the very epitome of how you felt
about vegetables when you were a child and people
made you eat them because they were supposed to be
good for you: the next thing to medicine! But fresh
young brussels sprouts are delicate, a little sweet, and,
if you don't overcook them, a little crunchy—lilliputian
cabbages fit for a doll-sized king. Take the trouble
to go to a good produce store or outdoor market to find
them fresh and young, and you won't regret serving
them. This recipe recognizes that they work well with
nuts. The red pepper is partly for looks and can be dispensed
with if you are busy.

———⟳———

1 pound brussels sprouts
1 large red bell pepper
2 tablespoons butter or oil
2 tablespoons mustard, preferably the
    coarse-grained kind
½ cup toasted cashews
2 tablespoons lemon juice
freshly ground pepper

Clean and trim the sprouts and cut a little *X* in the bottom of each one.
Steam or microwave them just until they are al dente. They are easy to
overcook, so give them 3 minutes in the microwave, or 6 minutes in a
steaming basket, and then test them. Spread them out to cool and cut
them in half when you can handle them. Heat the butter or oil in a skillet,
cut the pepper into strips, and sauté for 3 minutes. Stir in the mustard,
then add the sprouts and cashews. Stir to coat, add the lemon
juice and pepper. There's no salt in this recipe; I don't think it needs
any. Diners can add it at the table if they want, or you can lightly salt the
peppers as you fry them. You can also use olive oil and serve this dish as
a salad, at room temperature. Serves 6 to 8.

Parsnip-Squash Purée

I am suddenly very partial to parsnips in November.
They can of course be cooked, dressed with a little butter and parsley, and served on their own, but it is fun to
combine them with other vegetables. Celeriac, for instance, or, as in this case, my beloved isquotersquash:

1 large acorn squash
1 pound parsnips
3 tablespoons butter or margarine
salt and pepper
nutmeg

Cut the squash in half, season it with salt, pepper, and nutmeg, and
bake or microwave it until it is very tender. Peel the parsnips, cut them
into chunks, and put them in a pan of cold, salted water. Bring the
water to a boil and cook the parsnips about 10 minutes.

Put the squash flesh and the cooked parsnips in a food processor with
the butter and process until just smooth. Taste for seasoning. This dish
can be set aside and reheated just before serving. Six to 8 servings.

Sweet Potatoes with Apples

An attractive combination. The little bit of vinegar is
my addition, to cut the sweetness.

3 apples, peeled, cored, thinly sliced, and
   tossed with 1 tablespoon lemon juice
2 pounds sweet potatoes, peeled, halved
   lengthwise, and thinly sliced

> ½ cup cider or apple juice with 1 tablespoon
> cider vinegar or balsamic vinegar added
> 2 tablespoons butter or margarine

Preheat the oven to 350°. Arrange the potato and apple slices in layers in a baking dish. With a little extra effort you can make an attractive pattern here, like a pinwheel. Pour the cider-vinegar mixture on and dot with the butter. Cook the casserole for an hour covered, then uncovered for 15 more minutes. Serves 8.

●

Small Chestnut Riff

As I said in the November chapter, I prefer to roast chestnuts over an open fire. It's convivial, it smacks of long tradition, it imparts a wonderful smoky, roasted flavor to the chestnuts, and it distributes among the partakers the one thing that is a nuisance about chestnuts: the task of peeling them. Since everyone peels his or her own, the cook can relax and sip a little red wine, the perfect accompaniment.

You may not have a fireplace, however, or you may want to integrate chestnuts into a meal, as a companion to vegetables (the brussels sprouts recipe above, for instance, could use cooked, chopped chestnuts instead of cashews), or as part of a stuffing for a fowl, or in the form of a dessert. In that case you need to cook them and peel them. The traditional way is to cut an X in the fat side of the chestnut, using a sharp paring knife. Marcella Hazan prefers a cut that begins on the flat side, goes around the fat part, and over to the other flat side. You don't want to cut the meat, but you want the cooked chestnut to open up enough that you can peel off the shell and the inner skin, which is the part that often resists you most. Try to get someone to help you—this is definitely more fun if the chore is shared —and work with the chestnuts while they are still warm. You can cook the nuts that resist you a little longer to make them open their shells more.

Cooking chestnuts works well in the microwave. Score them in 1 of the 2 ways described above, then put them in a shallow dish. Cook them uncovered according to Barbara Kafka's times: 6 minutes for $\frac{1}{2}$ pound, 8 minutes for 1 pound, 11 minutes for $1\frac{1}{2}$ pounds. Peel as soon as they're cool enough to handle, and zap any reluctant ones for another minute.

You can also boil them. One way is to put them in a pot of cold water, add a little salt, a celery stalk, and a bay leaf, bring to a boil, and cook, covered, over low heat, for an hour. They should peel easily and can then be served as a side dish (Italians like them with pork and sautéed greens) or added to stuffings. They are also puréed for this purpose, with a little butter and broth added.

Moving on into the dessert mode, you can boil the chestnuts in a cup or so of red wine, adding a bay leaf. After an hour covered, take off the lid and let the liquid reduce to a kind of syrup. Peel the chestnuts and return them to this syrup; you can add sugar and lemon zest if you want to make it a little more dessertlike, but you shouldn't need to—the natural sweetness of the chestnuts marries marvelously with the acidity of the reduced red wine, so further sweetening or souring should be undertaken cautiously.

One more dessert idea: if you roast the chestnuts on the fire (or in a heavy skillet, shaking and stirring a lot), you can put them in some white wine for a few minutes before peeling. After peeling them you can put them in a fireproof dish or pan with some sugar and rum, ignite them, stir as they burn and caramelize, and then serve them along with a sweet wine (*vin santo,* as the Italians call it), port, or just plain red wine. I take this version from a new cookbook I just acquired, Anne Bianchi's *From the Tables of Tuscan Women.* She notes that this is a very ancient recipe, from the hills of northern Tuscany, so there must be versions of it that use the fiery home-made grape brandy called grappa rather than rum. If you use grappa, up the sugar a little.

DECEMBER

White Snow Falling without Wind

. . . .

Each season, in my understanding of the matter, is allotted three months: March, April, and May for spring; June, July, and August for summer; September, October, and November for fall. That makes December the first in the winter triad. It is also the most festive of its three, partly because of all the celebratory activities that have grown up around the winter solstice and the Christian calendar, and partly because winter, before we begin to tire of it, has its own exhilarations and delights. As the official end of the year, December always brings a sense of finishing an old thing and starting a new one. It seems to speed up, like the last grains of sand in an hourglass, headlong toward the winter solstice, then Christmas and, at the narrow neck of the glass, the last grains hurtling through on New Year's Eve.

When we were children, anticipating Christmas and presents, it couldn't go fast enough. Now, trying to fit in the gift buying, the party going, and all the other end-of-the-year responsibilities, we might wish it to slow down, hoping for more time to savor its peculiar taste. That flavor is compounded of the fascination of the depth of winter (in this part of the world, anyway), the slowing and stilling of life's pulses, counterpoised with all the rituals and stories that speak of rebirth and

288

. .

hope. A bear will hibernate as though it is climbing into the grave; in spring it will rise to new life again. So it is with the plants and roots. So it is with the gods we have invented to act out these seasonal rhythms and their life-and-death meanings.

I am almost embarrassed to admit how much the snow enchants me when it first comes in its full winter abundance, arriving to stay. I feel like a child, or like a lover in that first flush, giddy and intoxicated. Booted and scarved, outside to fill the bird feeders, I pause, in the early dusk of a December afternoon, to take in the ways in which snow transforms the world. As it comes down it lends both depth and substance to the air, falling close up and far away, often at a slight slant, as far as the eye can see. As the wind varies, the slant will change, and when the wind ceases, the snow will fall straight down, with a kind of slow-motion dreaminess. Then the world seems weightless for a time, and it's as if we suddenly witness its true essence, its molecules and atomic particles, taking the form of crystals.

Snowflakes form when dust particles attract the water molecules that constitute the mist of clouds. At the right temperature, the attraction produces ice crystals. As the crystals grow larger, their weight makes them fall, and the falling sets up chain reactions of crystals breaking, re-forming, compounding, and generating themselves in ever larger numbers. Down they come, tiny hexagons, dendrites, columns, needles, and bullets, often changing shape and size as they go. Since their weight is just barely adequate to make them fall, their lightness, featheriness, is what we most notice.

Sometimes snow will seem to be contradictory in its fallings, as when there's a fascinating crisscross, with the snow nearby slanting, for instance, to the right, and the snow farther off slanting to the left. Is this a pattern, an anomaly, or an illusion? And then there are odd times when just as many flakes seem to be drifting upward as are falling earthward, as if the snow from the ground were sifting itself back up to the clouds to replenish what is falling, an experience that again provides some of the strangeness, the heightened reality, of a dream. We all loved those snow-globes we could shake and then watch when we were children. They re-created this extraordinary experience, this weightless moment in a heavy world.

The snow eddies and gusts, swirls and races. We are seeing wind, seeing air's basic turbulence when we watch these movements, all its crosscurrents and upsurges, its sudden gusts and pauses. The air is made visible to us, as if our sight were suddenly more acute and powerful. Surely one part of winter experience is an unparalleled shower of wonder, an endless rain of beauty and light.

For snow also means illumination and brilliance. What falls is light, crystals of milk and chalk and frost and bleach, electric-white powder, light that will rim the trees and branches, light that blankets the ground and shines even in our protracted winter nights, blue in the moonlight as we sleep and the owl hunts the mouse and shrew and rabbit. When there is snow around and the wind blows, even a little and even on a uniformly gray day, puffs of light explode from the trees. Some chunks fall straight down, breaking up as they go, others dissipate as bursts of powder across the line of sight. Wind blows and piles and drifts this light all around us. Snowplows push brilliant heaps of luminescence into larger and larger mounds and rumble along the highways behind spectacular white fountains. The powerful incandescence cakes roofs and cars and fence posts. Children build forts of light and pile up glow-balls as ammunition.

It's not warm light, of course. It has no orange or yellow hues. It's the dead white of fluorescent lights, of frost and icebergs, a kind of corpse-pallor that drains the world of color and replaces it with a substance that smacks of both purity and absence, of the dark void that is its twin. The albino squirrel who comes to knock down my suet feeder and rummage through the birdseed on the ground is positively ivory, warm white on cold white, glowing with life against the snow. The sheets of paper I compose or print on are not so blank and insistent as the blanched expanse of my yard, unmarked at the moment even by footprints. When the sun shines, the shadows of this snow will be blue, colder and remoter somehow than ordinary shadows. When the light of sunrise or sunset falls across it, the warmth of the light will skip off and away rather than changing it.

The glacial look of snow—snowfall and snow cover, by day and by night—is beautiful but deadly. William Carlos Williams compares it to the lethal embrace of the polar bear:

THE POLAR BEAR

his coat resembles the snow
deep snow
the male snow
which attacks and kills

silently as it falls, muffling
the world
to sleep that
the interrupted quiet return

to lie down with us
its arms
about our necks
murderously a little while

That sense that the quiet and death snow brings are the true reality, a silence that life has only managed to interrupt temporarily, is one we have all experienced in the presence of snowfalls and snowscapes. It does not take a blizzard to remind us of life's precarious situating in the midst of an absence of life that is much, much larger.

❧

I always approach Christmas through two gateways: my own birthday on the fourteenth, followed, one week later, by the solstice. Over the years, the former has mattered less and less, the latter more and more. Counting my own years—I just passed through the fifty-ninth—has gotten a little boring, while contemplating the meanings and associations of the earth-sun relationship continues to deepen my consciousness, and enrich my life. Awareness of time is one thing when you measure it in terms of your own years, quite another when it comes informed with both the linear and the cyclical, with a rich weight of human experience and communal tradition.

I'll give an example: when Christmas came in 1973, we were living in London, in Chelsea. The children were attending a small state-run Church of England school in our neighborhood. Because Newell sang in their little choir, we attended some Christmas services to hear them. My son had a pure, vibrant soprano voice, and it was a thrill to hear him perform a solo. I was especially struck with the words of "The Holly and the Ivy":

> *Oh the holly and the ivy,*
> *Now both are full well grown,*
> *Of all the trees that are in the wood,*
> *The holly bears the crown.*
>
> *Oh the rising of the sun,*
> *The running of the deer,*
> *The playing of the merry organ,*
> *Sweet singing in the quire.*

The verses go on to connect the attributes of holly with Christmas iconography: its white blossom recalls the lilies associated with Mary, its red berry recalls the blood of Jesus, its prickle symbolizes his crown of thorns, and the bitterness of its bark, paradoxically, transforms into the recognition that "Mary bore sweet Jesus Christ, / For to redeem us all." Thus the carol is safely enfolded into Christian tradition, the meanings of the plant translated into the meanings of the Nativity and Passion. But one can easily trace its older origins. The holly and ivy were both sacred, as plants that did not lose their green in winter months, to the pre-Christian European religions organized around worship of the sun and the wheel of seasons. The first two lines of the chorus seem to me frankly pagan, relating to the solstice and the hunt, the hope of the sun's continuance and endurance and the need for food during the hard winter. These are juxtaposed to, and thereby simply equated with, the music of the organ and the singing of the choir. It is as though the carol is saying that on the right level of understanding all these apparent differences—sun and earth, pagan and Christian, animal world and human world, events in nature and in the realm of human art—are not really different at all. They have an equivalency of being and value, a relationship to cherish and celebrate.

Unpacking that carol pleased me almost as much as did hearing my son sing it. I had always felt that Christmas exceeded Christianity in its meanings and values. You could say that Christianity appropriated previous meanings of the solstice. You could also say that it joined itself to a larger and older chorus of human celebration that is tied to the solstice. Either way, it enlarged the spiritual horizon and made more sense both of that carol and of my sitting in that small church listening to it, a proud parent, my spine tingling with joy and affirmation as Newell's clear voice rose out over the seated congregation.

For years we have cooked a goose at Christmas. Goose at Christmas, for my father, always invokes Dickens. "There never was such a goose," he will quote, recalling Scrooge's transformation and the happy ending of *A Christmas Carol*. That story, along with Dylan Thomas's recording of his "A Child's Christmas in Wales" were things we often listened to, over the years, along with the carols we sang and played. The very familiarity of these special texts, associated with the holiday and its hopefulness, made them welcome, year after year, though I eventually began to find it hard to listen to them, especially the Thomas. You get so you know every joke, every image, every bon mot, before it arrives, and that is hard, at least for a writer. It's like tasting the goose before you even put it in your mouth, a sensation that defeats the purpose.

I am going to propose another Christmas text, one that has made less frequent, but nevertheless very important, appearances in my life. I think of it as my alternative to Dickens's *Christmas Carol,* and while that may at first seem strange, I think I can make the connection plausible.

The text is Joyce's "The Dead," the final story in his collection *Dubliners.* It's a melancholy story in many ways. Gabriel Conroy and his wife Greta go to a Christmas dinner given annually by his aunts. His social unease and self-preoccupation are the filter through which we witness the various events of merrymaking and feasting. There is singing and conversation, and there is a wonderful description of the food and drink set out on the table. Gabriel carves the fat brown goose and eventually makes the little speech he has been nervously rehearsing to himself throughout the evening. At the end, full of desire for his wife as they go to the hotel where they are to spend the night, Gabriel learns, when she bursts into tears, she has been thinking not of him but of her youthful lover, Michael Furey, whose presence in her life and memory he has never known about. A song has triggered her recollection of the young man's melancholy life, illness, and death.

Gabriel feels humiliated by his misperception and selfishness. At the end of the story, as Greta sleeps, he stares at the window, watching the snow fall, and his ego is consumed and overwhelmed by a vision of death and the dead, the "vast hosts" he is of course destined to join. There's a beautiful fin de siècle melancholy about the ending, an unforgettable picture made up of the loneliness of the individual, the communal bond of death, and the beauty of falling snow—*bianca neve scender senza vente,* we might say, which is my chapter's title, translated from a beautiful line by Guido Cavalcanti.

How much of the story's ending can I quote here? Gabriel is still awake, wondering "at the riot of emotions of an hour before." He thinks ahead to the death of his aunt, who had looked haggard at the Christmas supper. He imagines how her funeral will be and recognizes its imminence. Then he lies down, almost as if to his own death:

> *The air of the room chilled his shoulders. He stretched himself cautiously along under the sheets and lay down beside his wife. One by one they were all becoming shades. Better pass boldly into that other world, in the full glory of some passion, than fade and wither dismally with age. He thought of how she who lay beside him had locked in her heart for so many years that image of her lover's eyes when he had told her that he did not wish to live.*
>
> *Generous tears filled Gabriel's eyes. He had never felt like that himself*

*toward any woman, but he knew that such a feeling must be love. The
tears gathered more thickly in his eyes and in the partial darkness he
imagined he saw the form of a young man standing under a dripping
tree. Other forms were near. His soul had approached that region where
dwell the vast hosts of the dead. He was conscious of, but could not appre-
hend, their wayward and flickering existence. His own identity was fading out into a grey, impalpable world: the solid world itself, which these
dead had one time reared and lived in, was dissolving and dwindling.*

The latter half of the second paragraph, above, could be from some
symbolist narrative, intent on transcendence, or a translation of Homer or some other archaic text, like *Beowulf* or *Gilgamesh*. That Joyce
moves so easily among stylistic levels is a tribute to how far he has
brought his narrative. And now there comes the snow:

*A few light taps upon the pane made him turn to the window. It had
begun to snow again. He watched sleepily the flakes, silver and dark,
falling obliquely against the lamplight. The time had come for him to
set out on his journey westward. Yes, the newspapers were right: snow was
general all over Ireland. It was falling on every part of the dark central
plain, on the treeless hills, falling softly upon the Bog of Allen and,
farther westward, softly falling into the dark mutinous Shannon waves.
It was falling, too, upon every part of the lonely churchyard on the hill
where Michael Furey lay buried. It lay thickly drifted on the crooked
crosses and headstones, on the spears of the little gate, on the barren
thorns. His soul swooned slowly as he heard the snow falling faintly
through the universe and faintly falling, like the descent of their last
end, upon all the living and the dead.*

It was years before I noticed the parallels to Dickens, which may
or may not have been deliberate on Joyce's part. Ebenezer Scrooge is
visited by ghosts—his business partner and the ghosts of Christmas
past, Christmas present, and Christmas yet to come—and is made to
recognize his own selfishness and isolation. He is then allowed to wake
and begin his life again, given, in effect, a resurrection and a second

chance. We don't know whether this will happen to Gabriel Conroy. He may be chastened by his revelation, in which, as Joyce puts it, "his soul swooned softly." He may survive to a better life, as Scrooge does.

I've taught the story many times. I remember that a student once broke down in class and cried uncontrollably when we came to that magnificent ending. I've read those last paragraphs out loud at the funeral of a colleague who loved them. And I have read some critics who pick away at Gabriel's precarious self-esteem and self-preoccupation as if it had nothing to do with them or their lives, no relation to their own preening and posing egos. If we can't admit that we share Gabriel's failings, all of us, we can't read the story fully and well.

So the ambiguity and darker emphasis of Joyce feel appropriate to a modern, as opposed to a Victorian, text, and while I doubt that Joyce's "The Dead" will ever replace the Dickens as a Christmas classic, read aloud on Christmas Eve or performed in theaters, its beautiful confrontation with the chthonic, with our mortality, with the problems of egotism and excessive self-consciousness that most of us face, can be as cathartic and uplifting in its own way as the story of Scrooge. I see, looking back, why it has threaded its way through my life, off and on, ever since my college years.

Am I wrong to let this be my Christmas vision, joining a darker strain to ebullient Dickens and nostalgic Dylan Thomas? I do not see it as morose or morbid. Its beauty includes our mortality, true; but it is a hymn to the natural world and to our first and last place in it that never fails to move and compel me with its truth and its music. Joyce's "Christmas Carol" will remain mine, I think, until I, too, join those shades, those vast hosts who surround us even as we feast and feel quick, feel vital, feel connected, at Christmas.

One more thing to tell, now. On Chloe's last Christmas, 1984, we decided to read "The Dead" out loud on Christmas Eve. Chloe was within six weeks of her death, but we didn't know that. I knew that she was very ill, between the cancer and the toll taken by chemotherapy, and that the burden of nursing her and trying to keep her spirits up, along with my own, was considerably lightened by the arrival of the children, home from college and full of excitement about all the things they had been doing: Newell was then a sophomore at Vassar, Margaret a freshman at Yale. That was a particularly fine Christmas, in which we felt close and happy as a family and tried not to let Chloe's weakness and slowness diminish our festivities and our joy at being together. On Christmas Eve, as we sat around in the living room, by the fire and next to the Christmas tree, it began to snow heavily. We turned on an outside floodlight so we could see the dance of falling and blowing snow in the backyard.

9

I'm watching the brown tangle of tomato vines
in our December garden. They don't move.

If everything is moving
even beyond our senses
and even if it's mad and random,
that must help explain consciousness,
perched in the body, bird in a tree,
chirps, preens, looks wildly about,
even when dozing is alert,
metabolism racing,
beady-eye, singsong, flutter and shit—

If consciousness could match the body better
and be a bear
and even hibernate?

Oh then it would miss fine things!

On Christmas Eve it snowed
as if we lived in a greeting card.
The snow blowing off the roof
and through the backyard floodlight
as we watched from around the fire
made intricate patterns: scallops, loops,

tangles and alphabets. We're seeing the wind,
we realized, dressed
in powdery snow. Nothing to worship,
but something to wonder at,
a little epiphany, in season.

Pigeons in Buffalo, Holub told me,
can hear the Concorde landing in New York.
So what do we think we know? All of our dancing
is done in the dark, on the ceiling, the page, over the gorge
on the bridge of rotten rope and sturdy instinct.

I think I did worship that wind.

Belief is a move from branch to branch.
It doesn't much matter where you perch.
You may be hearing the Concorde. You may not.

That memorable snowfall coincided with our reading "The Dead" out loud around the fire, the first and last time we did that as a family.

Sometimes things happen to us, or we do things, that we marvel at later, asking "Did I really do that?" Did I read "The Dead" out loud to my family on the Christmas Eve that was also the evening of the long night that would be Chloe's death and absence? Did it snow, unexpectedly and beautifully? Events can assume mythic proportions. As they do, it grows harder to separate fact from fiction. I offer a fact that bothers me still: that it may have been an error to read that story to someone who was ill, frightened, and close to death. If it was, am I making it fiction when I suggest that we all came to terms, quietly and without speaking about it, with Chloe's death and with our own deaths? I don't know the answer to that question. Memory wraps events, softening their outlines, but it also illuminates their meanings.

Maybe around midnight, when we went to bed, the wind dropped and the snow fell tranquilly. Light in the darkness. White snow falling without wind. Maybe not. Maybe because the nearness of death at the end of the story is everyone's, past, present, and future, there is a comfort in the closure that surpasses our fear, her fear, all my doubt and sorrow. Maybe not. All of our dancing is done in the dark. That's the way it is.

⟳

Winter is also a time when I happen to see a lot of sunrises, a process that crystallizes in December. Some mornings the sunrise is almost imperceptible, just a gradual lightening of the world. Other days there is faint flush of rose beyond the high school and its limp flag, or through and then above the trees across the creek. And once in a while the sky floods with a wild, stirring pink or a deep, surprising pomegranate.

Around the winter solstice, sunrise seems to come at just about the same time for quite a while. The days start to grow longer in the evening, after the twenty-first, but not in the morning. The sunrise is almost exactly at the same time, around 7:50, each morning, for most of December and well into January. I try to picture why that would be, but my mind can't hold the picture of the earth's position with relation to the sun; it's too difficult to conceptualize, at least in a way that would explain these daily sunrises at the same time.

The snow creaks under my boots. The dog surfs through high drifts. The world is almost soundless except for the occasional call of a bluejay or a crow. Very often, at these moments, four lines from Shakespeare's *Much Ado about Nothing* go through my head, and I recite them softly:

> *Good morrow, masters. Put your torches out.*
> *The wolves have preyed, and look, the gentle day,*
> *Before the wheels of Phoebus, round about,*
> *Dapples the drowsy east with spots of gray.*

The lines are much less famous than the sunrise moment in *Hamlet,* when Horatio says, after the ghost's departure, "But look, the morn in russet mantle clad / Walks o'er the dew of yon high eastward hill," or the lines that Romeo is given in *Romeo and Juliet:*

> Look, love, what envious streaks
> Do lace the severing clouds in yonder East.
> Night's candles are burnt out, and jocund day
> Stands tiptoe on the misty mountain tops.

Nevertheless, my particular fondness for this quatrain, this moment characterizing the break of day, persists. "The wolves have preyed" stands in for all the sorrow and terror and death that can be associated with darkness and night and sheer human error. There is deep word-play at work as well. Claudio and Don Pedro have been praying for for-giveness. It seems likely, as my friend Tom Van Nortwick has suggested to me, that the wolves have also "prayed," calling on some pagan god of their own to bring forth the dawn. Like "the running of the deer" in the carol, the phrase links the human world and animal world in reso-nant fashion. If it's a matter of wolves doing what is natural to them, then it is an ordered and reassuring world, after all. The glance toward myth, with the wheels of Phoebus's chariot getting ready to roll forth from the east, acknowledges how long human beings have been finding honorific ways to characterize the meaning and power of the sun and its progress through the day and the year. It reminds me that I ended my long poem "Night Thoughts" with a jubilant summer sunrise. But a winter sunrise feels a little more like this one in *Much Ado,* a sunrise in the midst of considerable pain and peril, dappling the drowsy east with spots of gray.

DECEMBER RECIPES

Three More Winter Pasta Dishes

I put 3 of these in the January section. Here are 3 more, all classics, all easy, and all wonderful in cold weather.

●

Woodcutter's Penne

The name is a translation of *alla bosciola.* I suppose the idea is that the woodcutter has a good chance of finding the mushrooms and building this dish around them.

1 pound penne or similar pasta

1 celery stalk

1 carrot

1 onion

4 tablespoons olive oil

5–8 ounces mushrooms—fresh porcini would be
    ideal; failing that, dried porcini, soaked in hot water
    for 20 minutes, or a mixture of dried and fresh
    mushrooms such as portobello or shiitake

1 small can tomatoes (8-ounce), drained and chopped

3 tablespoons chopped parsley

2 ounces heavy cream

Boil a pot of salted water for the pasta. You can make the sauce almost while the pasta's cooking. Chop the celery, carrot, and onion together (food processor makes this easy), and cook them briefly in the olive oil. Add the mushrooms and cook for a few minutes (fresh mushrooms will sweat, or give off their liquid, when ready). Add the tomatoes and parsley and cook for a few more minutes. Add the cream and simmer for a minute or 2. Add the cooked pasta to the skillet, stir well, and serve.

●

Spaghetti with Tuna and Anchovy

I suggest always having the ingredients for this on hand. It's a great dish for emergencies or when you haven't had time to shop. Of course, fresh parsley improves it enormously (as does a little fresh basil, if you get lucky in the winter and happen to find some), but freeze-dried works well and is good to have on hand.

—⦿⦿⦿—

1 pound spaghetti (or linguine or fettuccine)
2 tablespoons olive oil
2 cloves garlic
pinch of red pepper flakes
1 large or 2 small cans tuna fish
4–5 anchovy fillets from a can
3–4 tablespoons parsley (and 2 tablespoons
    fresh basil if you have it)
salt and pepper
a dozen capers

Again, you can make the sauce as the pasta cooks. Heat the olive oil and cook the crushed, peeled garlic cloves until they are brown. Discard them. Add the pepper flakes, fry them for 30 seconds, then add tuna and the anchovies, mashed or chopped. Stir well and add the parsley.

Cook for a few minutes to let the flavors blend, season with salt and pepper, then add the capers (chopped if they are the large kind, whole if they're the small kind). Again, if your pan is big enough, dump the cooked spaghetti in and mix well.

Three variations on this dish: (1) A small can of tomatoes, added when the parsley goes in. (2) Lemon juice and grated Parmesan, added when the capers go in. (3) Leave out the anchovies, if salt bothers you, and just salt very lightly.

●

Thunder and Lightning
(*Tuone e lampe*)

It's true, I can't resist the name. Does it come from the digestive effects, as Diane Seed suggests in her *The Top One Hundred Pasta Sauces*? Or is it a fanciful visual rendition? In any case, the combination is very healthy and very tasty.

———

1 pound tagliatelle or similar pasta
2 cloves garlic
1 celery stalk
1 carrot
1 onion
6 tablespoons olive oil
2 cans (15-ounce) chickpeas
1 small can (8-ounce) tomatoes
2 tablespoons chopped parsley
large pinch hot pepper flakes
salt and pepper

Chop the garlic, onion, celery, and carrot together (food processor) and sauté them in the oil. Open the chickpeas, drain and rinse. Add the tomatoes and cook for 15 to 20 minutes, adding water if necessary. Stir in the chickpeas, parsley, and red pepper, cook for a minute or 2, add salt and pepper, and remove from the heat. At this point some people would add boiling water to the chickpea mixture and cook the pasta in it, draining the whole thing at the end. I prefer to cook the pasta separately and to add it to the chickpea mixture after draining it.

A Christmas Goose

This is adapted from Craig Claiborne and Pierre Franey's *The New New York Times Cookbook*.

10–12-pound goose
2–3 cups chopped celery, onion,
    and carrot
2 garlic cloves, unpeeled
1 bay leaf
1 cup water

Stuffing

2 tablespoons butter

1 cup chopped celery

2 cups chopped onion

goose liver and heart

1 clove garlic, chopped

1 cup white wine

3 sage leaves, crumbled

1 bay leaf

1 cup parsley

1 cup raisins or prunes

3 cups peeled, seeded apples,
    thinly sliced

1 cup bread crumbs

2 eggs, lightly beaten

salt and pepper

Preheat oven to 400°. To make the stuffing, cook the celery and onion in the butter. Purée the liver and heart in a food processor and add to the celery-onion mixture. Add the garlic, wine, sage, bay leaf, and parsley. Cook stirring for a few minutes, then remove from the heat and add the raisins or prunes, the apples, bread crumbs, eggs, and salt and pepper to taste. Stuff both cavities of the goose with this mixture (one cavity is likely to have the neck in it; be sure to remove that and set it aside). Sprinkle the goose liberally with salt and pepper. Truss it if necessary.

Set the goose in a shallow roasting pan in the oven and bake for an hour. It will throw off fat you can use for basting every 10 to 15 minutes. Remove from the oven and drain off the fat (save it if you are planning to make a cassoulet with the leftover goose—see p. 307). Scatter the chopped onion-celery-carrot mixture, the unpeeled garlic cloves, and the bay leaf around the goose. Add the neck to the pan. Return to the oven and cook for another hour, basting frequently.

At the end of 2 hours you'll have a nice brown goose. If you think it's getting too brown, cover it with aluminum foil. It will need about another ½ hour if it's the size I've suggested, up to 1 hour if it's larger.

Put the goose on a warm platter and take off most of the fat from the roasting pan. Add the cup of water and deglaze the pan, stirring. Strain the resulting liquid and serve as sauce. Carve the goose and serve it.

●

Alsatian Red Cabbage

A fine accompaniment to a roast goose. Also, of course, a great color.

—◦◦◦—

1 head red cabbage
4 tablespoons vegetable oil
3–4 whole cloves
2–3 tablespoons red wine vinegar
2–3 tablespoons brown sugar
salt and pepper
3–4 tablespoons butter

Trim the cabbage and shred it finely (food processor works well). Heat the oil in a very large skillet, then add the cabbage. Cook, stirring frequently, for about 5 minutes. Add the cloves (crushed in a mortar), the vinegar, sugar, and salt and pepper to taste. Cook for 10 to 15 minutes. Stir frequently. Add the butter just before serving.

●

The Rest of the Christmas Dinner

I'm not going to add more recipes here, just suggest what I think goes well with the goose, the stuffing, and the red cabbage. I would add a dish of garlic mashed potatoes (mashed potatoes with some roasted garlic mixed in), a dish of cranberries, and maybe a couple of side dishes of things like green olives and celery stalks. I would serve a French red wine, something in the Burgundy family perhaps, or maybe a good California or Oregon pinot noir.

●

Cassoulet with Leftover Goose

A wonderful use for any leftover goose meat and goose fat is cassoulet, the great French peasant bean dish that basically uses 3 to 4 meats—roast pork, lamb, preserved goose, and sausage—for the incredible flavoring of the baked beans. I suppose it must be said that any set of recipes that emphasizes great peasant cooking must have this formidable classic. It was very fashionable to serve at dinner parties at one time, in the sixties and seventies, and now one doesn't hear much about it. It is rather a heavy dish, true, and there's no shortage of meat and fat in it, but it's still, most of all, a really great bean dish, made in the winter with available meats, preserved, stewed, or in the form of sausage. The variations are probably endless, but the basic idea is to cook the beans, in their final form, interspersed with roasted and stewed meats, so that their flavor becomes rich and aromatic.

The goose in a real French cassoulet is confit, preserved goose cooked and then put up for the winter in its own fat. I tried this once, with a fresh goose I bought from a local farmer, because I was curious about a really authentic cassoulet. The result was indeed truly memorable, but I don't think, realistically, that many people are going to cut up a goose, boil it in its own fat (and additional lard, if necessary), put it up in jars of fat, and then employ it in cassoulet. It's worth the extra effort, and you can find a recipe for doing it in the Claiborne and Franey book mentioned above. But you can also use the fat and leftover meat from your Christmas goose in a cassoulet, which means you have 1 less key ingredient to worry about, even if it's roast goose rather than confit of goose.

My cassoulet recipe combines several sources but owes most to Julia Child and Craig Claiborne and Pierre Franey. This is a very large dish because it's complicated and only worth doing if you want to make a lot. That's one reason why it's so good to serve to company and so good reheated for days and days after you first make it. Fresh bread and salad are the natural accompaniments. You probably won't want anything more than a pear or a tangerine for dessert.

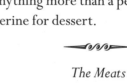

The Meats

1 small pork roast (2–3 pounds center cut pork loin)

salt and pepper

2–3 pounds stewing lamb (shoulder or breast), cut in large chunks

3 tablespoons goose fat, if you have it, or cooking oil

soup bones, lamb or beef

1 cup chopped onions

4 garlic cloves, smashed and peeled

1 6-ounce can tomato paste

1 14-ounce can tomatoes

1 cup white wine

1 bay leaf

2 cups beef stock or water

2 cups roast goose meat

1 pound sausage meat

Salt and pepper the pork roast and cook it in a hot (425°) oven for about an hour, turning 2 or 3 times. After it cools, slice it into neat slices. Pour off the fat and deglaze the roasting pan with a little water or white wine.

Meanwhile, brown the lamb chunks in the goose fat, salt and pepper them, and remove to a plate. Brown the bones and add to the lamb. Cook the onions in the fat, then put the meat and bones back in, add the garlic, tomato paste, and tomatoes, white wine, bay leaf, and stock or water. Cover and cook slowly, either on the stove or in the oven, for about 1½ hours, or until the lamb is tender. Remove the lamb chunks with a slotted spoon, discard the bones, skim the fat, and save the cooking liquid.

Your goose meat should have been stripped from the carcass and cut into bite-sized chunks. The sausage should be shaped into cakes and fried lightly, then drained on paper towels.

The Beans

2 pounds (about 5 cups) dry white great northern
    or similar beans, soaked overnight or boiled
    for 5 minutes and allowed to stand in their
    water for at least 1 hour

at least 3 quarts water

1 large onion, stuck with cloves

piece of salt pork (about ½ pound)

2 carrots, trimmed

2 cups bread crumbs

1 cup chopped parsley

Cook the beans in the water with the onion, salt pork, and carrots for about 1½ hours, or until fairly tender. Drain, reserving the liquid and the piece of salt pork.

Put a layer of beans in the bottom of a large casserole. Add a layer of sliced pork. A second layer of beans, then the lamb stew. Another layer, then the sausage cakes. Another layer, and the goose meat and the salt pork, diced finely. Now take the lamb cooking liquid, the deglazed pork pan liquid, a cup or more of the bean cooking liquid, combine them, and pour over the casserole. The amount of liquid should be generous enough that it almost comes up to the top layer of beans. Add more bean cooking liquid if necessary and have some on hand to add later on if the beans seem to be getting too dry. Sprinkle the bread crumbs and parsley over the top and drizzle with melted goose fat if you have some.

The casserole cooks uncovered in a 375°–400° oven for about 45 minutes. Julia Child recommends that you turn the oven down to 350° when a light crust forms on the top of the casserole, and that you break up this crust and baste the top with the cooking liquid a couple of times, leaving it alone the last 10 or 15 minutes to form a final crust. Serve from the casserole, hot and bubbling. This is unbelievably good, at least to my palate. It combines all the virtues of peasant cooking—it's hearty, sensible, economical—with some of the features of fancy cuisine—it's imaginative, poetic, and combines apparently unlikely ingredients in a harmonious whole. And just think: every Christmas you can enjoy first a goose and then, a couple of days later, this amazing bean dish, which will last you for meals right into the new year!

Three Other Delicious but
Less Time-Consuming Bean Dishes

December is a great time to eat beans, so I will conclude my seasonal recipes with 3 favorite winter bean
dishes. Beans are often thought of as the quintessential
peasant food because they are so cheap, so easily stored,
and subject to so many interesting variations. Hence
their place of honor here, where subsistence eating and
gourmet delight dance a tango.

●

White Beans
with Parsley and Garlic

There is something magical about the simple combination of the 3 ingredients in this dish, which can be a
soup or a side dish, depending on how thin or thick you
care to make it. Hats off once more to Marcella Hazan,
who introduced me to this recipe in volume 1 of *The
Classic Italian Cook Book.* She calls this "a bean lover's
bean soup."

2 cups dried white beans (I use great northern;
    Hazan suggests white kidney beans), soaked
    overnight and cooked for 1 hour in water to
    cover by 2 inches, on the stove or in the oven
½ cup olive oil
2 cloves garlic, chopped
2 tablespoons chopped parsley
salt and pepper
1 cup broth or stock

The beans sit in their cooking liquid until you are ready to finish them. Put the olive oil in a pot and sauté the garlic until it starts to brown. Add the parsley, stir well, then add the drained, cooked beans. Season with salt and pepper, cover and simmer for 5 minutes.

At this point you can go in several directions. You can purée some or all of the beans. If you want to serve soup, do about a cupful in the food processor or through a food mill, put the puréed beans back in the pot and add the cup of stock or broth. Simmer for a while and serve over slices of Italian bread, toasted.

You can purée all the beans if you want to and serve the mixture, reheated, as a side dish (especially good with roast lamb or grilled sausages). You can make a soup that is very smooth by puréeing all the beans and then adding as much liquid as you need to get the consistency right, again serving it over toast if you like that combination.

If you are really short of time you can use canned white beans and simply begin with the sautéing of the garlic. The result won't be as tasty, but it will still be very appealing and, of course, incredibly quick and easy.

If you make this recipe and use, say, only half of it, here is something nifty to do with the leftovers: make a white sauce with 3 to 4 tablespoons butter, 3 to 4 tablespoons flour, and 1 cup of milk. Separate 2 eggs and add the yolks to the white sauce off heat, then mix the beans in. Beat the egg white until stiff and fold the bean and white sauce mixture in. Butter and bread crumb a mold of appropriate size, put the mixture into it, and bake it in a 350° oven for 25 minutes. You can un-mold it and serve it in slices. (This last suggestion is taken from Anne Bianchi's *From the Tables of Tuscan Women*.)

●

Wild West Beans with Flank Steak

Are cowboys peasants? Perhaps not, but their cuisine has a kind of subsistence character of its own, as in this recipe from Montana, adapted from a *New York Times* article by Molly O'Neill on organic beef ranchers.

———

1 pound dried pinto beans
5–6 tomatoes, halved
4 peppers or chilies (banana peppers,
    Anaheim chilies, etc.), halved
    lengthwise and seeded and cored
1 jalapeño pepper
2 tablespoons olive oil
1 onion, minced
1 tablespoon dry mustard
3 tablespoons molasses
3 tablespoons salt
1 tablespoon freshly ground black pepper
1 flank steak, about 1 pound
2 teaspoons coarse salt
3 tablespoons chopped coriander (optional)

The beans need to be rinsed, placed in water to cover by 2 inches, boiled for 3 minutes, and allowed to stand, covered, for at least 2 hours.

The tomatoes and peppers (or chilies) are to be roasted, skin side up, in a 400° oven for about 24 minutes. The peppers will have been seeded and cored. Meanwhile, the jalapeño should be seeded and sliced, but not roasted. The tomatoes, peppers, and the jalapeño should be put in a food processor and puréed until smooth.

Cook the minced onion in the olive oil for a few minutes, then add the drained beans. Add enough fresh water to just cover them. Add the molasses, mustard, salt and pepper, and the roasted vegetable mixture. Stir well and bring to a boil. At this point you can cover the pot and bake the beans for 1½ to 2 hours, checking to make sure they have enough liquid. Or you can simmer them on the stove, which makes the liquid checking a little easier.

About 15 minutes before the beans are done, cook the steak in the following fashion: heat a cast-iron skillet very hot, with salt (coarse salt, e.g., kosher or sea salt, is best) sprinkled over the bottom. Sear the steak in the hot skillet for 2 to 3 minutes per side. Let it stand for a few minutes and check to see if it's done. If it seems too rare, cook it a minute longer in the microwave or put it back in the pan. Put a mound of beans on each plate and top with slices of steak. Sprinkle with chopped fresh coriander if you have it.

●

Beans like Little Birds

The name of this dish translates *fagioli all uccelletto,*
denoting that the seasoning pattern is the same as that
used for cooking small birds, a combination of sage,
rosemary, and tomatoes. I made this recently, when
short of time, with canned beans, and people loved it.
Imagine how good it would have been if I could have had
dried, soaked beans, or even, wonder of wonders, fresh
white haricots or cannellini!

—∽∾∿∽—

1 pound white beans (fresh, or dried and soaked
overnight, or canned) such as cannellini,
great northern, or white haricots

2 cloves crushed garlic
2 tablespoons olive oil
2 tablespoons sage
6 whole peppercorns
6 tablespoons olive oil
2 cloves garlic, crushed
2 tablespoons chopped sage, fresh or dried
1 tablespoon minced rosemary, fresh or dried
1 14-ounce can tomatoes, chopped, with
    their liquid
1 cup stock or broth
salt and pepper

After soaking overnight, the beans should be cooked very slowly in plenty of water, to which crushed garlic, olive oil, sage, and peppercorns are added. Italians would cook them *nel fiasco,* in a flask, until they were dry and tender. I suggest a casserole in a very slow oven. You can go up to 3 hours if your heat is low enough.

To finish, heat the 6 tablespoons of olive oil in a skillet, add the garlic, the sage, and the rosemary, and cook briskly for a minute. Add the tomatoes and the stock or broth and bring to a boil. Add the beans and season to taste with salt and pepper. Cook for about 15 minutes, stirring frequently.

I've made this often in the past, but I just got a new twist on it from a cookbook given to me for Christmas, Anne Bianchi's *From the Tables of Tuscan Women*. She notes, "In certain towns in Versilia, it is customary to add 2 tablespoons of strong balsamic vinegar just before serving. Try it." I did. It was terrific.

A Reading List

. . . .

This list combines favorites mentioned in passing with books I consulted or cited along the way while writing this one. Tom Sherman's *A Place on the Glacial Till* (Oxford, 1997) came along in manuscript, a loan from the author, just as I was finishing up *Seasoning.* Our decisions to write about this area were arrived at independently, and the two books made for a wonderful coincidence. They complement each other in ways that have pleased both of us very much.

Bettoja, Jo, and Anna Maria Cornetto. *Italian Cooking in the Grand Tradition.*

Bianchi, Anne. *From the Tables of Tuscan Women.*

Bugialli, Giuliano. *The Fine Art of Italian Cooking.*

Chaucer, Geoffrey. *The Canterbury Tales.*

Child, Julia. *Mastering the Art of French Cooking.*

Claiborne, Craig, and Pierre Franey. *The New New York Times Cookbook.*

Coffey, Timothy. *The History and Folklore of North American Wildflowers.*

Conant, Roger, and Joseph T. Collins. *Reptiles and Amphibians: Eastern/Central North America.*

Curtis, Carlton C., and S. C. Bausor. *The Complete Guide to North American Trees.*

318

Davenport, Guy. *Charles Burchfield's Seasons.*

David, Elizabeth. *French Provincial Cooking.*

de Groot, Roy Andries. *The Auberge of the Flowering Hearth.*

Dickinson, Emily. *Collected Poems.*

Donne, John. *Collected Poems.*

Follain, Jean. *A World Rich in Anniversaries* (trans. W. S. Merwin).

Francis, Robert. *Collected Poems.*

Gilfillan, Merrill. *Moods of the Ohio Moons.*

Graham, Verne Ovid. *Mushrooms of the Great Lakes Region.*

Gray, Patience. *Honey from a Weed: Fasting and Feasting in Tuscany,
    Catalonia, the Cyclades, and Apulia.*

Grigson, Jane. *The Mushroom Feast.*

Hazan, Marcella. *The Classic Italian Cook Book* (volume 1).

————. *More Classic Italian Cooking* (volume 2).

Hieatt, A. Kent. *Short Time's Endless Monument.*

Herbert, George. *The Temple.*

Hillman, Howard. *The Cook's Book.*

Hopkins, Gerard Manley. *Selected Poems and Prose.*

Howe, Susan. *My Emily Dickinson.*

Joyce, James. *Dubliners.*

Kafka, Barbara. *The Microwave Gourmet.*

Keats, John. *Collected Poems.*

Kinnell, Galway. *Flower-Herding on Mount Monadnock.*

Kline, David. *Great Possessions.*

Kunitz, Stanley. *Selected Poems.*

Kurta, Allen. *Mammals of the Great Lakes Region.*

La Place, Viana, and Evan Kleinman. *Cucina Fresca.*

Leibenstein, Margaret. *The Edible Mushroom.*

Little, Elbert L. *National Audubon Society Field Guide to North American
    Trees.*

Marvell, Andrew. *Selected Poems.*

Meyer, Danny, and Michael Romano. *The Union Square Cafe Cookbook.*

Miller, Orson K., Jr. *Mushrooms of North America.*

Montale, Eugenio. *Selected Poems.*

Newell, Venetia. *An Egg at Easter.*

Norris, Kathleen. *Dakota.*

Peterson, Roger Tory. *A Field Guide to the Birds.*

Peterson, Roger Tory, and Margaret McKenny. *A Field Guide to Wildflowers.*

Petrides, George A. *A Field Guide to Trees and Shrubs.*

Rilke, Rainer Maria. *Sonnets to Orpheus* (trans. David Young).

————. *The Duino Elegies* (trans. David Young).

Roden, Claudia. *A Book of Middle Eastern Food.*

Romer, Elizabeth. *The Tuscan Year.*

Routhier, Nicole. *Foods of Vietnam.*

Schrecker, Ellen. *Mrs. Chiang's Szechwan Cookbook.*

Seed, Diane. *The Top One Hundred Pasta Sauces.*

Shakespeare, William. *A Midsummer Night's Dream.*

Sherman, Thomas Fairchild. *A Place on the Glacial Till.*

Smith, Alexander H. *The Mushroom Hunter's Field Guide.*

Snyder, Gary. *The Real Work.*

Sokolov, Raymond. *Why We Eat What We Eat.*

Spencer, Edwin R. *Just Weeds.*

Spenser, Edmund. *Collected Poems.*

Stafford, William. *Stories That Could Be True.*

Stevens, Wallace. *Collected Poems.*

Stokes, Donald. *Nature in Winter.*

Tatum, Billy Joe. *Wild Foods Field Guide and Cookbook.*

Thorne, John. *Outlaw Cook.*

Visser, Margaret. *Much Depends on Dinner.*

Wang Wei, Li Po, Tu Fu, Li Ho, and Li Shang-yin. *Five T'ang Poets* (trans. David Young).

Wilbur, Richard. *The Beautiful Changes.*

Willard, Nancy. *Swimming Lessons.*

Williams, William Carlos. *Spring and All.*

Wright, Charles. *The World of the Ten Thousand Things.*

Wright, James. *This Journey.*

Young, David. *Boxcars.*

————. *Earthshine.*

————. *Foraging.*

————. *The Names of a Hare in English.*

————. *Night Thoughts and Henry Vaughan.*

————. *The Planet on the Desk.*

————. *Something of Great Constancy: The Art of "A Midsummer Night's Dream."*

————. *Sweating Out the Winter.*

————. *Work Lights: Thirty-two Prose Poems.*

Credits

.   .   .   .

When not otherwise indicated, the author is David Young, and, in the case of the translations, when not otherwise indicated, the translator is David Young. Poems by David Young are courtesy of the following presses: University of Pittsburgh Press, Ecco Press, Cleveland State University Press, Wesleyan University Press, and Ohio State University Press. Translations by David Young are courtesy of Wesleyan University Press, W. W. Norton, and Oberlin College Press.

page

x–xi   "Ohio," *Boxcars* (1973), 37; *The Planet on the Desk, Selected and New Poems* (1991), 29.

2–3   Robert Francis, "Cold," *The Orb Weaver* (1960), 61. Reprinted by permission of Wesleyan University Press.

5   From "Water Diary," *Boxcars* (1973), 84; *The Planet on the Desk* (1991), 44.

5–6   Du Mu (Tu Mu), "Bian River Freezing Over," *FIELD*, no. 48 (Spring 1993): 18.

7   William Stafford, "Ask Me," *Stories That Could Be True: New and Collected Poems* (1977), 19. Reprinted by permission of HarperCollins.

8   "Root Vegetable Ghazal," *The Planet on the Desk* (1991), 142.

26   Robert Francis, "The Seed Eaters," *Collected Poems, 1936–1976* (1976), 193. Reprinted by permission of the University Press of New England.

34–35   Robert Francis, "Waxwings," *Collected Poems, 1936–1976* (1976), 188. Reprinted by permission of the University Press of New England.

35–36   From "Poem in Three Parts, II. Dancing in the Dark," *Earthshine* (1988), 44.

36–37   From "February," *Boxcars* (1973), 39–40.

51–52   William Carlos Williams, "Spring and All," *The Collected Poems of William Carlos Williams,* Vol. 1, 1909–1939 (1986), 183. Reprinted by permission of New Directions.

53–54   William Carlos Williams, "The Farmer," *The Collected Poems of William Carlos Williams,* Vol. 1, 1909–1939 (1986), 186. Reprinted by permission of New Directions.

54–55   From "Water Diary," *Boxcars* (1973), 72.

59–60   "Elegy in the Form of an Invitation," *Foraging* (1986), 39–40.

60   From "In My Own Back Yard," *Foraging* (1986), 3.

78–79   Wang Wei, "A Spring Day at the Farm," *Five T'ang Poets* (1990), 27.

80   "Putting It Mildly," *Sweating Out the Winter* (1969), 30.

82–83   From Rainer Maria Rilke, *Sonnets to Orpheus* (1987), 105.

84   "Easter Ghazal," *The Planet on the Desk* (1991), 144.

108–12   "Homing," *Boxcars* (1973), 8–14; *The Planet on the Desk* (1991), 18–21.

114   Tu Fu (Du Fu), "Spring Scene," *Five T'ang Poets* (1990), 89–90.

117   From Rainer Maria Rilke, *Sonnets to Orpheus* (1987), 83.

118–19   "Homage to William Carlos Williams," *Voices of Cleveland* (1996), 173.

132   From "The Small-Town Poets," *Sweating Out the Winter* (1969), 31.

132–33   From "In My Own Back Yard," *Foraging* (1986), 5.

135   From "Night Thoughts," *Night Thoughts and Henry Vaughan* (1994), 43–44.

144   From "Poem in Three Parts, III. The Light Show," *Earthshine* (1988), 51.

159–60   "Love Song," *Boxcars* (1973), 41.

160–62   "Three Walks," *Foraging* (1986), 46–47.

163   From "Water Diary," *Boxcars* (1973), 73.

163–64   "Woodrow Wilson," *Boxcars* (1973), 71.

164   From "In My Own Back Yard," *Foraging* (1986), 3.

166–67 From Rainer Maria Rilke, *The Duino Elegies, A New Translation* (1978), 24–25.

168–69 "The Day Nabokov Died," *The Names of a Hare in English* (1979), 16–18.

189 "Imaginary Polaroid," first section of "Vermont Summer: Three Snapshots, One Letter," *Foraging* (1986), 41.

191 From "Four about the Letter P," *Work Lights: Thirty-two Prose Poems* (1977), 12.

191–92 "Poem for Adlai Stevenson and Yellow Jackets," *New England Review* 15, no. 4 (Fall 1993): 169.

195, 196 Eugenio Montale, "News from Mount Amiata," *FIELD,* no. 27 (Fall 1982): 35–36.

197 "Late Summer: Lake Erie," *Sweating Out the Winter* (1969), 3.

212–13 "A Country Postcard," *Boxcars* (1973), 56–57.

214–15 "Poem about Hopping," *Sweating Out the Winter* (1969), 39.

215 From "Poem in Three Parts, II. Dancing in the Dark," *Earthshine* (1988), 36.

219 Tu Fu (Du Fu), "New Moon," *Five T'ang Poets* (1990), 102.

221 Jean Follain, "Dawn," *Transparencies of the World,* translated by W. S. Merwin (1969), 37.

222–23 "Suite for Jean Follain," *Foraging* (1986), 37–38.

236 "Evasions," *Sweating Out the Winter* (1969), 41.

239–41 "October Couplets," *Foraging* (1986), 17–19.

244–45, 246 From "Poem in Three Parts, III. The Light Show," *Earthshine* (1988), 53–55.

261 "Autumn Ghazal," *The Planet on the Desk: Selected and New Poems* (1991), 145.

263–64 From "Three Time-Trips," *The Names of a Hare in English* (1979), 14.

266–67 Galway Kinnell, from "Ruins under the Stars," *Selected Poems* (1982), 57–58.

268–69 From "Poem in Three Parts, II. Dancing in the Dark," *Earthshine* (1988), 37–38.

270–71 From "Poem in Three Parts, II. Dancing in the Dark," *Earthshine* (1988), 40.

291 William Carlos Williams, "The Polar Bear," *The Collected Poems of William Carlos Williams,* Vol. 2, 1939–1962 (1991), 395. Reprinted by permission of New Directions.

297–98 From "Poem in Three Parts, II. Dancing in the Dark," *Earthshine* (1988), 42–43.

324

Index of Recipes

· · · ·